Straight to the Point

ADO.NET

DINESH MAIDASANI

B.A., Dip. Comp. Sc.

FIREWALL MEDIA

(An Imprint of Laxmi Publications Pvt. Ltd.)

BANGALORE • CHENNAI • COCHIN • GUWAHATI • HYDERABAD
JALANDHAR • KOLKATA • LUCKNOW • MUMBAI • RANCHI
NEW DELHI • BOSTON, USA

Published by :
FIREWALL MEDIA
(*An Imprint of Laxmi Publications Pvt. Ltd.*)
113, Golden House, Daryaganj,
New Delhi-110002

Phone : 011-43 53 25 00
Fax : 011-43 53 25 28

www.laxmipublications.com
info@laxmipublications.com

Price : **Rs. 125.00** *Only.* *First Edition* : 2008

OFFICES

India

✆ **Bangalore**	080-26 61 15 61
✆ **Chennai**	044-24 34 47 26
✆ **Cochin**	0484-239 70 04
✆ **Guwahati**	0361-254 36 69, 251 38 81
✆ **Hyderabad**	040-24 65 23 33
✆ **Jalandhar**	0181-222 12 72
✆ **Kolkata**	033-22 27 37 73, 22 27 52 47
✆ **Lucknow**	0522-220 95 78
✆ **Mumbai**	022-24 91 54 15, 24 92 78 69
✆ **Ranchi**	0651-230 77 64

USA

Boston
11, Leavitt Street, Hingham,
MA 02043, USA

FST-2950-125-STTP_ADO.NET
Typeset at : Kalyani Computer Services, New Delhi.

C—14780/07/09
Printed at : Sanjeev Offset Press, Delhi.

Straight to the Point

ADO.NET

Contents

1 Introduction to ADO.Net

INTRODUCTION

ADO.Net technology is used for the interaction with the databases. You know that databases are used to store data. Also you can retrieve data from database whenever required. Databases usually work as a back-end, i.e., to interact with the database when required by some front-end such as Visual Basic, C#.Net, ASP.Net. etc. Thus, ADO technology works in between front-end and back-end. Back-end database can be created in MS Access, SQL Server, Oracle, etc., according to the requirement.

In this book we use ASP.Net as front-end technology. Visual Basic 2005 and Visual Studio 2005 as per requirement of chapters to teach different sections of ADO.Net.

To show you how fast we can create database oriented application using Visual Studio 2005 and ADO.NET, let's begin with the following example. Here we will create a database in MS Access and then use that Visual Studio.

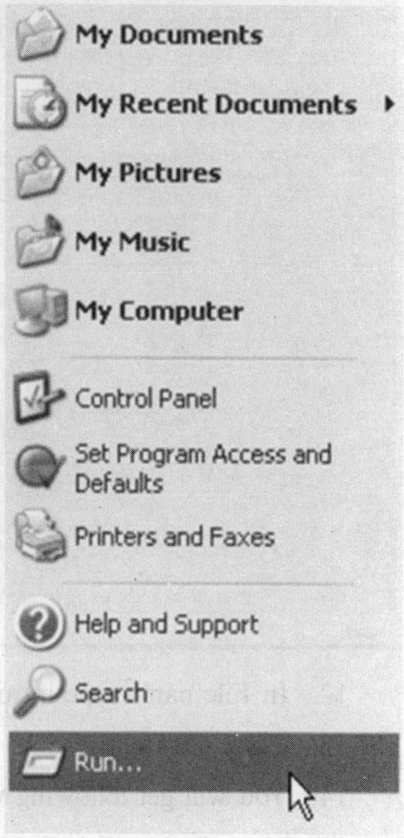

Creating database using MS Access

Perform the following steps for creating database in MS Access:

1. Click Start
2. Click Run
3. You will get Run dialog box
4. Type msaccess
5. Click OK
6. You will get Microsoft Access window:
7. On menu bar click File
8. Click New
9. In New File... click Blank database
10. You will get Save in dialog-box
11. Select C: drive

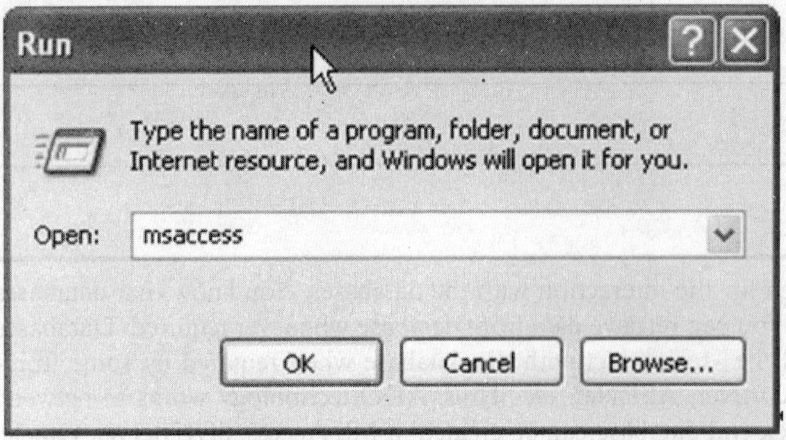

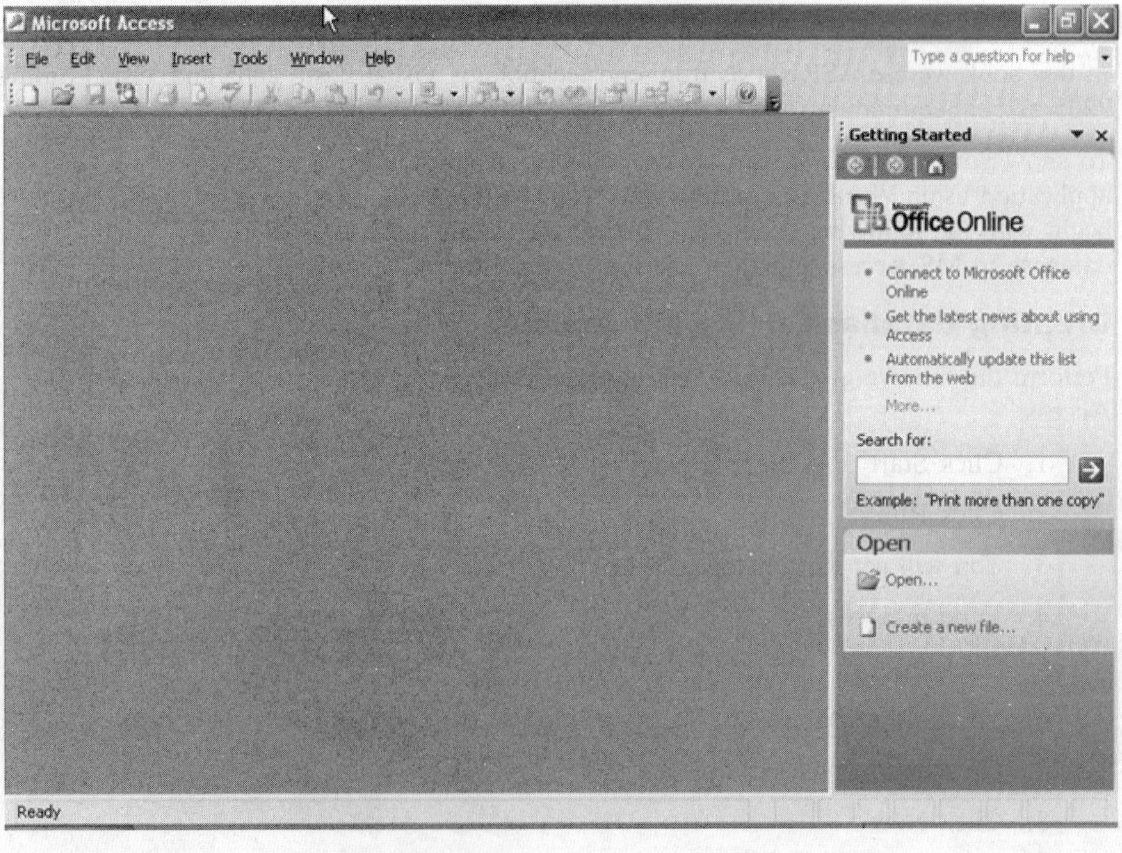

12. In File name type introdatabase
13. Click Create
14. You will get following window:
15. Now double-click Create table in Design view

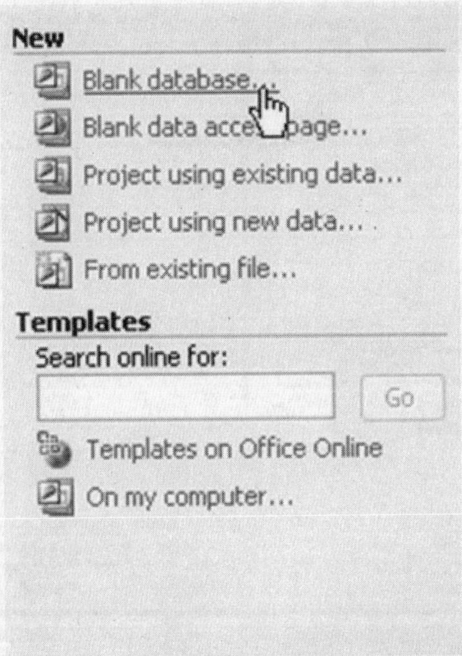
New
Blank database...
Blank data access page...
Project using existing data...
Project using new data...
From existing file...
Templates
Search online for:
Go
Templates on Office Online
On my computer...

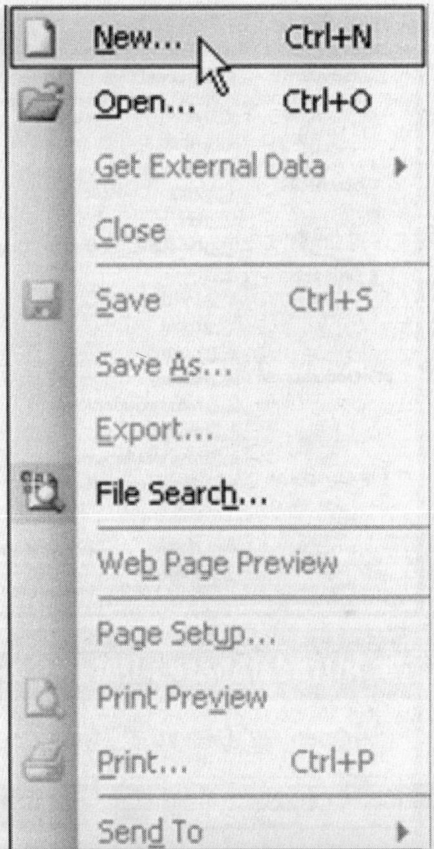
New... Ctrl+N
Open... Ctrl+O
Get External Data
Close
Save Ctrl+S
Save As...
Export...
File Search...
Web Page Preview
Page Setup...
Print Preview
Print... Ctrl+P
Send To

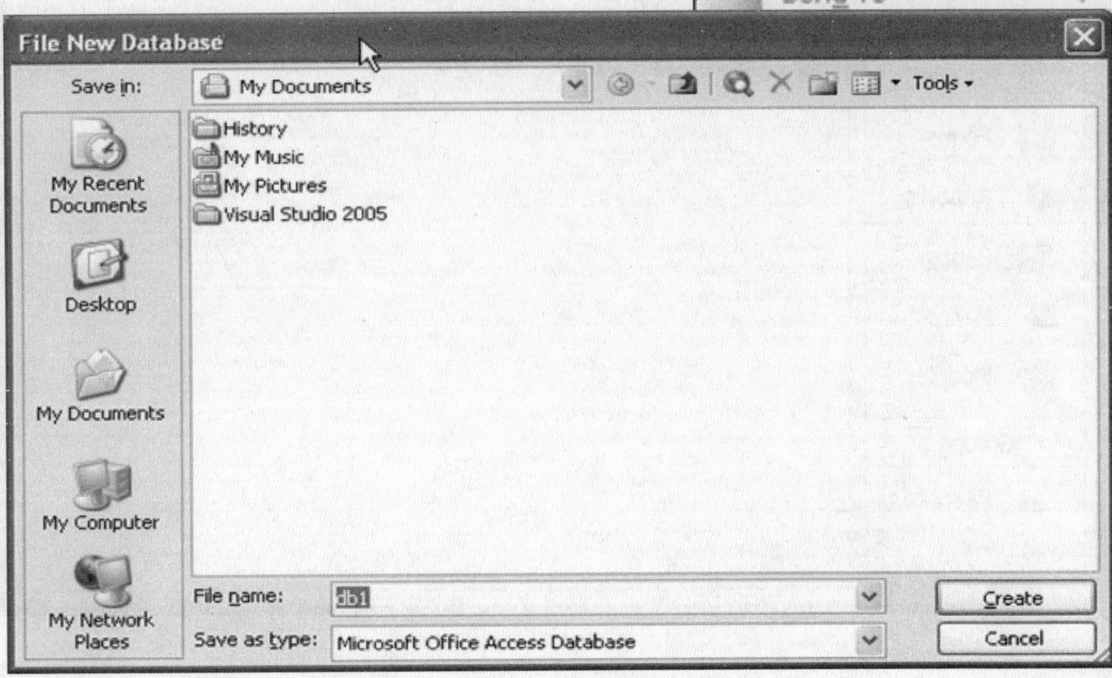
File New Database
Save in:
My Documents
Tools
History
My Music
My Pictures
Visual Studio 2005
My Recent Documents
Desktop
My Documents
My Computer
My Network Places
File name:
db1
Save as type:
Microsoft Office Access Database
Create
Cancel

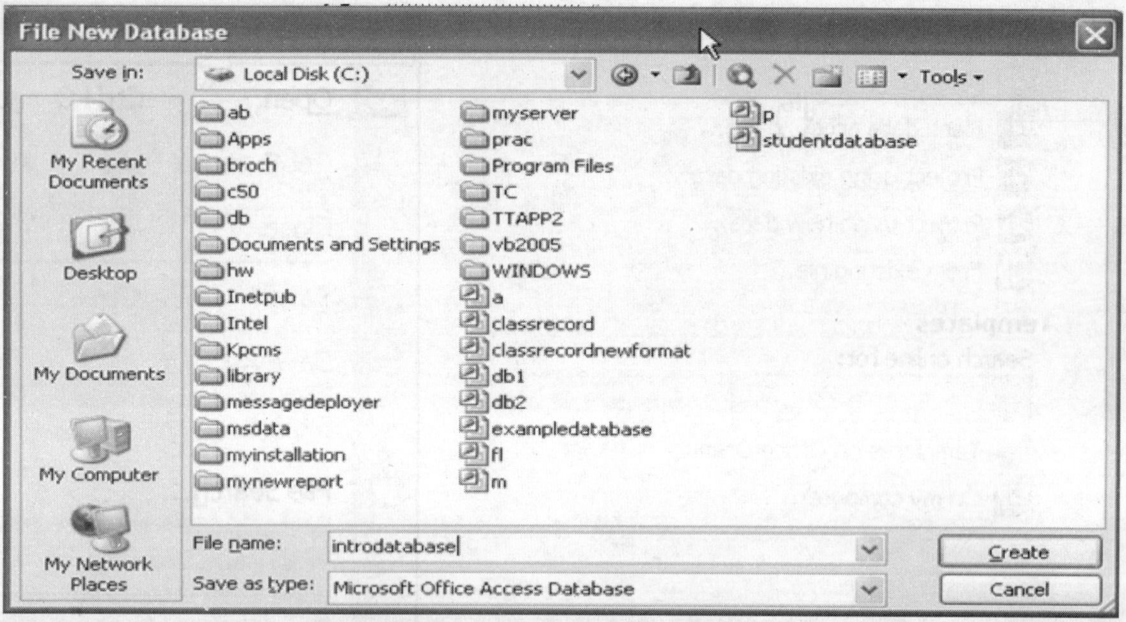
File New Database
Save in: Local Disk (C:)
Tools
My Recent Documents
Desktop
My Documents
My Computer
My Network Places
ab
Apps
broch
c50
db
Documents and Settings
hw
Inetpub
Intel
Kpcms
library
messagedeployer
msdata
myinstallation
mynewreport
myserver
prac
Program Files
TC
TTAPP2
vb2005
WINDOWS
a
classrecord
classrecordnewformat
db1
db2
exampledatabase
fl
m
p
studentdatabase
File name: introdatabase
Save as type: Microsoft Office Access Database
Create
Cancel

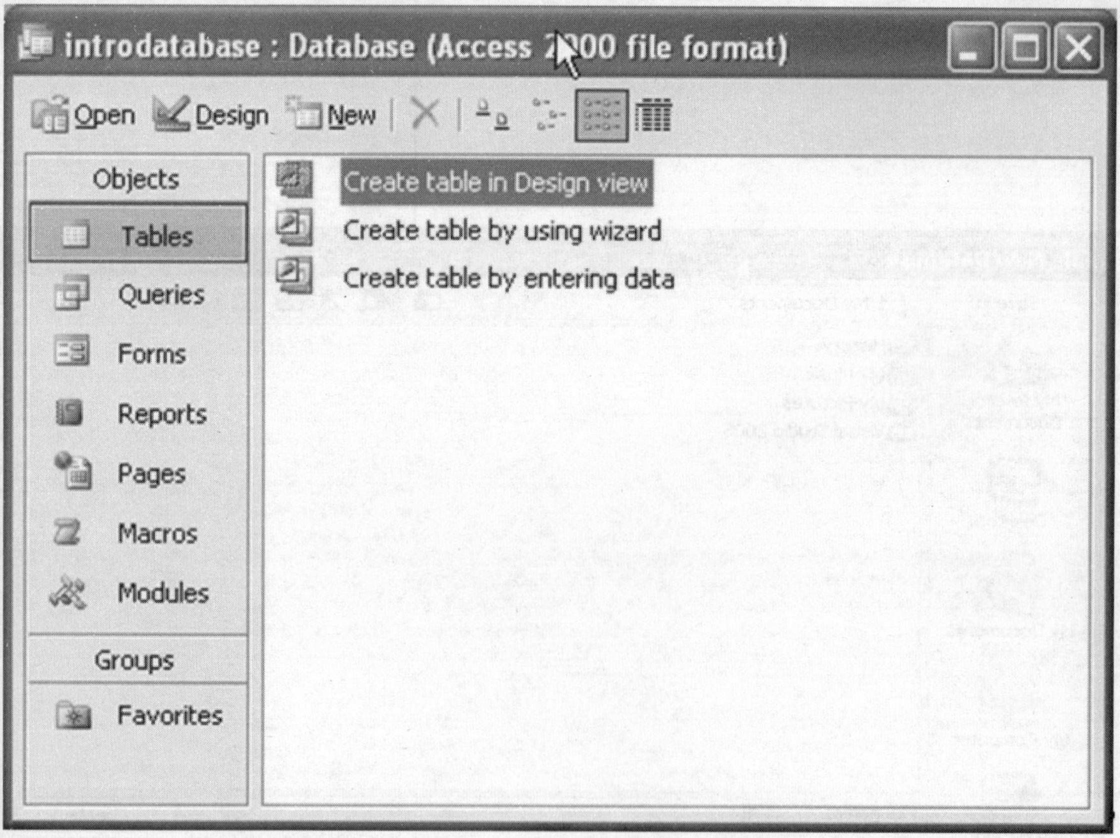
introdatabase : Database (Access 2000 file format)
Open
Design
New
Objects
Tables
Queries
Forms
Reports
Pages
Macros
Modules
Groups
Favorites
Create table in Design view
Create table by using wizard
Create table by entering data

16. You will get following window:

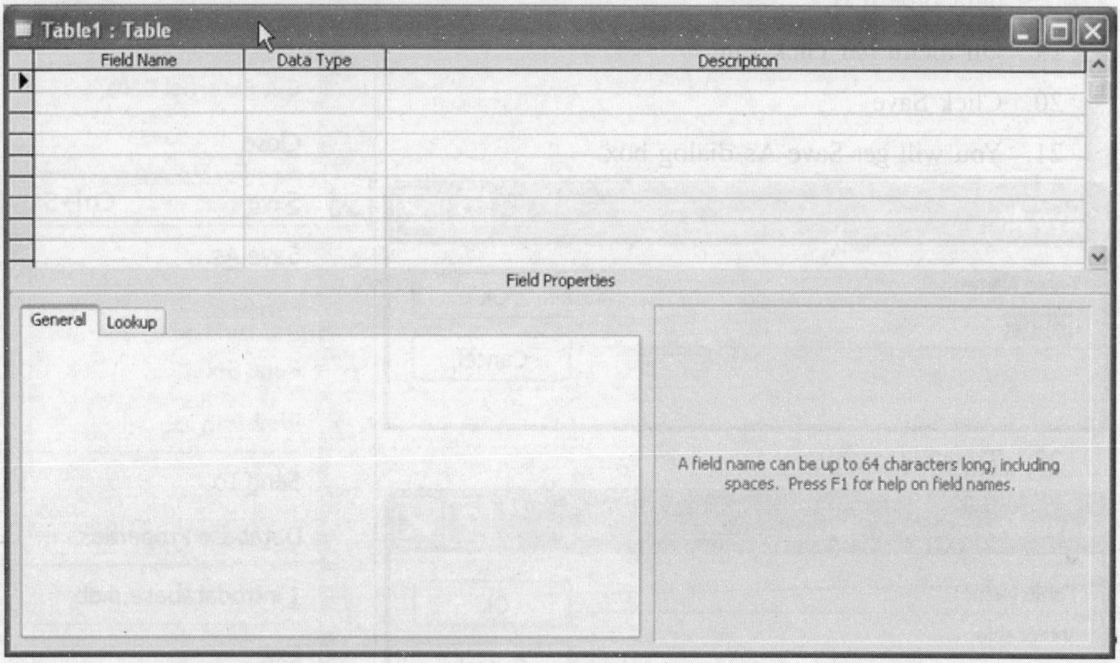

17. Type following details as shown in figure below:

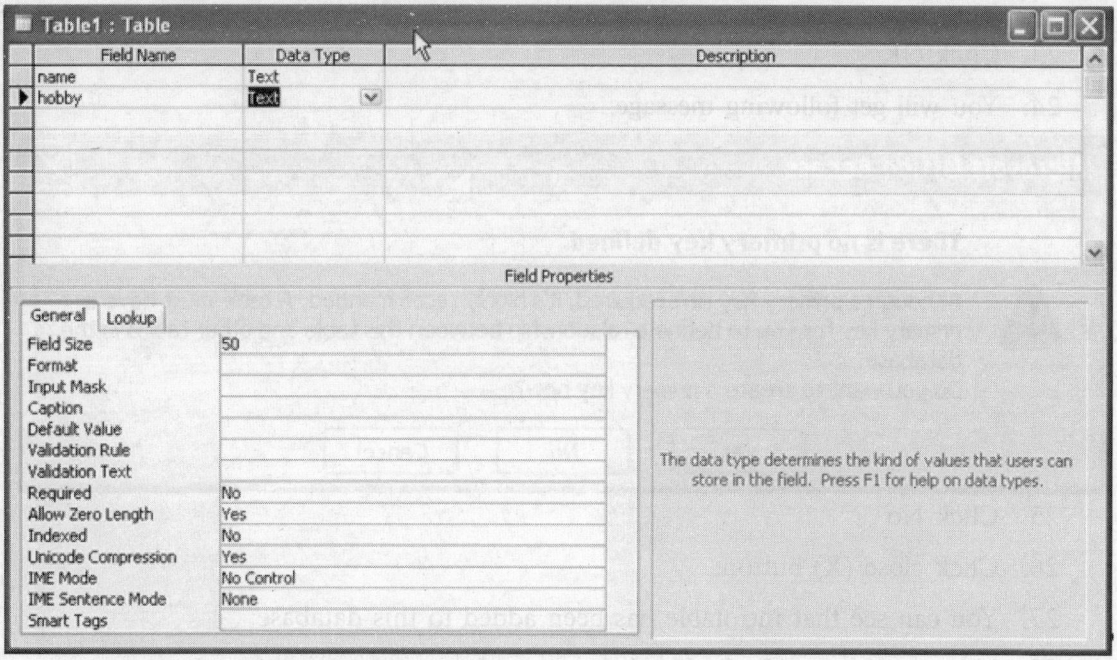

18. You have entered two fields name and hobby with data type text.
19. On menu bar click File

20. Click Save
21. You will get Save As dialog box.

22. Type introtable.

23. Click OK
24. You will get following message:

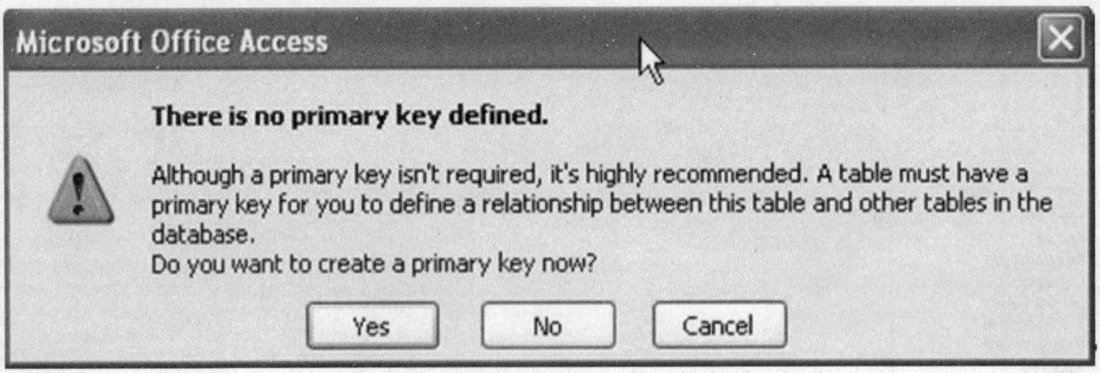

25. Click No
26. Click close (X) button.
27. You can see that introtable has been added to this database
28. Now to add records double-click introtable icon
29. You will get following window:

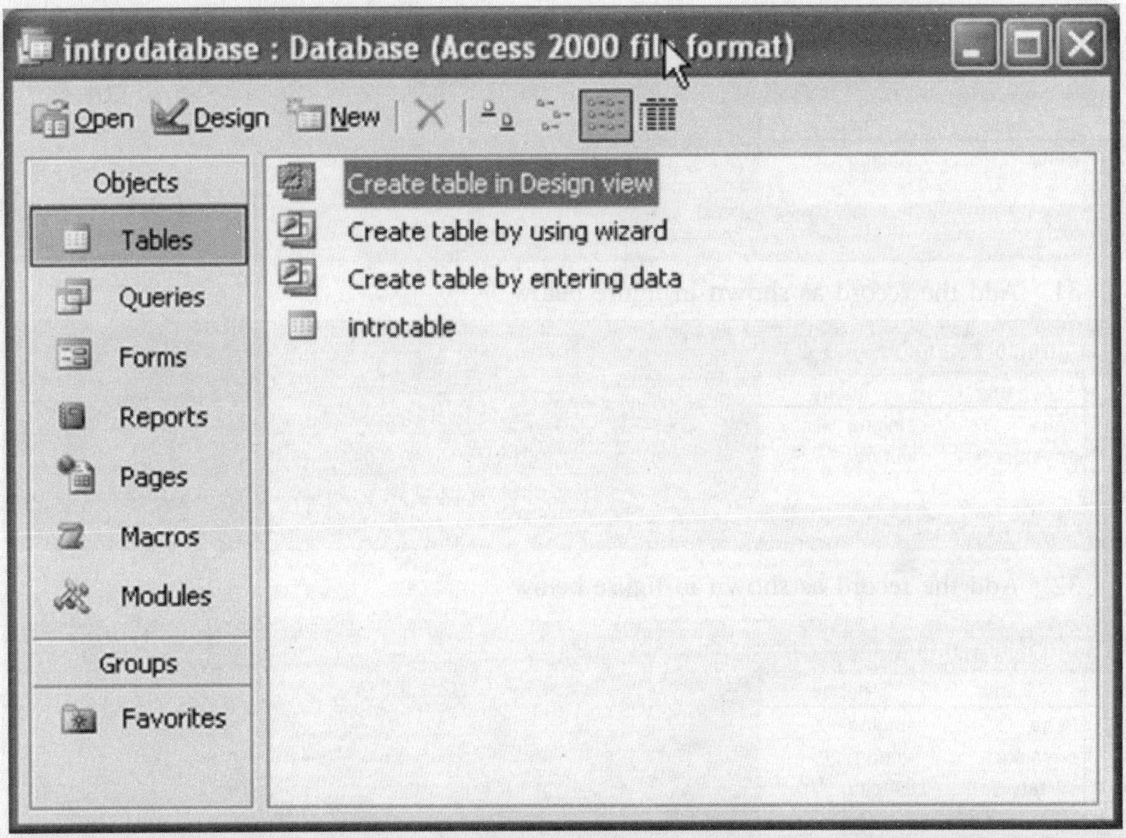
introdatabase : Database (Access 2000 file format)
Open
Design
New
Objects
Tables
Queries
Forms
Reports
Pages
Macros
Modules
Groups
Favorites
Create table in Design view
Create table by using wizard
Create table by entering data
introtable

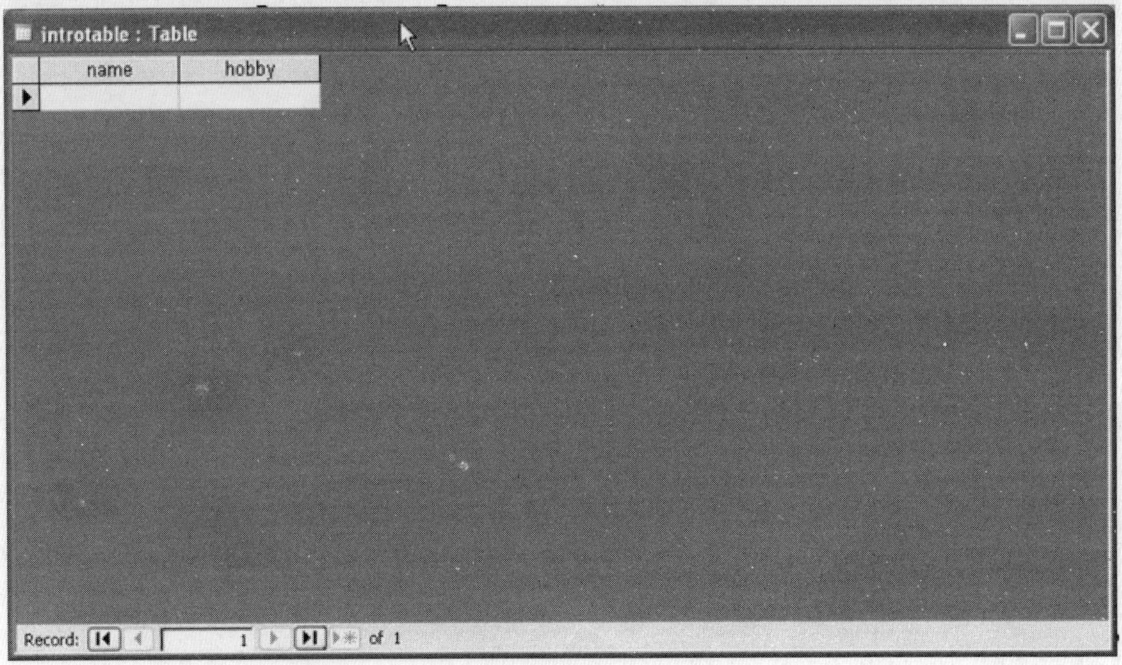
introtable : Table
name
hobby
Record:
1
of 1

30. Add the record as shown in figure below

name	hobby
neha	singing

31. Add the record as shown in figure below

name	hobby
neha	singing
priyanka	writing

32. Add the record as shown in figure below

name	hobby
neha	singing
priyanka	writing
sweety	dancing

33. Add the record as shown in figure below

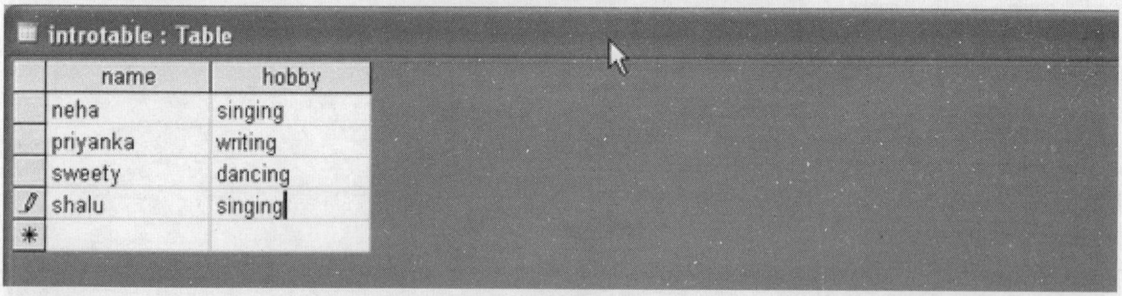

name	hobby
neha	singing
priyanka	writing
sweety	dancing
shalu	singing

34. Add the record as shown in figure below

name	hobby
neha	singing
priyanka	writing
sweety	dancing
shalu	singing
mahak	singing

35. Add the record as shown in figure below

36. Add the record as shown in figure below

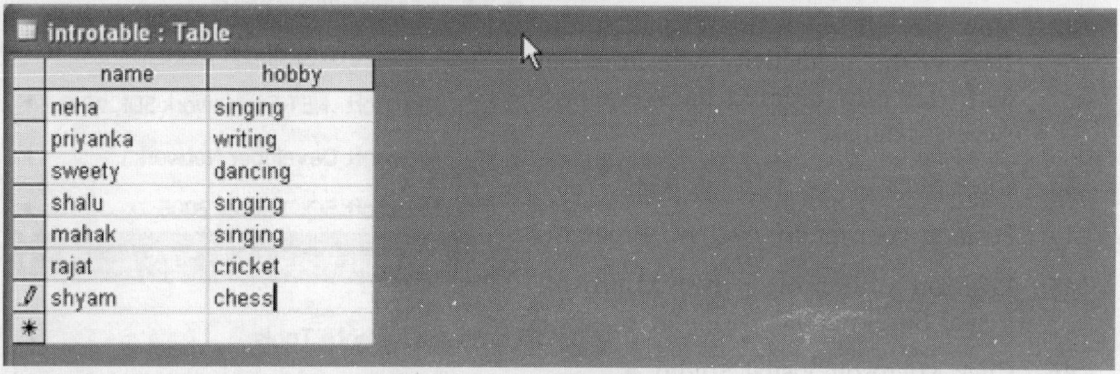

37. Add the record as shown in figure below

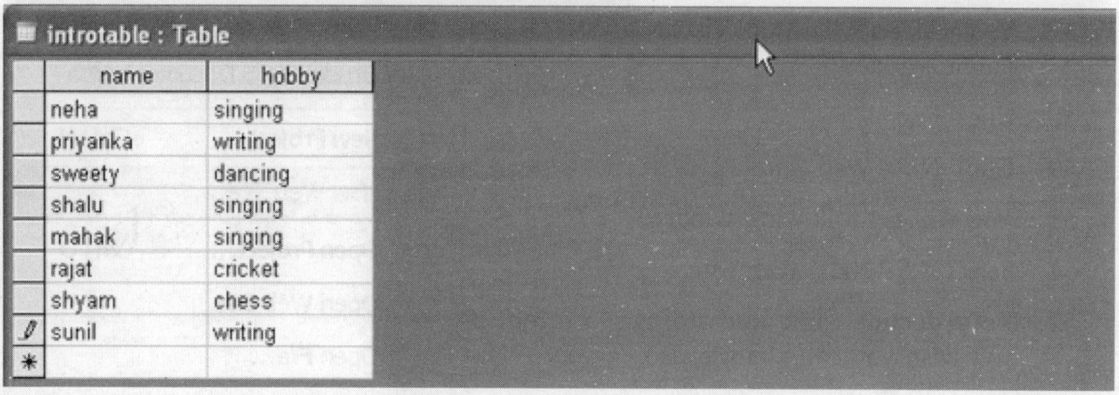

38. Add the record as shown in figure below
39. Now click close button
40. So we have added 9 records in our introtable which is located in introdatabase
41. We have successfully created the database, now click all Close button to close the MS Access

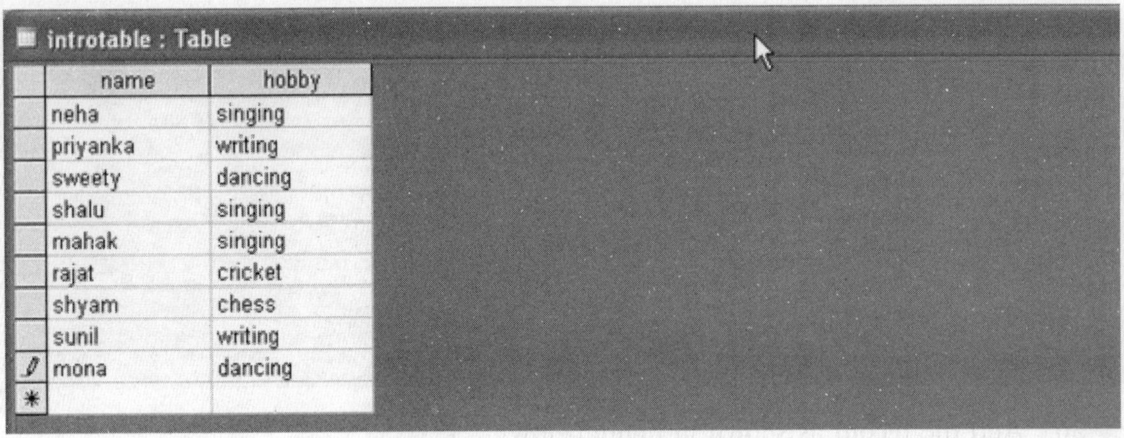

introtable : Table

name	hobby
neha	singing
priyanka	writing
sweety	dancing
shalu	singing
mahak	singing
rajat	cricket
shyam	chess
sunil	writing
mona	dancing

42. Now we will open the Visual Studio 2005 for the interactivity with front-end with our now created back-end MS Access database.
43. Click Start
44. Position your mouse over All Programs
45. Position your mouse over Microsoft Visual Studio 2005
46. Click Microsoft Visual Studio 2005
47. You will get Microsoft Visual Studio window
48. Click File
49. Click New Web Site...
50. You will get following window
51. Select ASP.NET Web Site
52. Keep default name and storage location, if you wish you can change also.
53. In Language field select Visual Basic
54. Click OK
55. On menu bar click View
56. Click Server Explorer

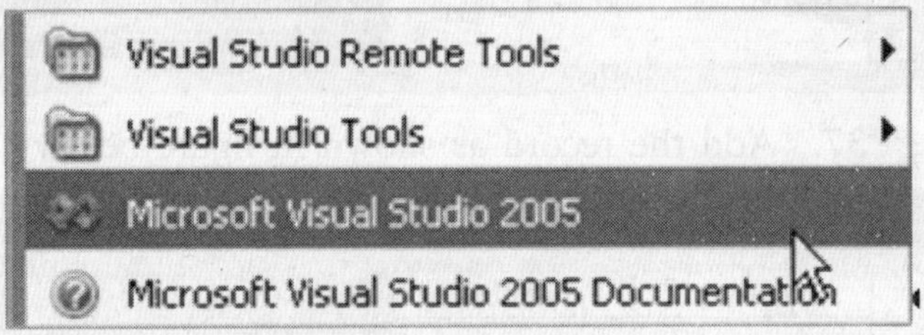

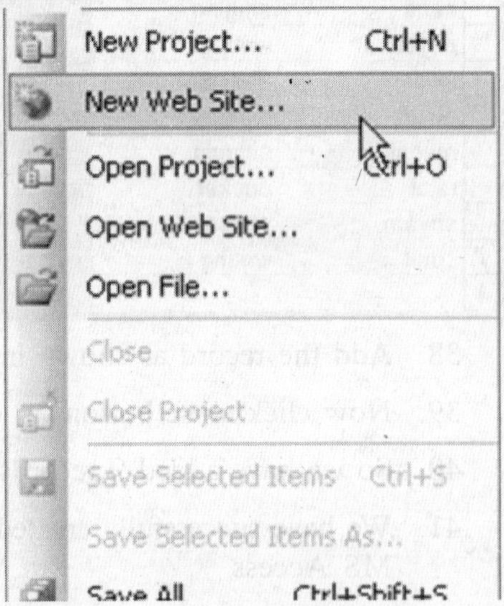

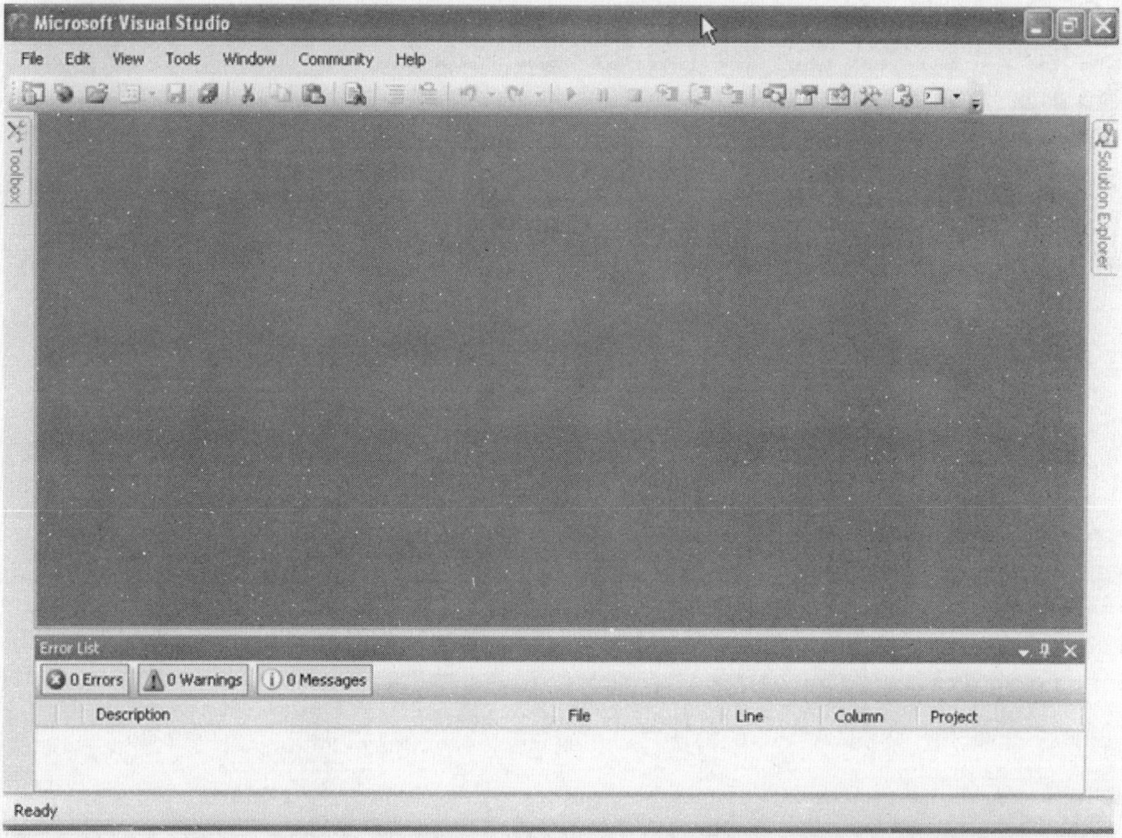

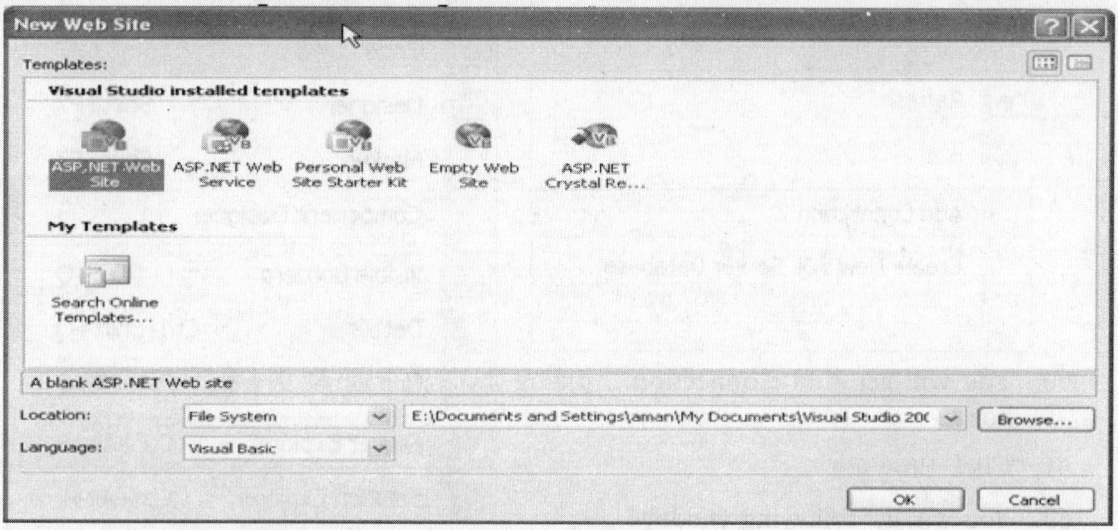

57. At present you have following scenario with Server Explorer window
58. In Server Explorer, right click on Data Connections.

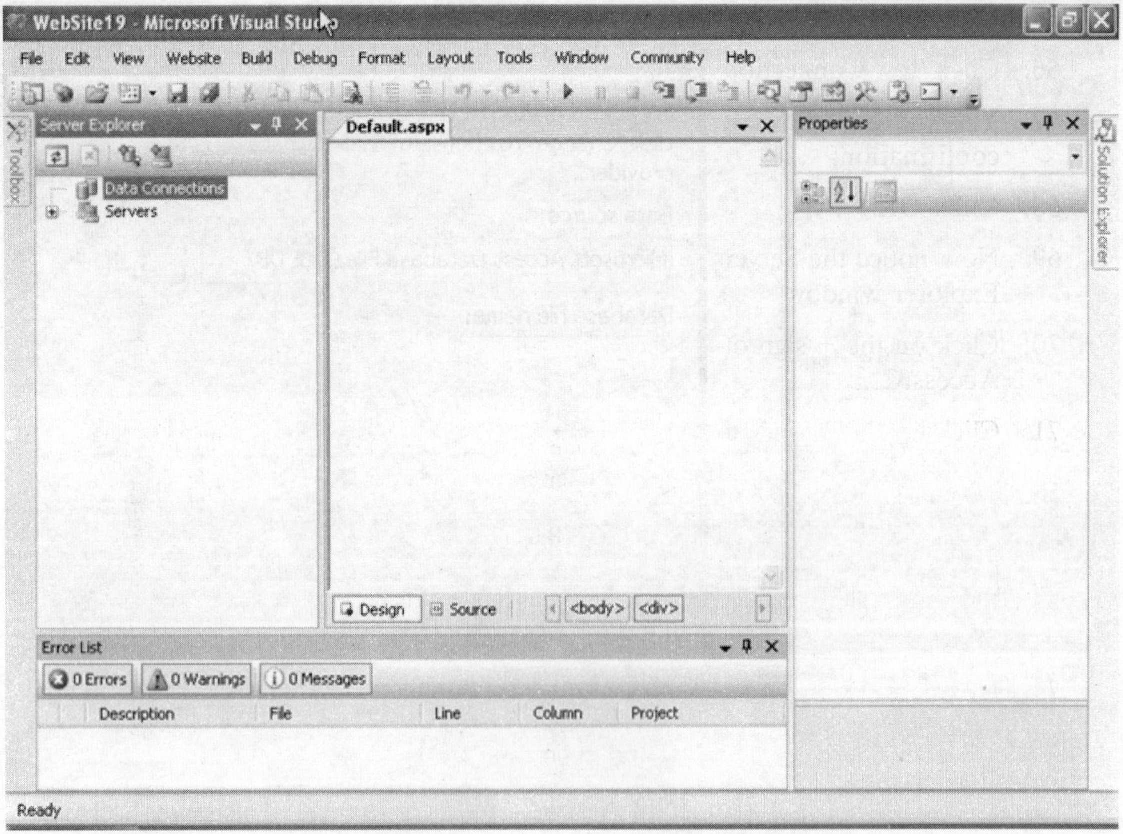

59. Click Add Connection…

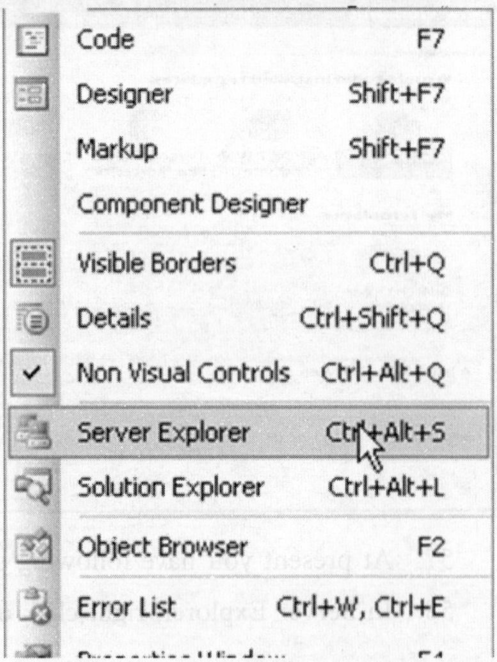

60. You will get Add Connection… dialog box
61. Click Browse
62. You will get following window:
63. Now select the C: drive
64. Select introdatabase

65. Click Open
66. Click Test Connection
67. You will get following confirmation:
68. Click OK
69. Now notice the Server Explorer window
70. Click on the + sign of Access.C...
71. Click on the + sign of Tables
72. Click on the + sign of introtable
73. You can see all fields here
74. Now single click on introtable to select it
75. Now drag it in between default.aspx page section, be sure that Design tab is selected.

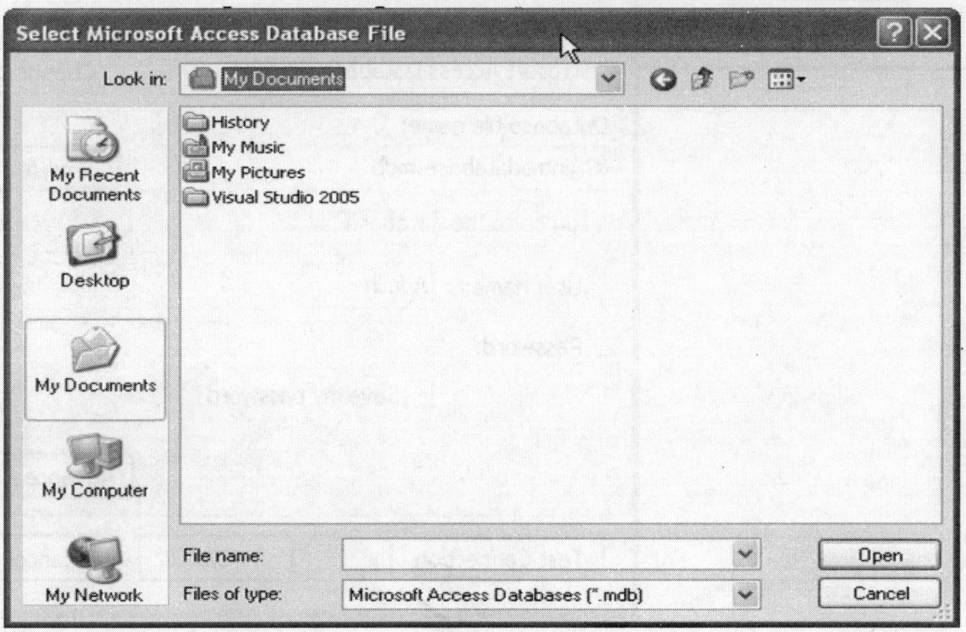

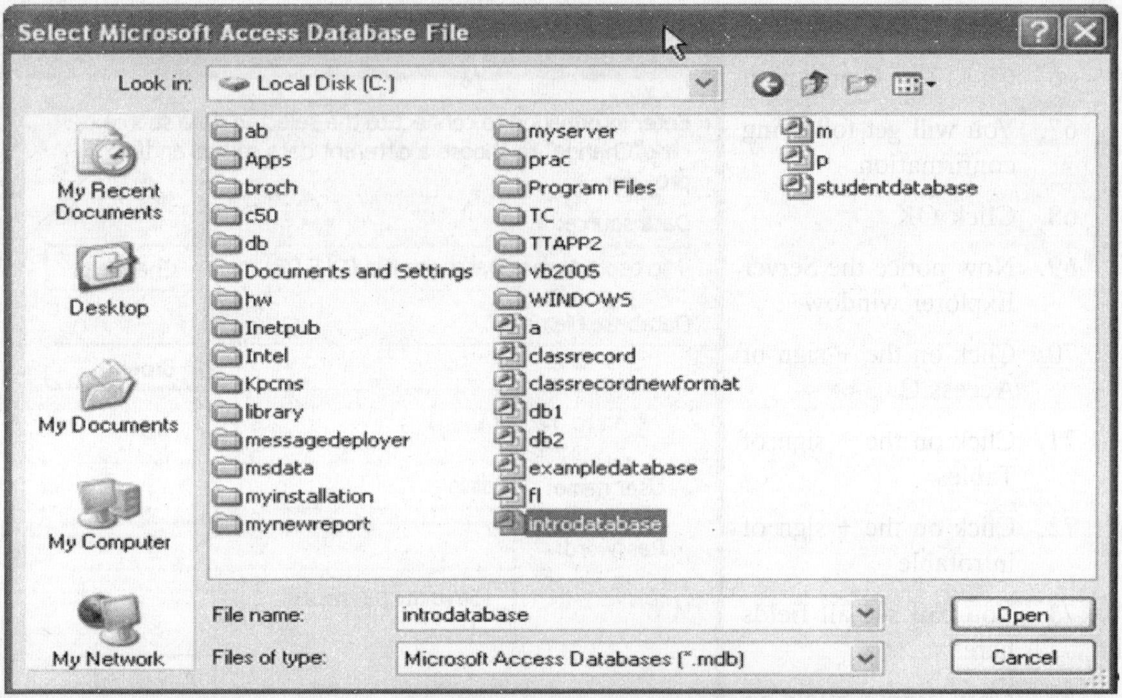
Select Microsoft Access Database File
Look in:
Local Disk (C:)
My Recent Documents
Desktop
My Documents
My Computer
My Network
ab
Apps
broch
c50
db
Documents and Settings
hw
Inetpub
Intel
Kpcms
library
messagedeployer
msdata
myinstallation
mynewreport
myserver
prac
Program Files
TC
TTAPP2
vb2005
WINDOWS
a
classrecord
classrecordnewformat
db1
db2
exampledatabase
fl
introdatabase
m
p
studentdatabase
File name:
introdatabase
Files of type:
Microsoft Access Databases (*.mdb)
Open
Cancel

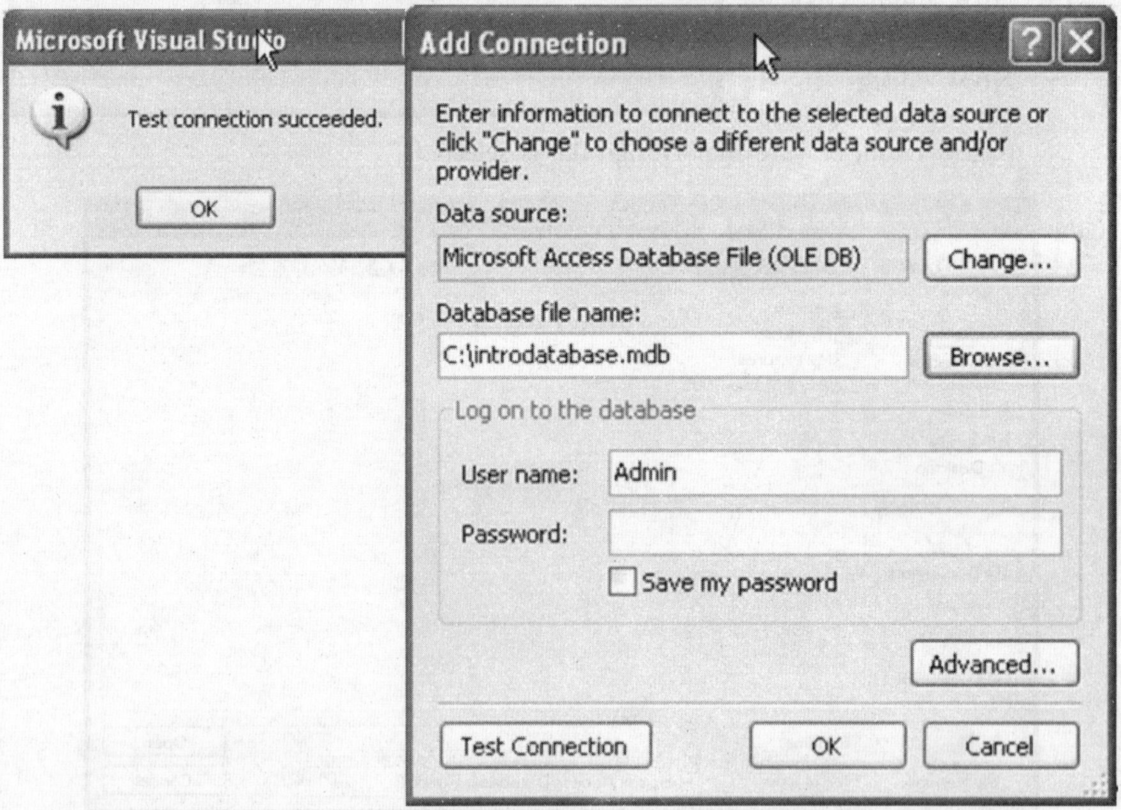
Microsoft Visual Studio
Test connection succeeded.
OK
Add Connection
Enter information to connect to the selected data source or click "Change" to choose a different data source and/or provider.
Data source:
Microsoft Access Database File (OLE DB)
Change...
Database file name:
C:\introdatabase.mdb
Browse...
Log on to the database
User name:
Admin
Password:
Save my password
Advanced...
Test Connection
OK
Cancel

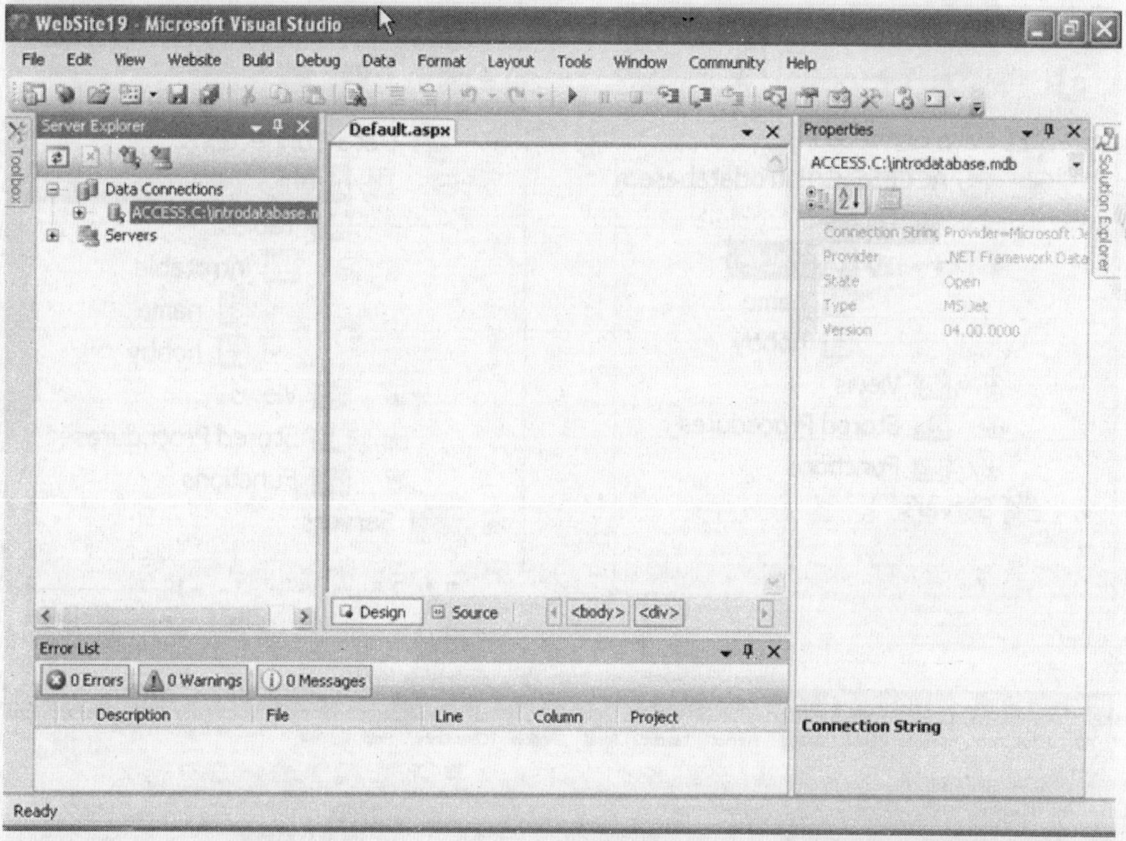

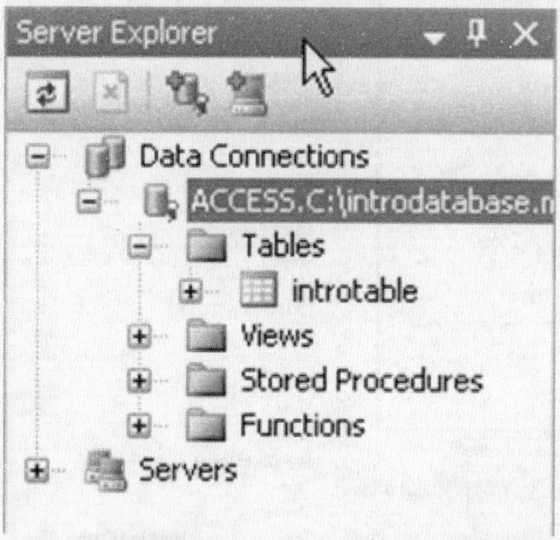

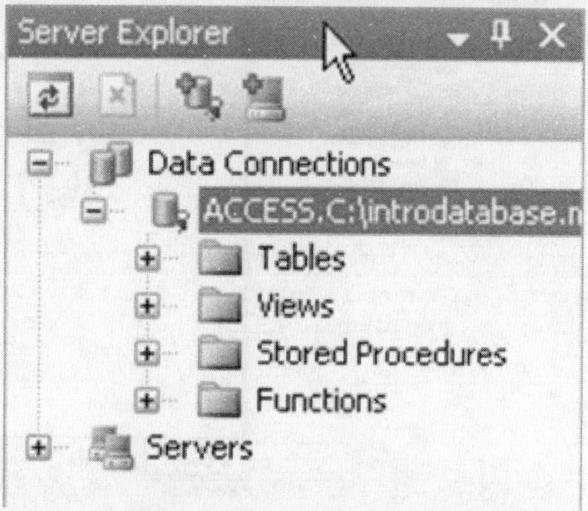

76. You can notice this that all fields are now located here:
77. You have written none a single code for this database interactivity program.
78. Now to run and check this program press F5 key on your keyboard.

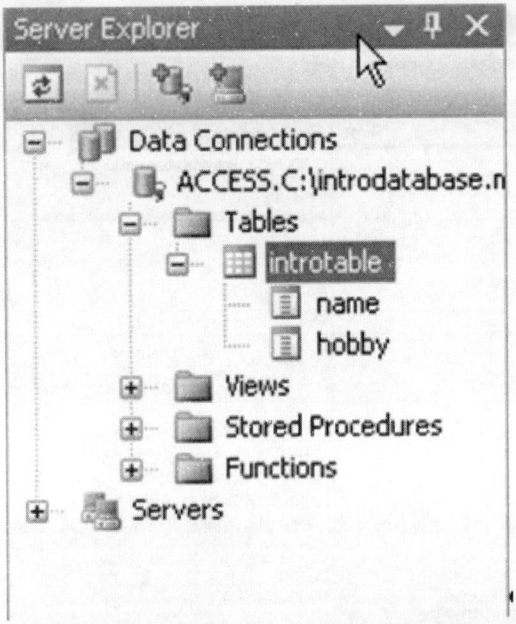
Server Explorer
Data Connections
ACCESS.C:\introdatabase.m
Tables
introtable
name
hobby
Views
Stored Procedures
Functions
Servers

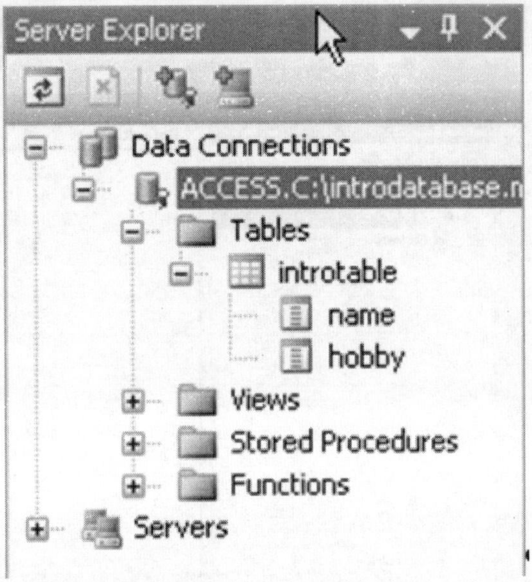
Server Explorer
Data Connections
ACCESS.C:\introdatabase.m
Tables
introtable
name
hobby
Views
Stored Procedures
Functions
Servers

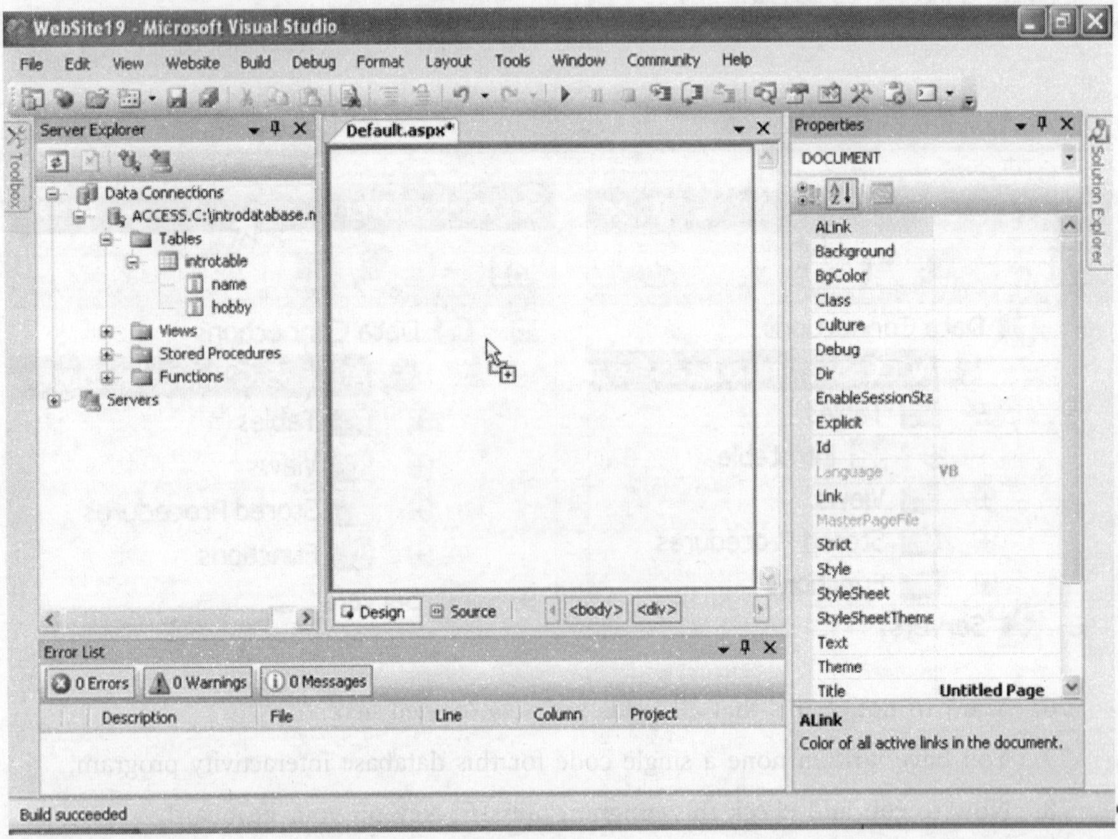
WebSite19 - Microsoft Visual Studio
File Edit View Website Build Debug Format Layout Tools Window Community Help
Server Explorer
Data Connections
ACCESS.C:\introdatabase.m
Tables
introtable
name
hobby
Views
Stored Procedures
Functions
Servers
Default.aspx*
Design Source <body> <div>
Properties
DOCUMENT
ALink
Background
BgColor
Class
Culture
Debug
Dir
EnableSessionSta
Explicit
Id
Language VB
Link
MasterPageFile
Strict
Style
StyleSheet
StyleSheetTheme
Text
Theme
Title Untitled Page
ALink
Color of all active links in the document.
Error List
0 Errors 0 Warnings 0 Messages
Description File Line Column Project
Build succeeded
Toolbox
Solution Explorer

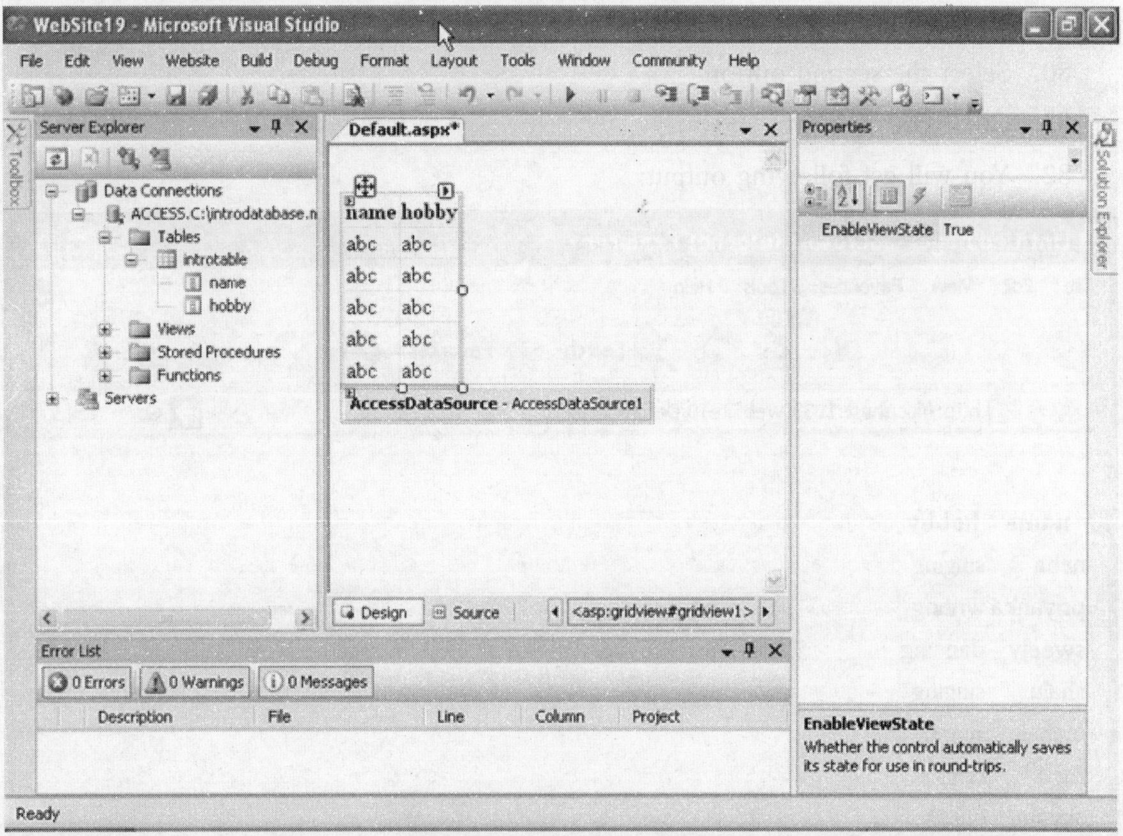
WebSite19 - Microsoft Visual Studio
File Edit View Website Build Debug Format Layout Tools Window Community Help
Server Explorer
Data Connections
ACCESS.C:\introdatabase.m
Tables
introtable
name
hobby
Views
Stored Procedures
Functions
Servers
Default.aspx*
name hobby
abc abc
abc abc
abc abc
abc abc
abc abc
AccessDataSource - AccessDataSource1
Design
Source
<asp:gridview#gridview1>
Properties
EnableViewState True
EnableViewState
Whether the control automatically saves its state for use in round-trips.
Error List
0 Errors
0 Warnings
0 Messages
Description
File
Line
Column
Project
Ready
Toolbox
Solution Explorer

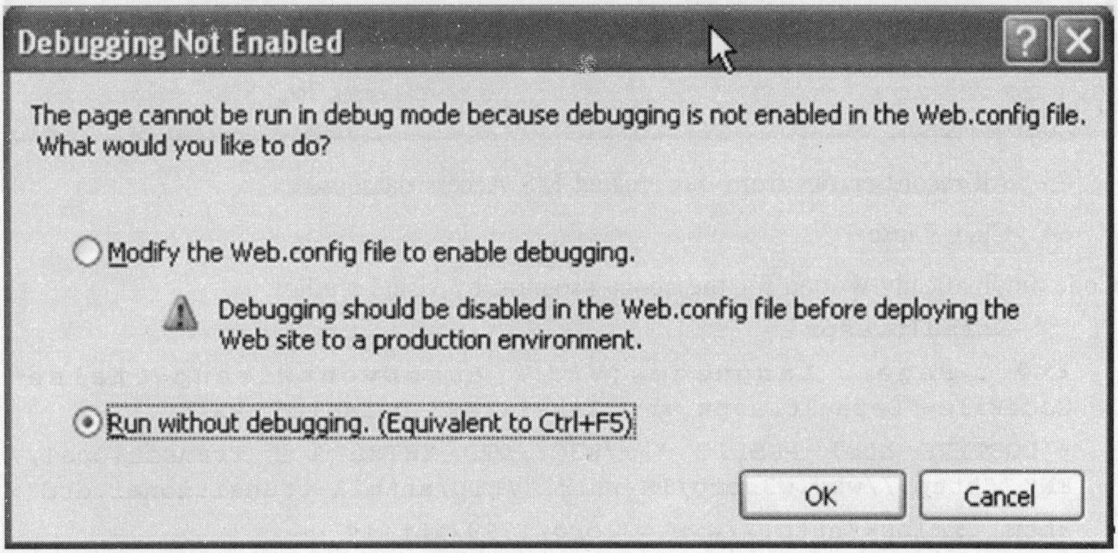
Debugging Not Enabled
The page cannot be run in debug mode because debugging is not enabled in the Web.config file. What would you like to do?
Modify the Web.config file to enable debugging.
Debugging should be disabled in the Web.config file before deploying the Web site to a production environment.
Run without debugging. (Equivalent to Ctrl+F5)
OK
Cancel

79. You will get following message
80. Select the second option
81. Click OK
82. You will get following output:

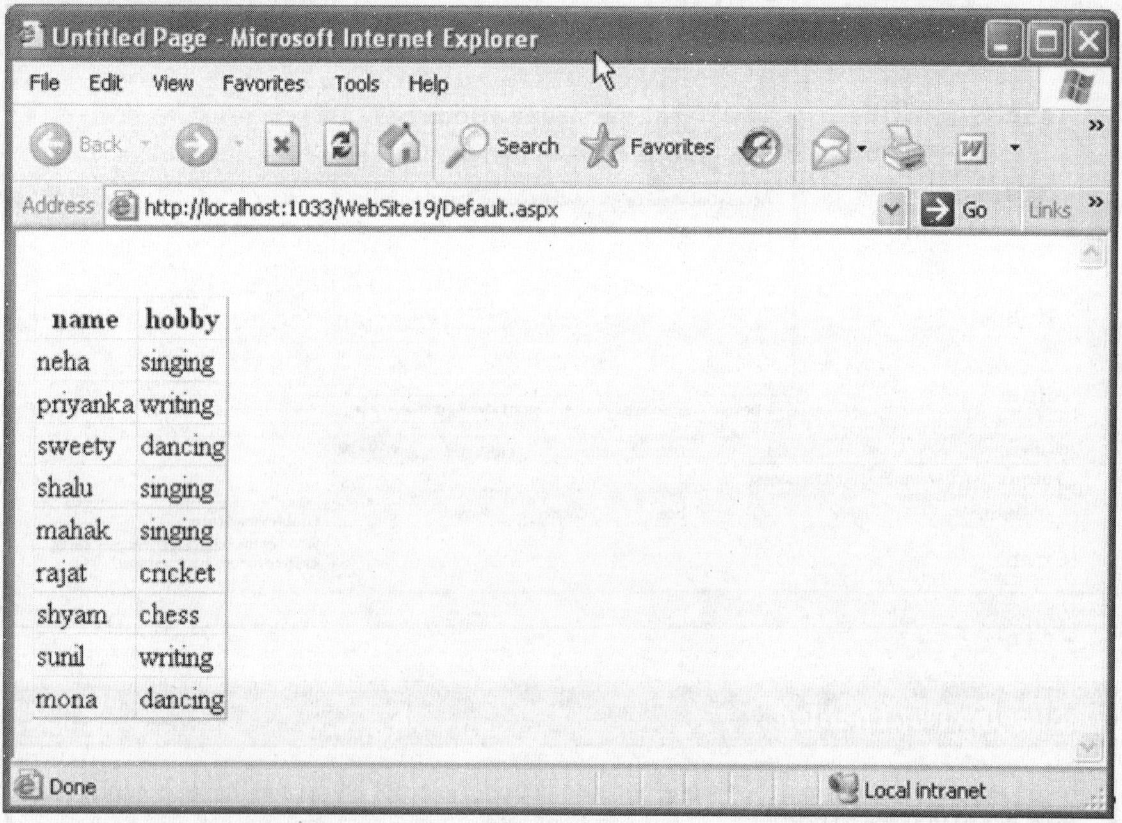

83. All record entries from our created MS Access database
84. Click Close

Code automatically written for the above program by visual studio:

```
-Default.aspx-
<%@ Page Language="VB" AutoEventWireup="false"
CodeFile="Default.aspx.vb" Inherits="_Default" %>
<!DOCTYPE html PUBLIC "-//W3C//DTD XHTML 1.0 Transitional//
EN" "http://www.w3.org/TR/xhtml1/DTD/xhtml1-transitional.dtd">
<html xmlns="http://www.w3.org/1999/xhtml" >
<head runat="server">
    <title>Untitled Page</title>
```

```
</head>
<body>

    <form id="form1" runat="server">
    <div>
         
            <asp:GridView ID="GridView1" runat="server"
AutoGenerateColumns="False" DataSourceID="AccessDataSource1"
                EmptyDataText="There are no data records to
display.">
                <Columns>
                    <asp:BoundField DataField="name"
HeaderText="name" SortExpression="name" />
                    <asp:BoundField DataField="hobby"
HeaderText="hobby" SortExpression="hobby" />
                </Columns>
        </asp:GridView>
            <asp:AccessDataSource ID="AccessDataSource1"
runat="server" DataFile="C:\introdatabase.mdb"
                SelectCommand="SELECT 'name', 'hobby' FROM
'introtable'"></asp:AccessDataSource>

    </div>
    </form>
</body>
</html>

    Default.aspx.vb
Partial Class _Default
Inherits System.Web.UI.Page
End Class
    Web.config
<?xml version="1.0"?>
<!—
```

Note: As an alternative to hand editing this file you can use the web admin tool to configure settings for your application. Use the Website->Asp.Net Configuration option in Visual Studio. A full list of settings and comments can be found in machine.config.comments usually located in \Windows\Microsoft.Net\Framework\v2.x\Config.

—>

```
<configuration>
    <appSettings/>
    <connectionStrings/>
    <system.web>
        <!—
        Set compilation debug="true" to insert debugging
        symbols into the compiled page. Because this
        affects performance, set this value to true only
        during development.
        Visual Basic options:
            Set strict="true" to disallow all data type conversions
            where data loss can occur.
            Set explicit="true" to force declaration of all
variables.
          —>
            <compilation debug="false" strict="false"
explicit="true" />
            <pages>
                <namespaces>
                    <clear />

    <add namespace="System" />
        <add namespace="System.Collections" />
        <add namespace="System.Collections.Specialized" />
        <add namespace="System.Configuration" />
        <add namespace="System.Text" />
        <add namespace="System.Text.RegularExpressions" />
        <add namespace="System.Web" />
        <add namespace="System.Web.Caching" />
```

```
    <add namespace="System.Web.SessionState" />
    <add namespace="System.Web.Security" />
    <add namespace="System.Web.Profile" />
    <add namespace="System.Web.UI" />
    <add namespace="System.Web.UI.WebControls" />
    <add namespace="System.Web.UI.WebControls.WebParts" />
    <add namespace="System.Web.UI.HtmlControls" />
      </namespaces>
      </pages>

  <!-
  The <authentication> section enables configuration
            of the security authentication mode used by
            ASP.NET to identify an incoming user.
        ->
        <authentication mode="Windows" />

  <!-
  The <customErrors> section enables configuration
  of what to do if/when an unhandled error occurs
  during the execution of a request. Specifically,
  it enables developers to configure html error pages
  to be displayed in place of a error stack trace.

  <customErrors                          mode="RemoteOnly"
defaultRedirect="GenericErrorPage.htm">

  <error statusCode="403" redirect="NoAccess.htm" />
  <error statusCode="404" redirect="FileNotFound.htm" />
     </customErrors>
     ->
     </system.web>
  </configuration>
```

You can check all files in Solution Explorer window

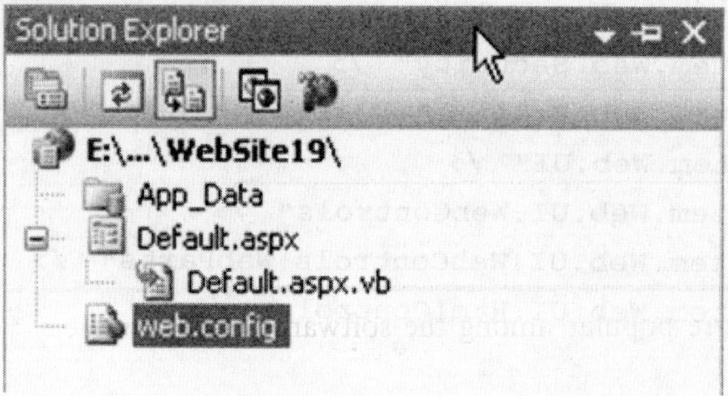
Solution Explorer
E:\...\WebSite19\
App_Data
Default.aspx
Default.aspx.vb
web.config

2 ADO.Net and ASP.Net

INTRODUCTION

The features which make ADO.Net more popular among the software developers are:

- Statelessness
- XML integration
- Scalability

To work with ADO.NET you need to understand following objects:

- Connection
- Command
- DataAdapter
- DataReader
- DataSet

Inside a DataSet you can find tables, columns, views, etc., but DataSet is not aware of the location or source of the data. You can say this that DataSet works as a standalone entity. DataSet is used to store and program against the relational data, flat data and XML data.

DataAdapter role is to provide connectivity with database. DataAdapter also plays the role of mediator for retrieving and saving the data between DataSet and data source. Since DataSet does not know about the source of the data, so you have to manage the provider which connects and fills the DataSet.

You need to understand SQL Server.Net data provider and OLE DB data provider. SQL Server.Net data provider deals with Microsoft SQL Server and OLE DB data provider deals with any OLE DB provider. Both provide following objects:

Connection

This is used for database connection and transaction

Command

This is used for giving SQL commands

DataAdapter

It is used for retrieving and saving the data between DataSet and data source.

DataReader

From a SQL Server data source it is used to read a forward-only stream of data records

When you deal with SQL Server.Net data provider you have to use System.Data. ...SQLClient class and when you deal with OLE DB data provider you deal with System.Data..OleDb class.

This is the right time to show you one practical example, that will do database connection and then we will add Grid view control onto the web form to display that data.

For this perform the following steps:

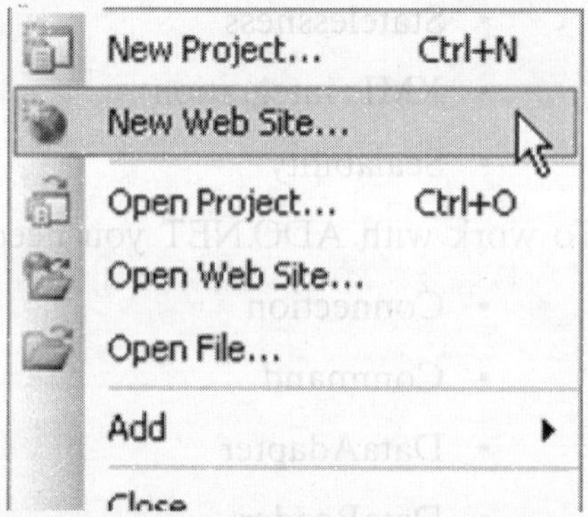

1. Start Visual Studio 2005
2. On menu bar click File
3. Click New Web Site...
4. You will get following window:
5. Select ASP.NET Web Site
6. In Language field select Visual Basic
7. Click OK

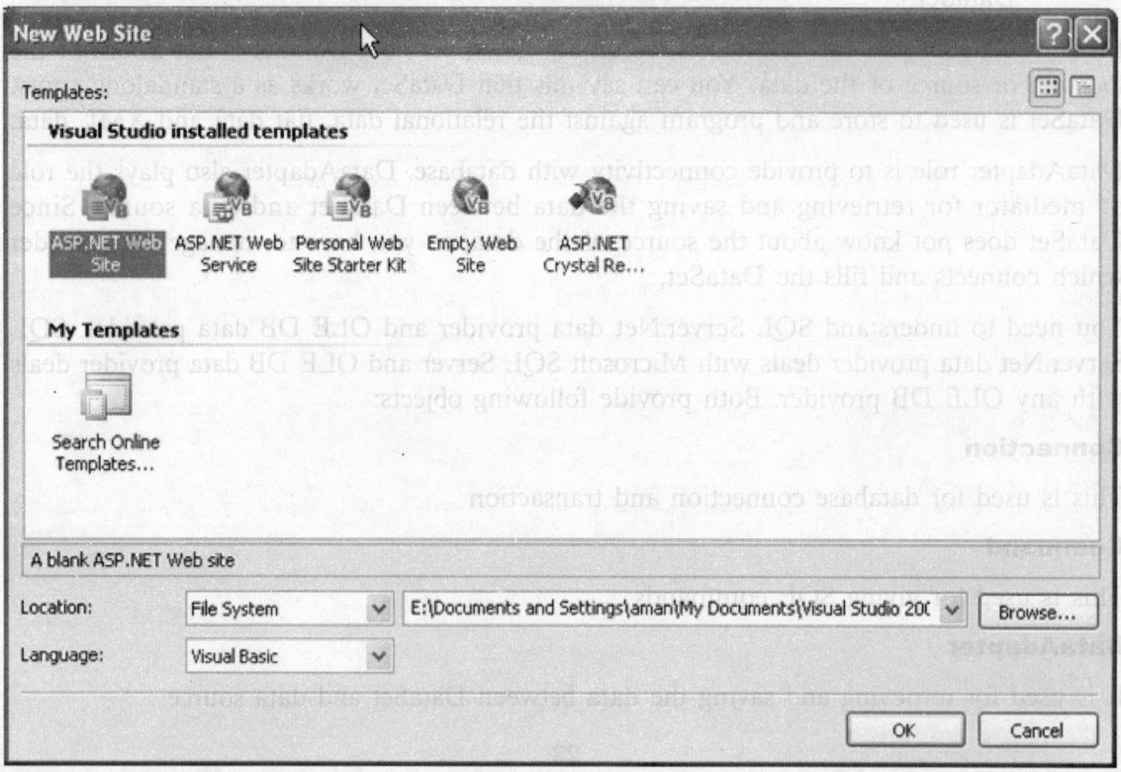

8. To bring Server Explorer, on menu bar click View
9. Click Server Explorer
10. To bring Solution Explorer, on menu bar click View
11. Click Solution Explorer
12. At present your screen may appear like this:

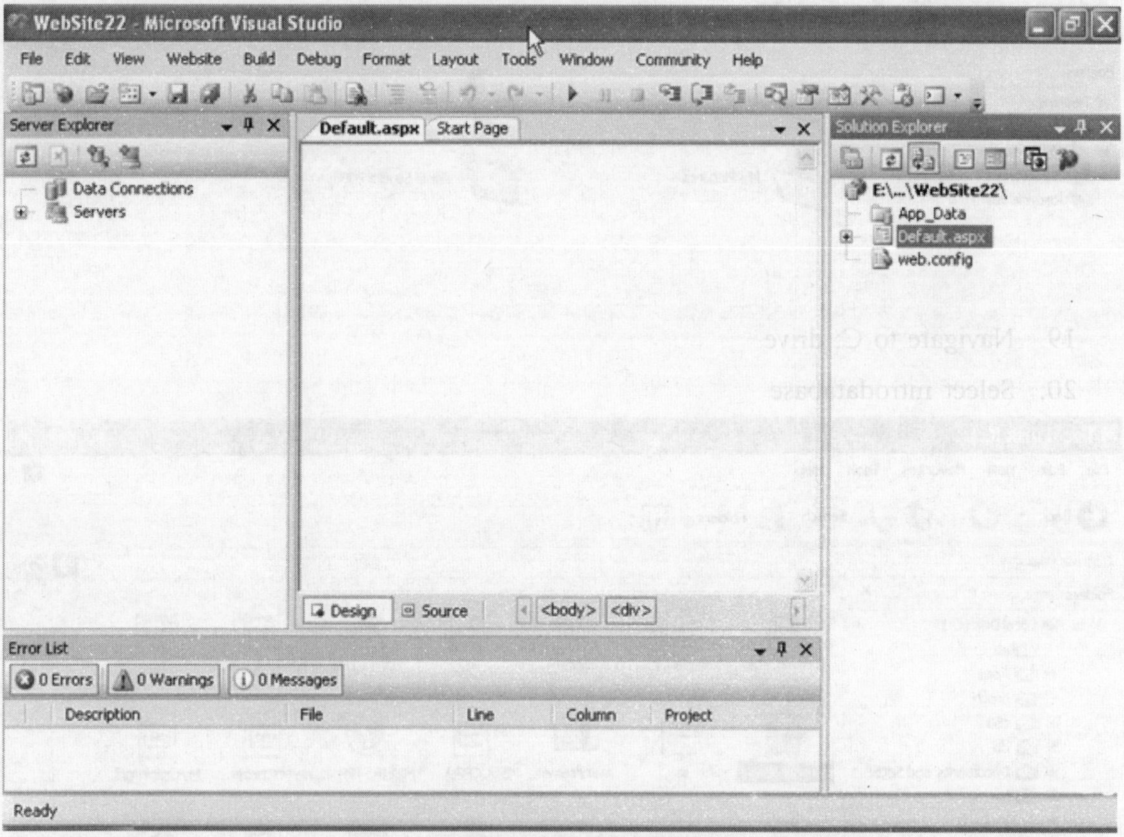

13. Now open Window Explorer, for this click on Start button
14. Now click on Run

15. You will get Run dialog box.

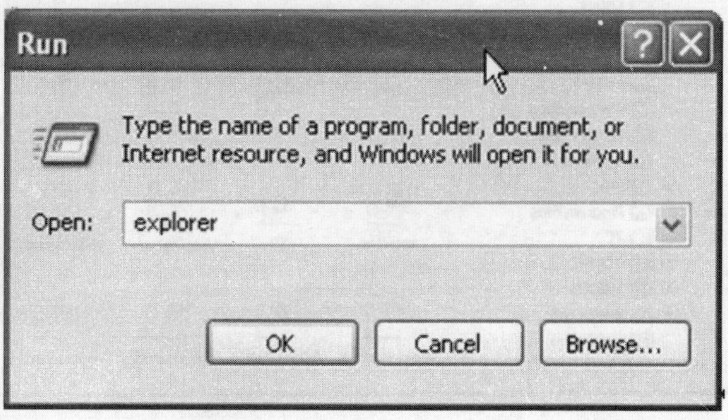

16. In Open field type explorer
17. Click OK
18. You will get Window Explorer

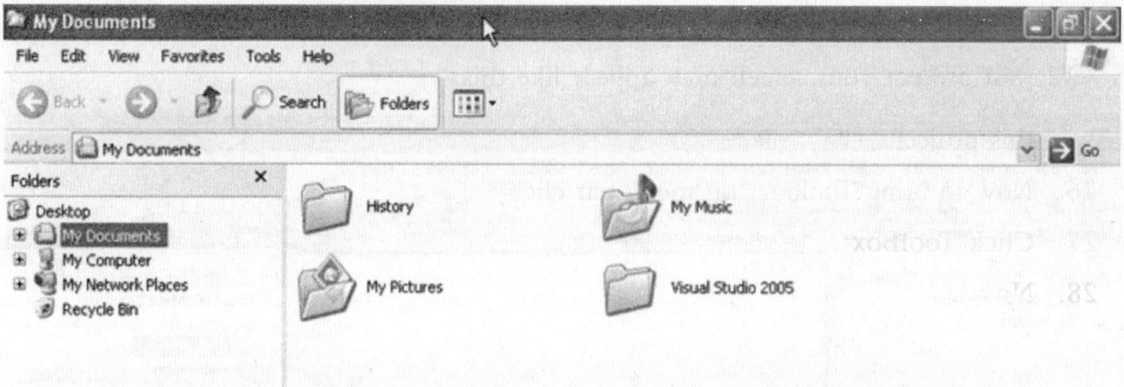

19. Navigate to C: drive
20. Select introdatabase

21. Now right-click on introdatabase
22. Click Copy
23. Now switch back to Visual Studio 2005
24. Select the Solution Explorer by clicking on its title bar.
25. Now press Ctrl + V shortcut key on your keyboard, it will copy the ms access database file and make this a part of this project.

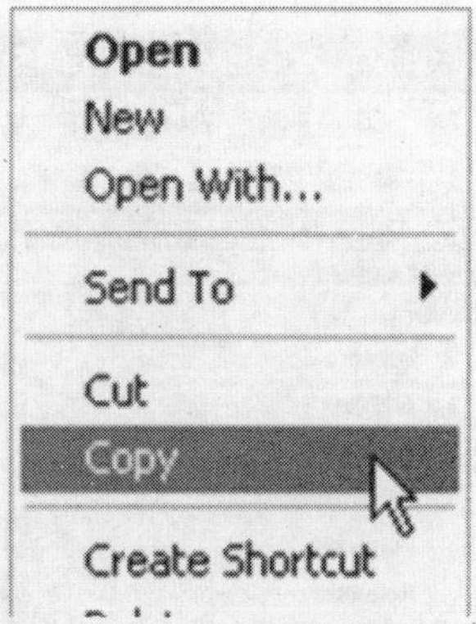

26. Now to bring Toolbox, on menu bar click View
27. Click ToolBox
28. Now in ToolBox in Data section, select GridView
29. Now add the GridView control onto the web form.
30. Now position your mouse over gridview control

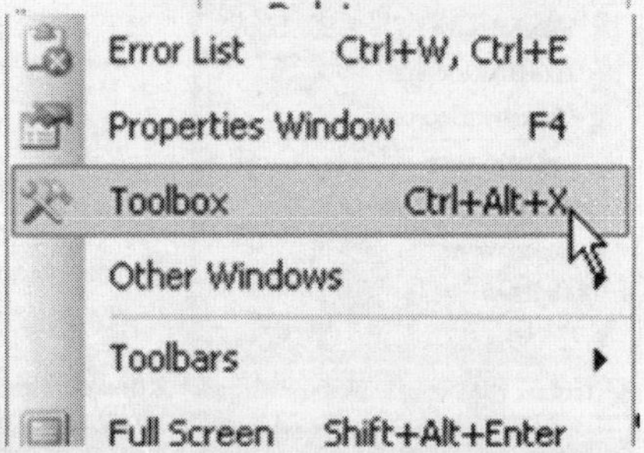

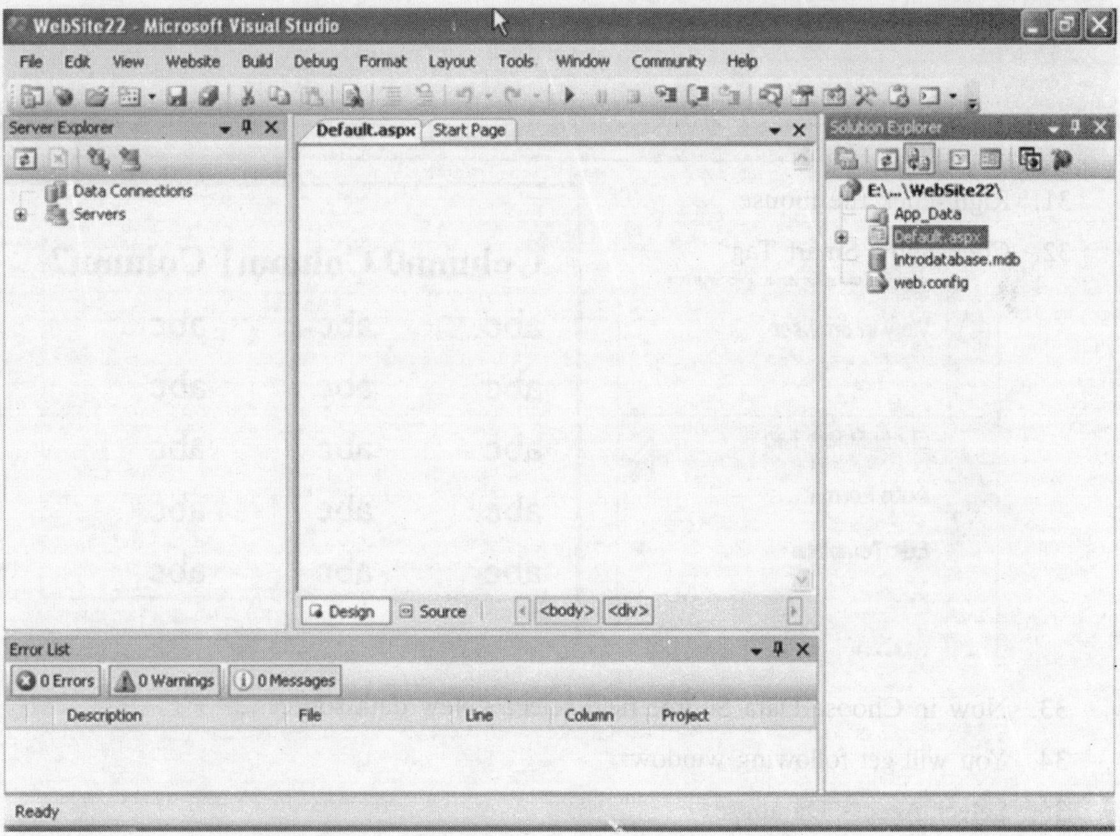

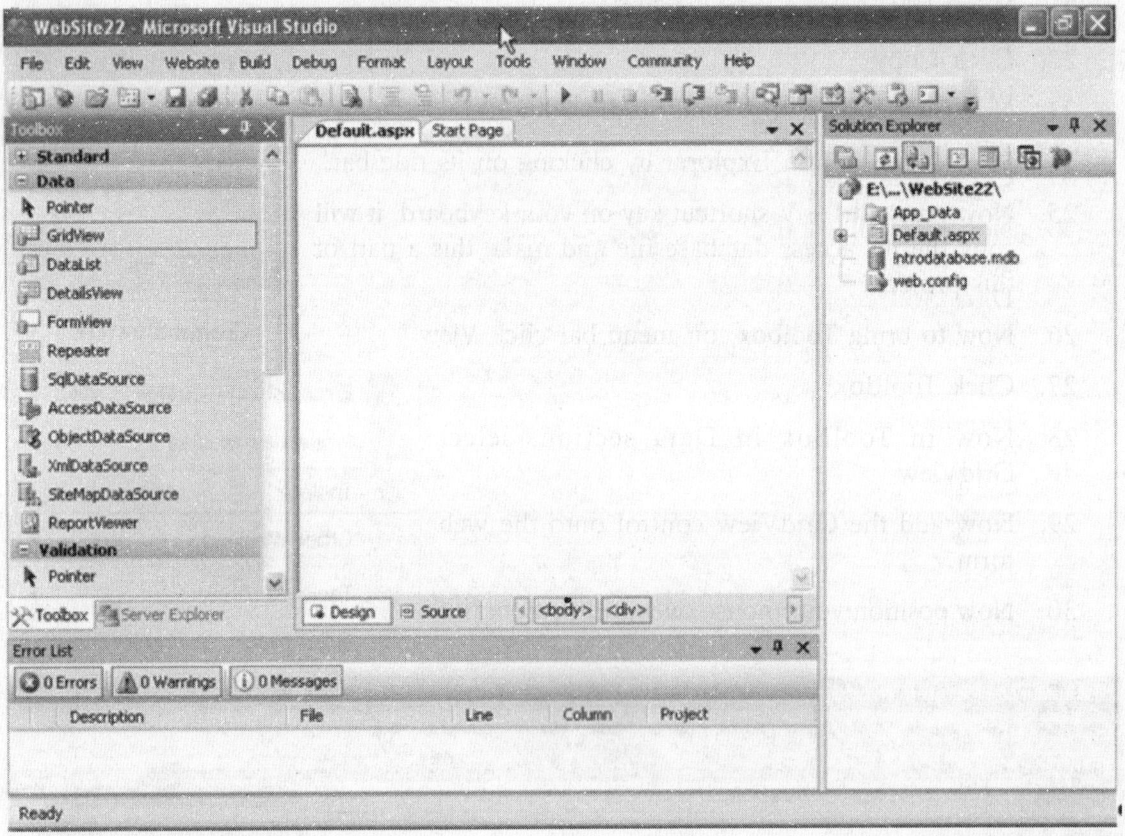

31. Right-click the mouse
32. Click Show Smart Tag

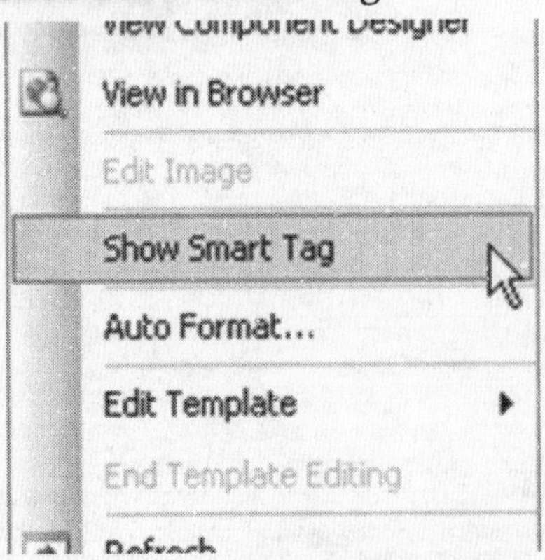

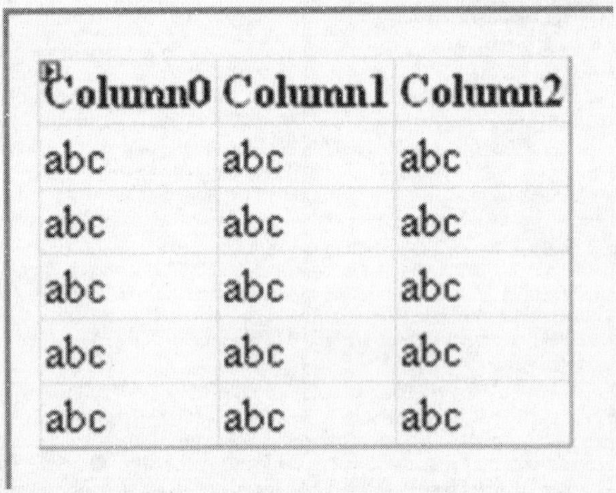

33. Now in Choose Data Source field select <New data source…>
34. You will get following window:
35. Select Access Database

36. Keep default ID name for the data source
37. Click OK
38. Now you will get Configure Data Source window
39. Click on Browse button
40. You will get following window
41. Select the introdatabase.mdb
42. Click OK
43. Click Next

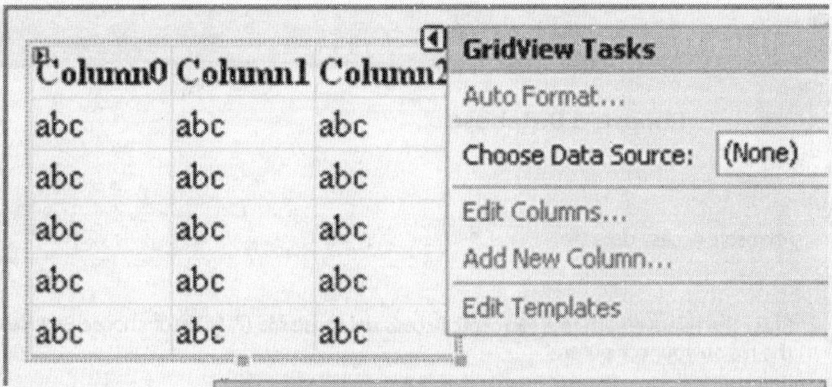

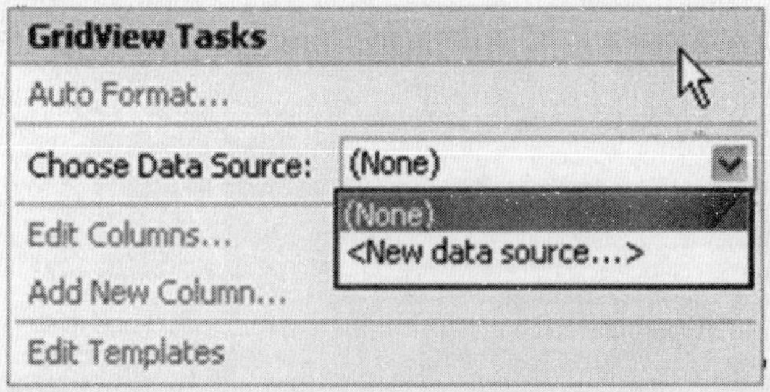

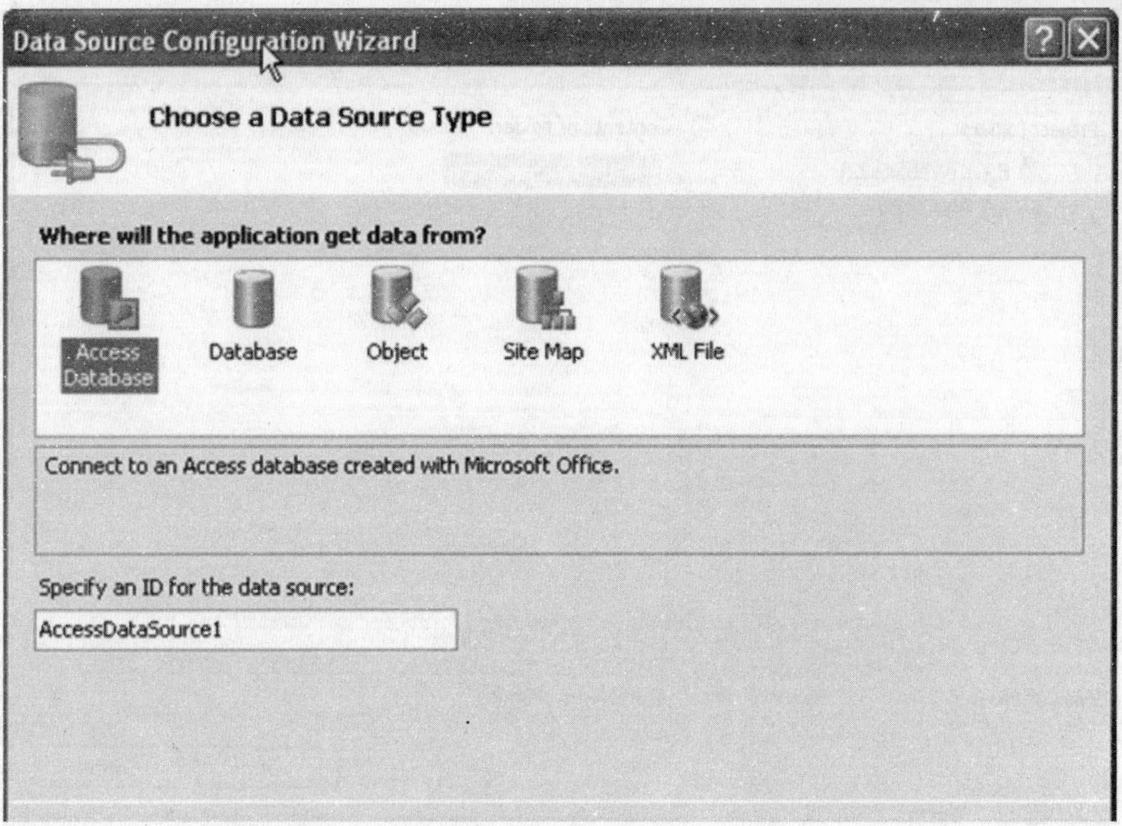

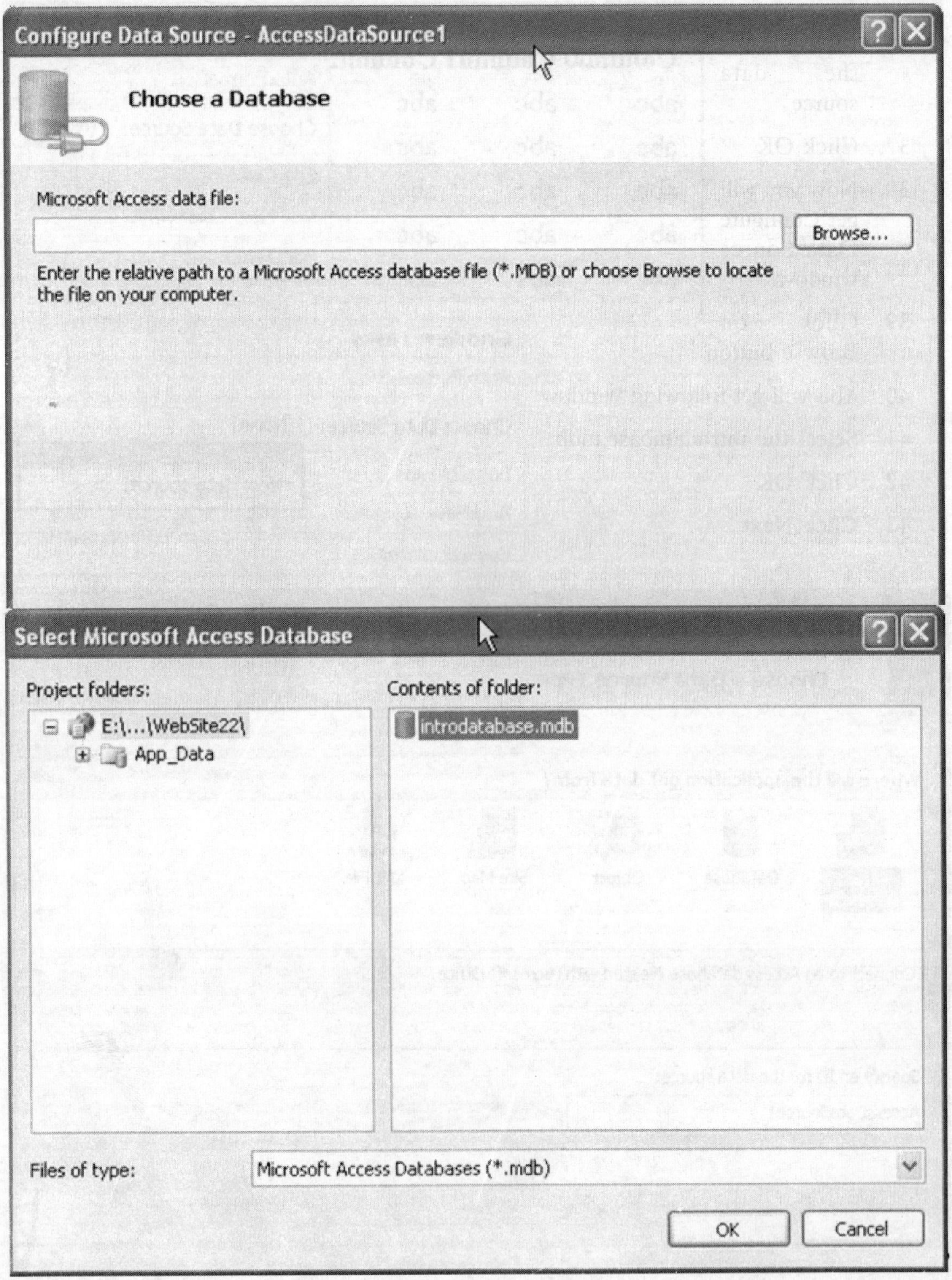
Configure Data Source - AccessDataSource1
Choose a Database
Microsoft Access data file:
Browse...
Enter the relative path to a Microsoft Access database file (*.MDB) or choose Browse to locate the file on your computer.
Select Microsoft Access Database
Project folders:
Contents of folder:
E:\...\WebSite22\
App_Data
introdatabase.mdb
Files of type:
Microsoft Access Databases (*.mdb)
OK
Cancel

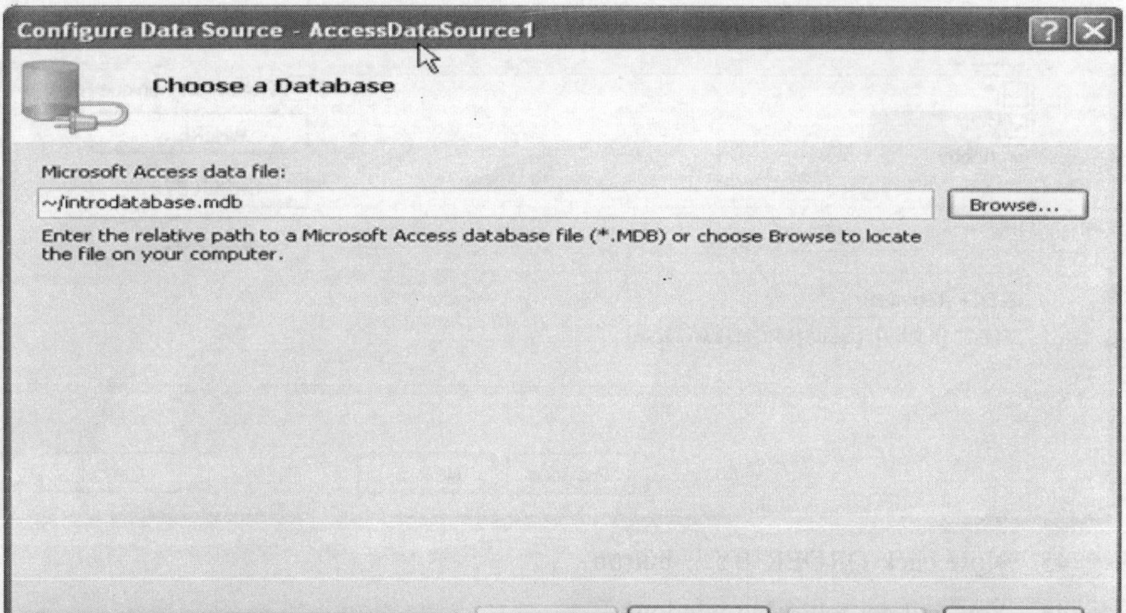
Configure Data Source - AccessDataSource1
Choose a Database
Microsoft Access data file:
~/introdatabase.mdb
Browse...
Enter the relative path to a Microsoft Access database file (*.MDB) or choose Browse to locate the file on your computer.

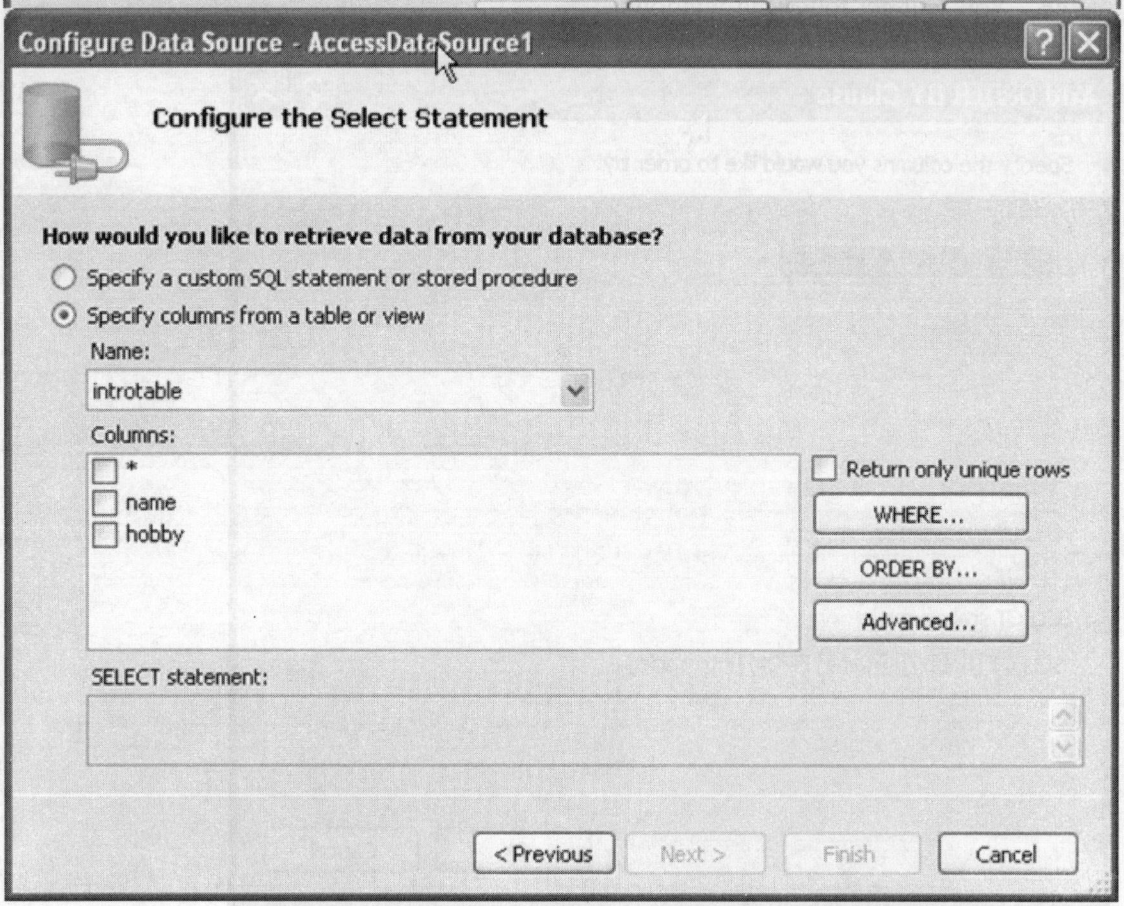
Configure Data Source - AccessDataSource1
Configure the Select Statement
How would you like to retrieve data from your database?
Specify a custom SQL statement or stored procedure
Specify columns from a table or view
Name:
introtable
Columns:
*
name
hobby
Return only unique rows
WHERE...
ORDER BY...
Advanced...
SELECT statement:
< Previous
Next >
Finish
Cancel

44. Select both fields name and hobby

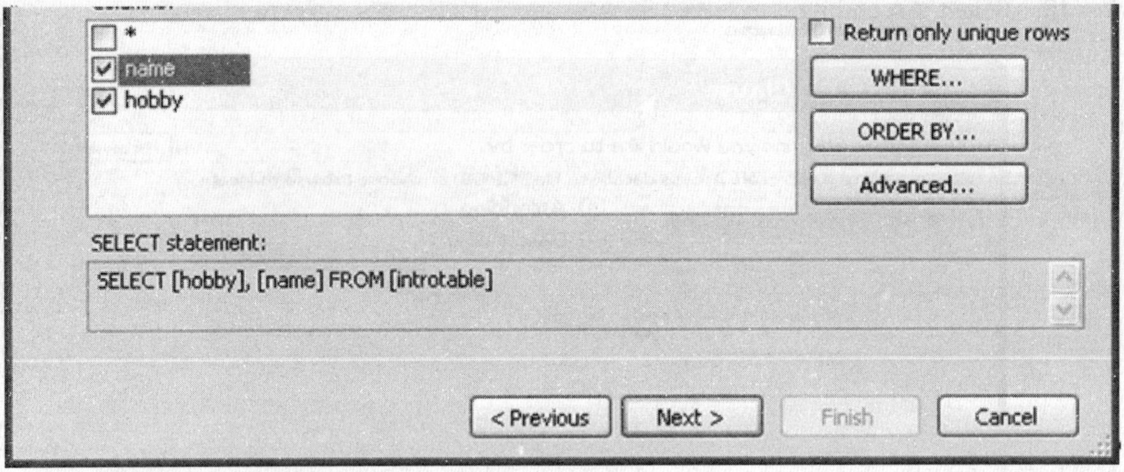

45. Now click ORDER BY... button

46. You will get following window:

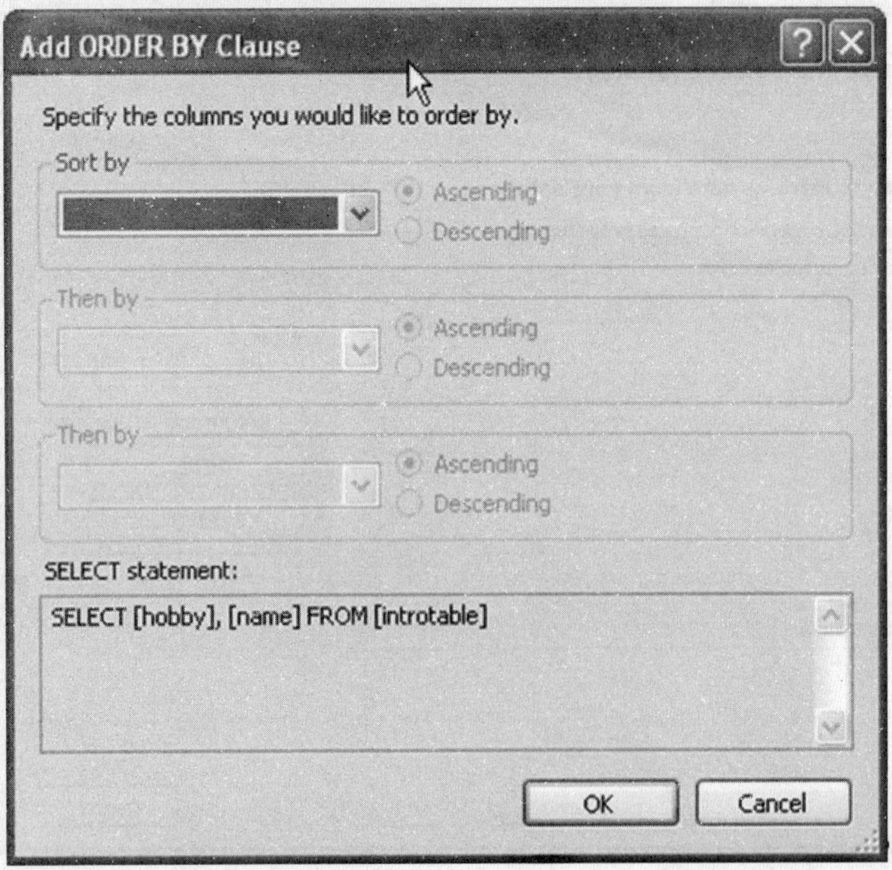

47. In Sort by field select name

48. Select Ascending

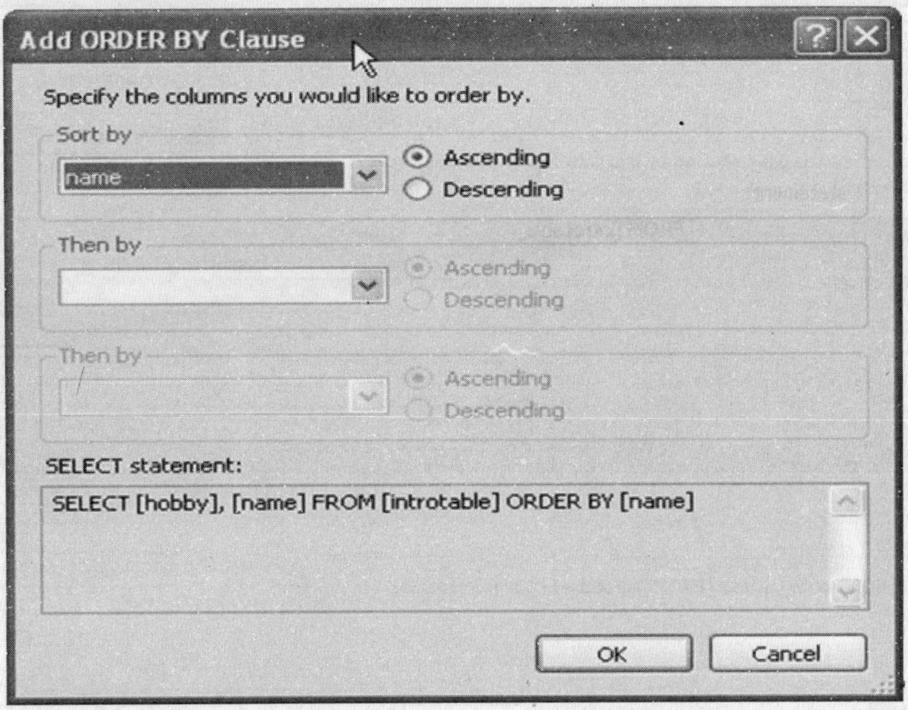

49. Click OK

50. You can see the query at bottom

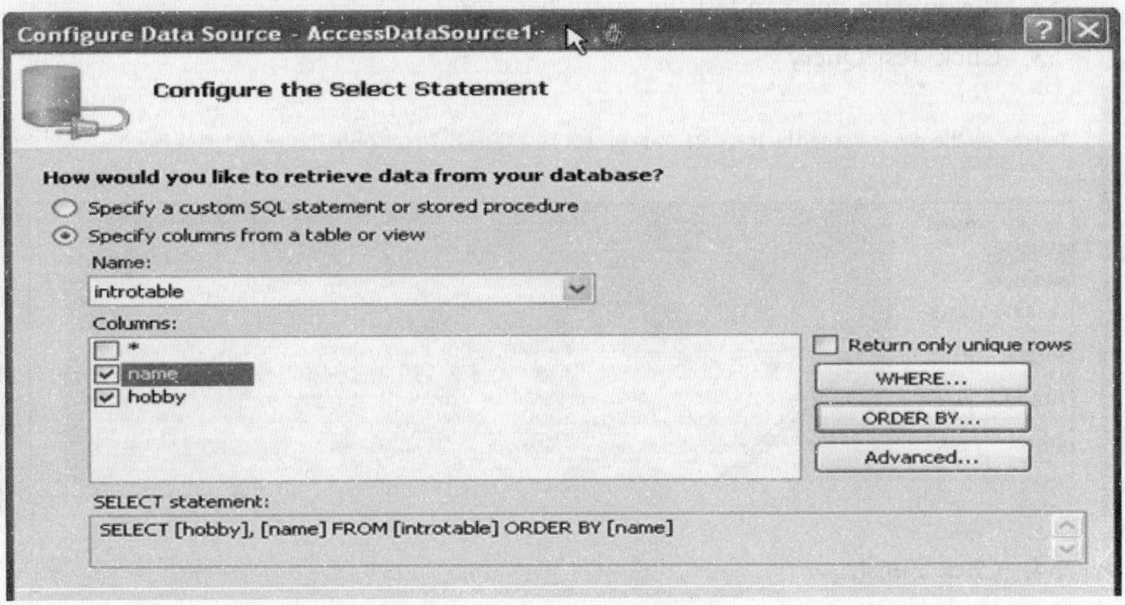

51. Click Next

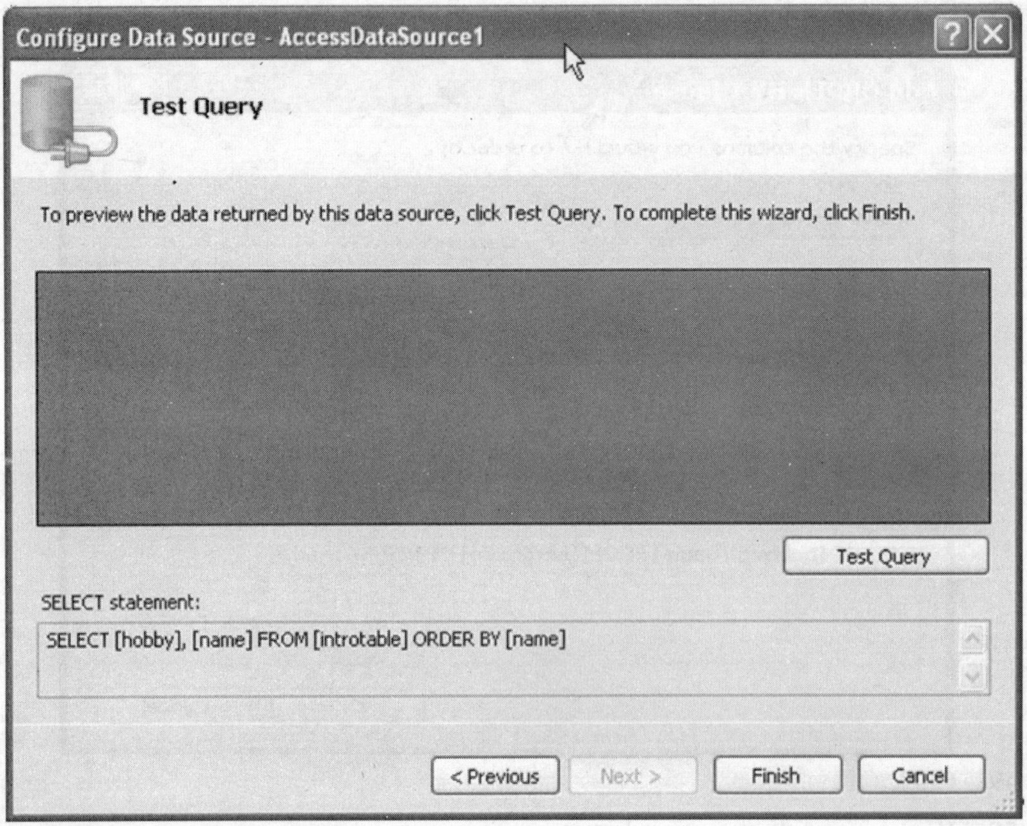

52. If you wish you can test the query here too.

53. Click Test Query

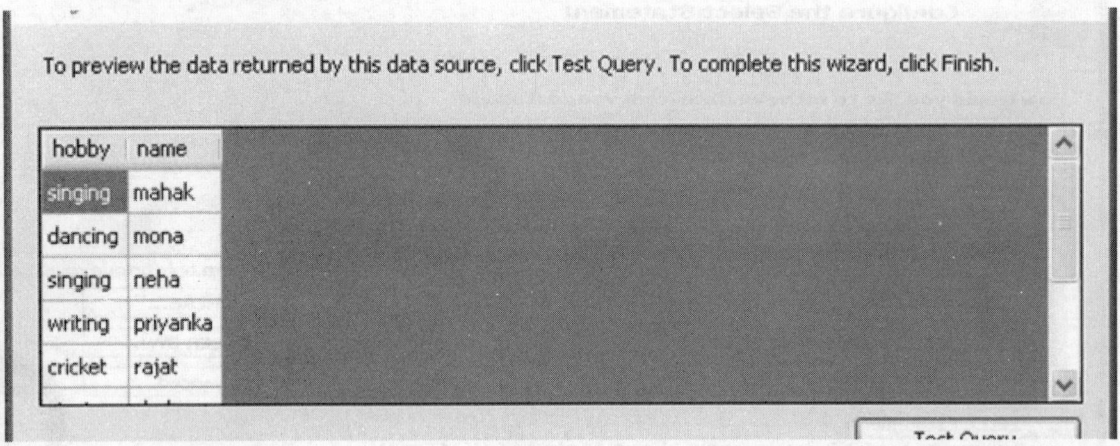

54. Click Finish

55. You will not see the result here in design time

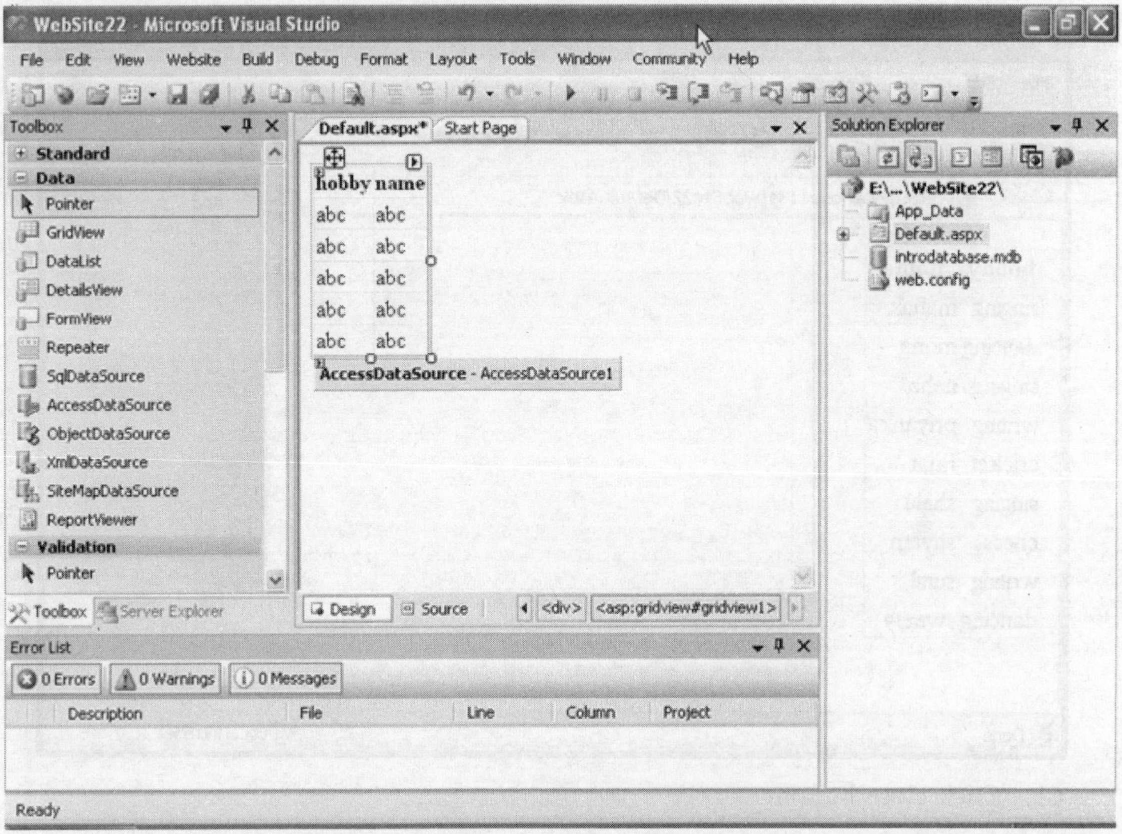

56. Now this is the right time to test this program, press F5 key on your keyboard

57. You will get following message

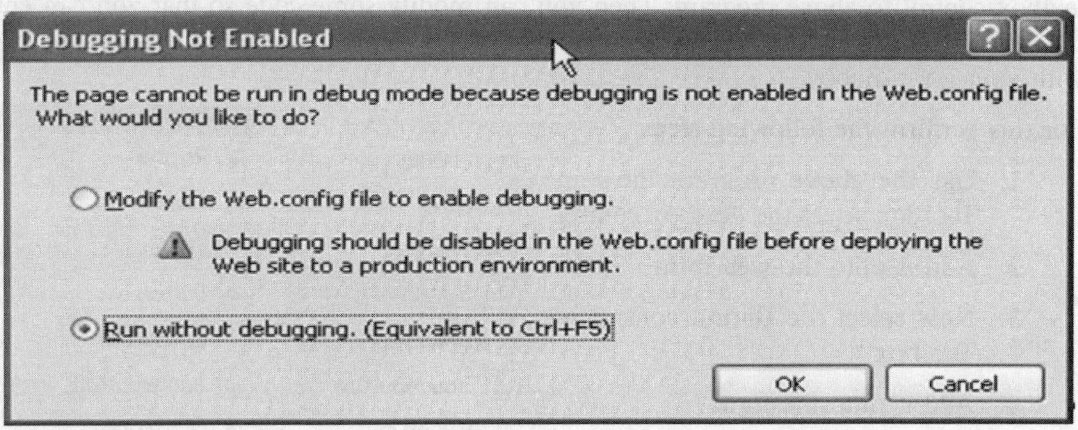

58. Select the second option.

59. Click OK

60. You will get following output

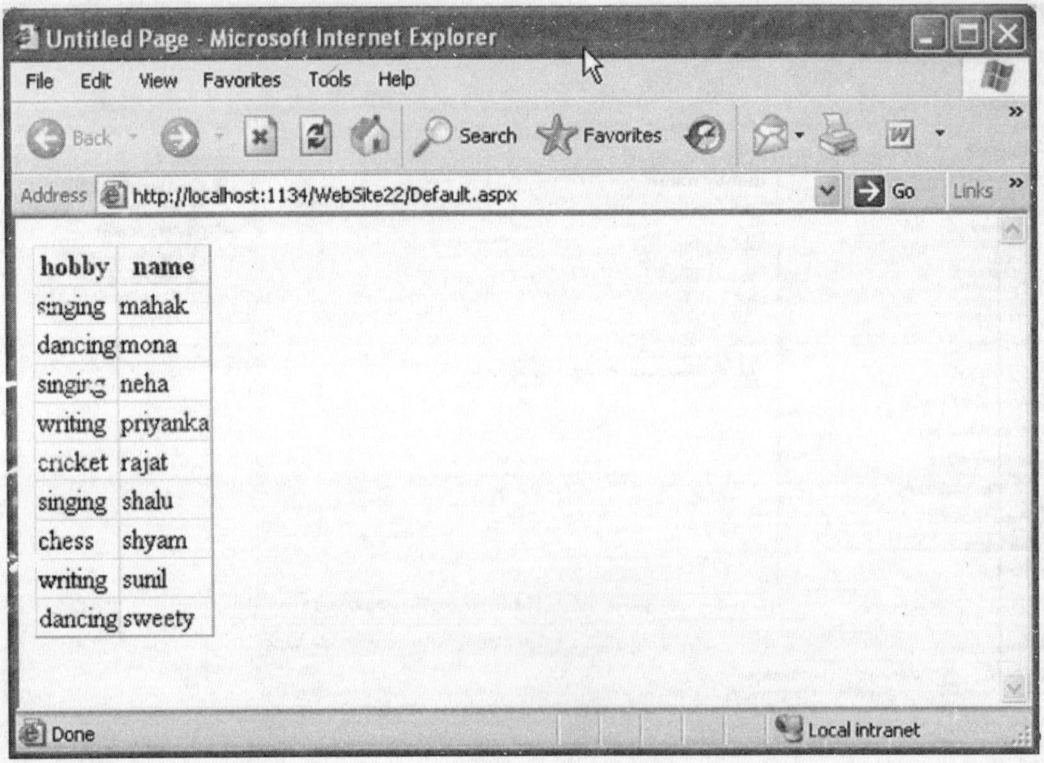

61. Click close button

Parameterized Filter

At this stage you can specify the criteria for a particular field. For example you can add the textbox control to above program. Then you can modify some code so that you can enter the hobby records and only those records should get display whose hobbies are matched with your given hobby.

For this perform the following steps:

1. Use the above program, now in ToolBox select the Textbox control
2. Add it onto the web form
3. Now select the Button control in Toolbox
4. Add it onto the form
5. Your screen should appear like this as shown in below figure

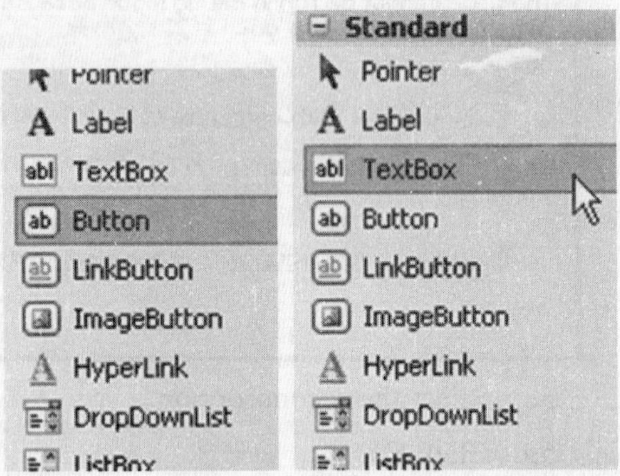

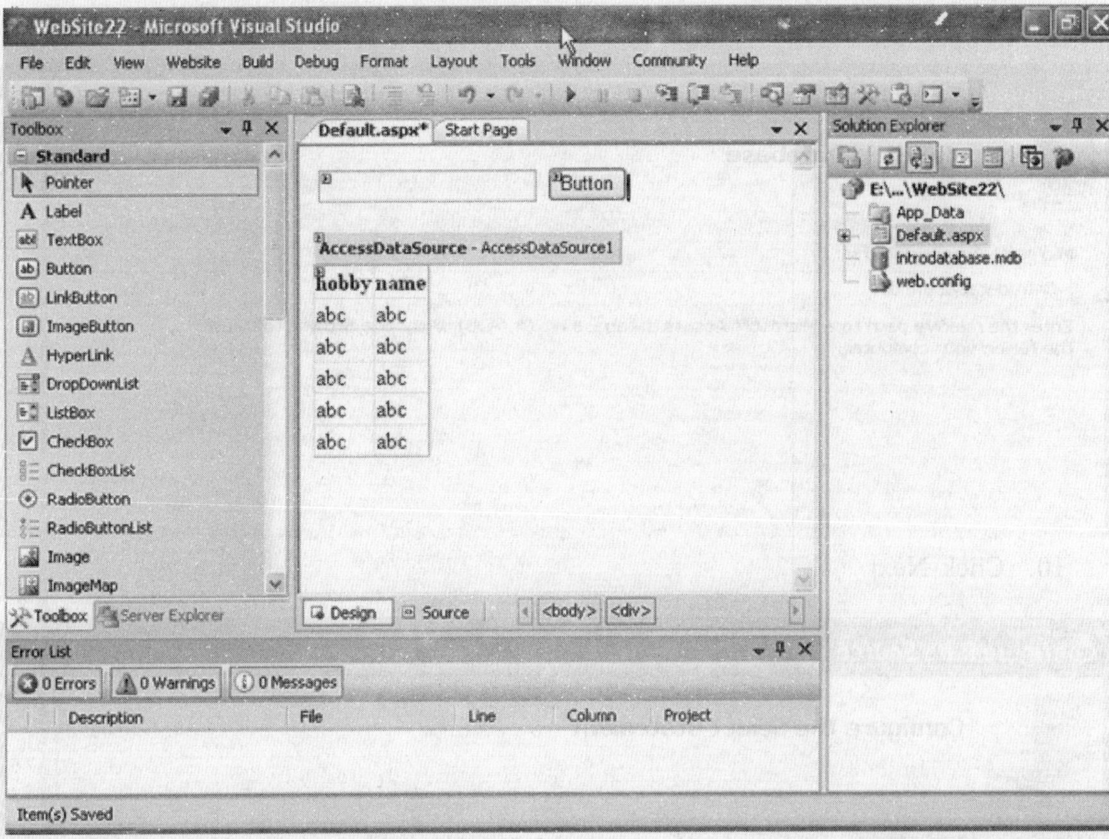

6. Now right click on the Gridview control
7. Click Show Smart Tag
8. Now click Configure Data Source...

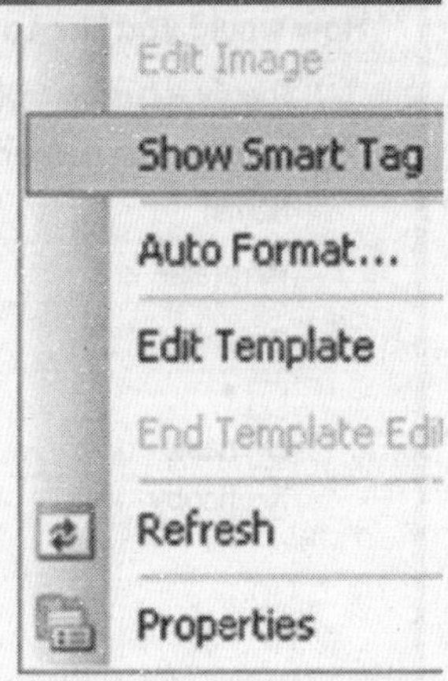

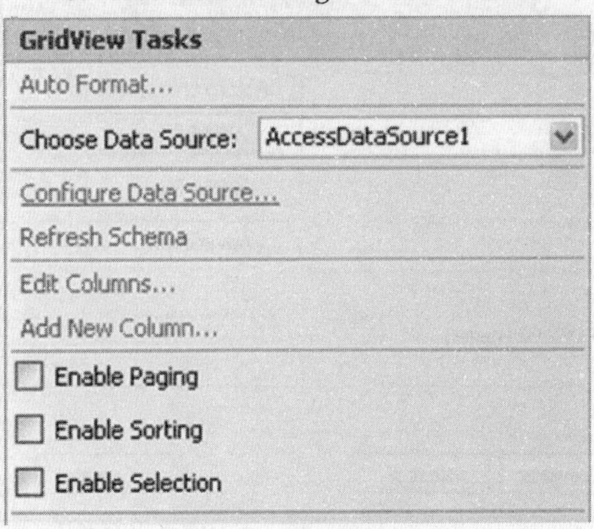

9. You will get following window

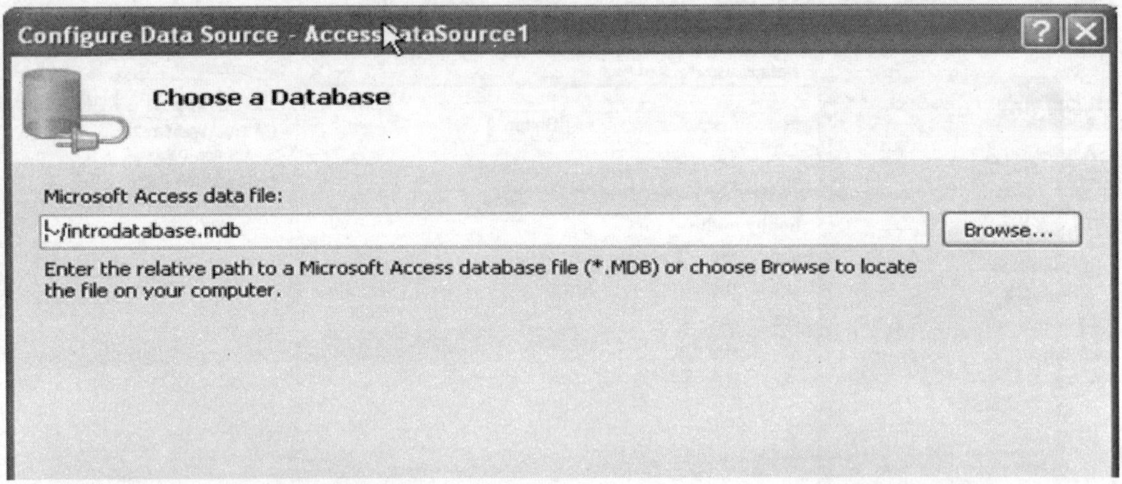

10. Click Next

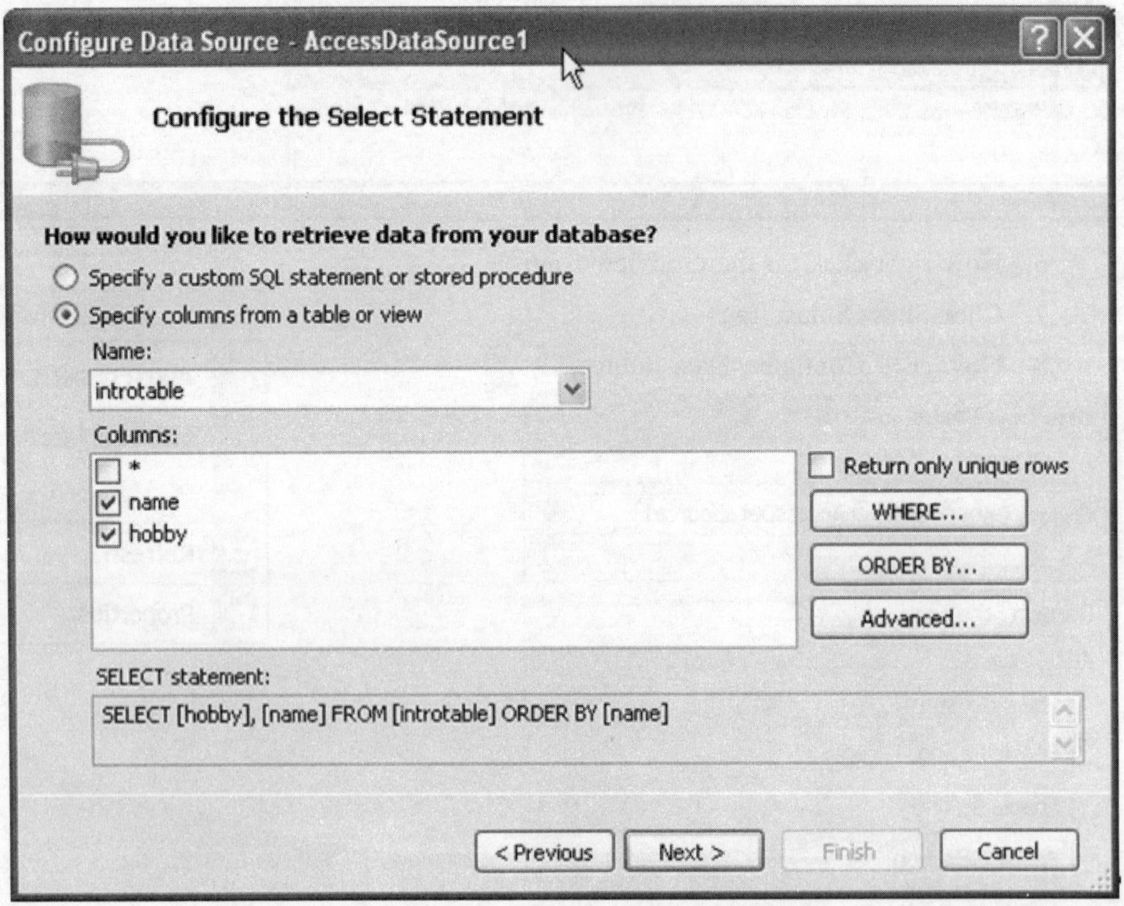

11. Now click Where... button
12. You will get following window:

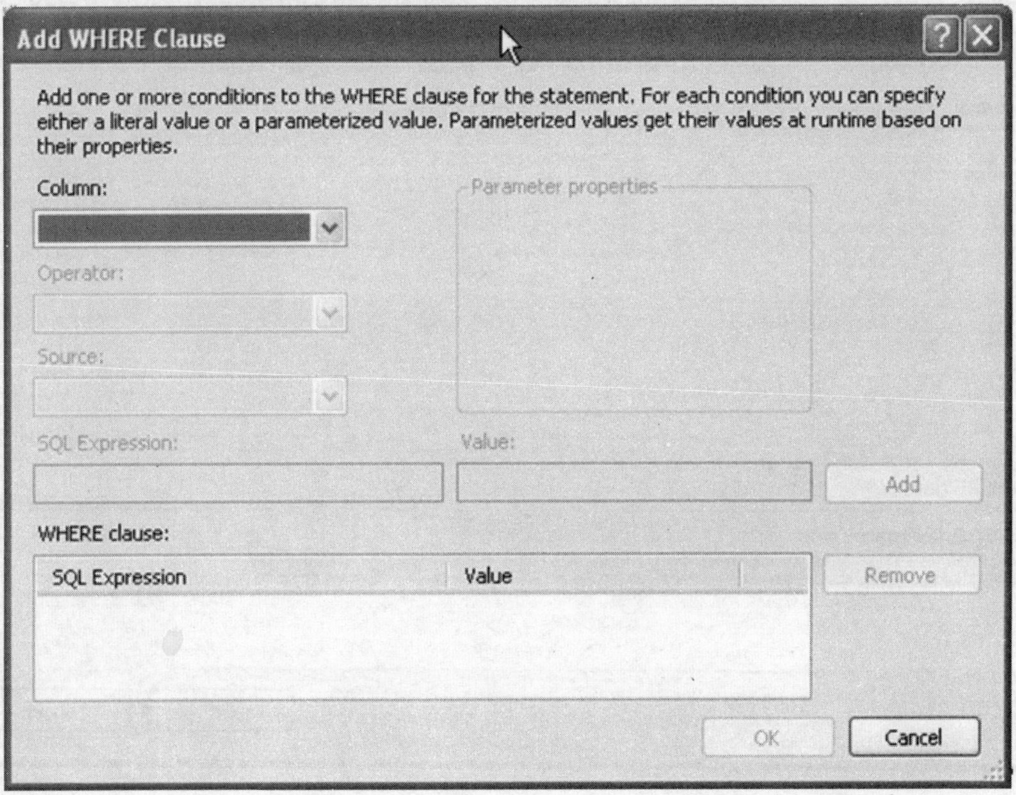

13. In Column field select hobby
14. In Operator field select =
15. In Source field select Control
16. In Control ID field select TextBox1
17. Click ADD
18. Click OK
19. Click Finish
20. Now you are back to design time.
21. Press Ctrl + F5 to run the program
22. At present you will get following output:
23. In textbox type writing

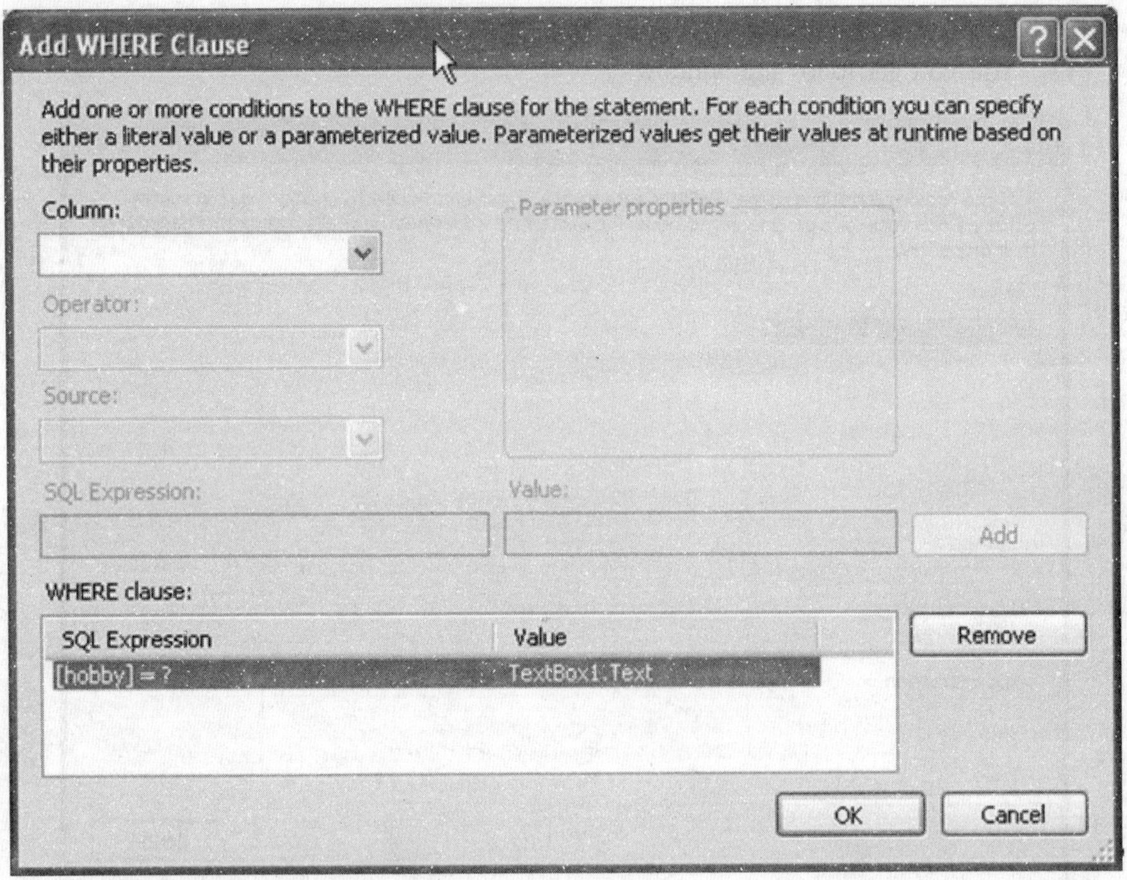
Add WHERE Clause
Add one or more conditions to the WHERE clause for the statement. For each condition you can specify either a literal value or a parameterized value. Parameterized values get their values at runtime based on their properties.
Column:
Operator:
Source:
Parameter properties
SQL Expression:
Value:
Add
WHERE clause:
SQL Expression
Value
[hobby] = ?
TextBox1.Text
Remove
OK
Cancel

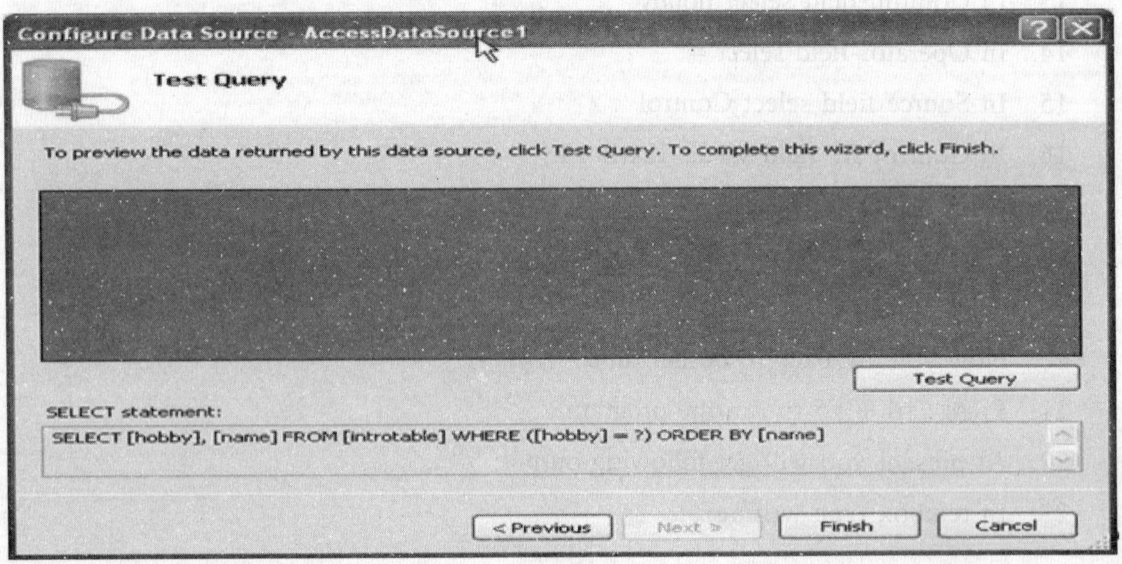
Configure Data Source - AccessDataSource1
Test Query
To preview the data returned by this data source, click Test Query. To complete this wizard, click Finish.
Test Query
SELECT statement:
SELECT [hobby], [name] FROM [introtable] WHERE ([hobby] = ?) ORDER BY [name]
< Previous
Next >
Finish
Cancel

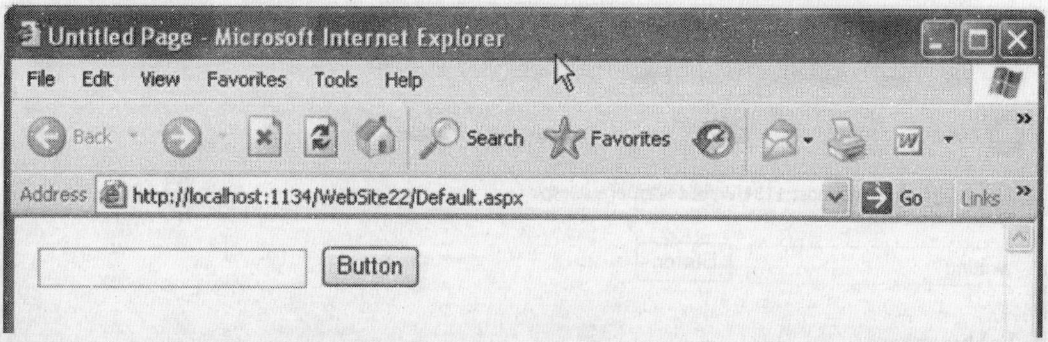

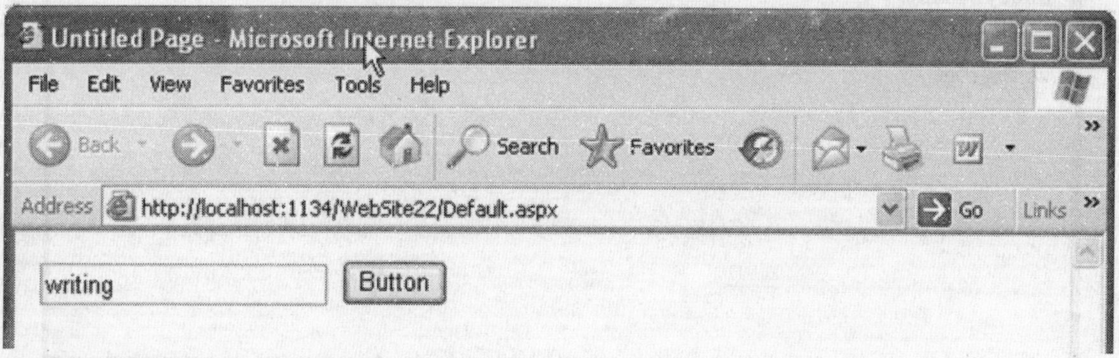

24. Click Button control
25. You will get following output:

Following is the source code:

— Default.aspx —

```
<%@  Page  Language="VB"  AutoEventWireup="false"
CodeFile="Default.aspx.vb" Inherits="_Default" %>
<!DOCTYPE html PUBLIC "-//W3C//DTD XHTML 1.0 Transitional//
EN" "http://www.w3.org/TR/xhtml1/DTD/xhtml1-transitional.dtd">
<html xmlns="http://www.w3.org/1999/xhtml" >
<head runat="server">
<title>Untitled Page</title>
</head>
<body>
<form id="form1" runat="server">
<div>
      <asp:TextBox ID="TextBox1" runat="server"></
asp:TextBox> 
     <asp:Button ID="Button1" runat="server" Text="Button" /
><br />
```

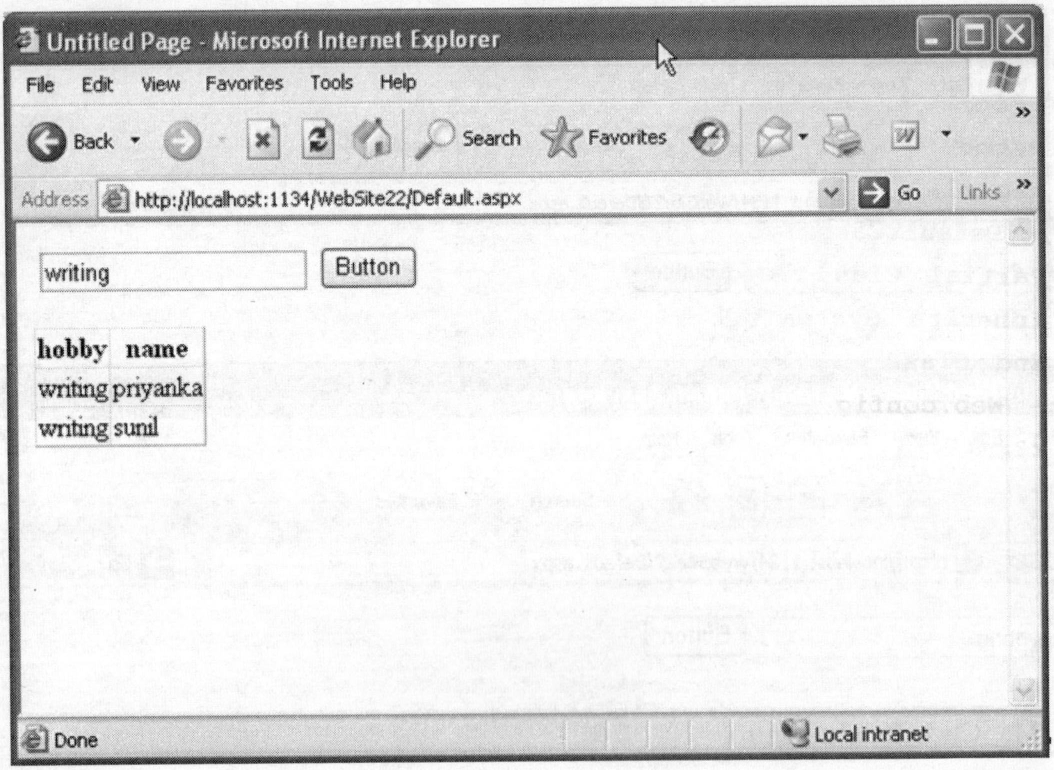


```
    <br />
    <asp:AccessDataSource ID="AccessDataSource1" runat="server"
DataFile="~/introdatabase.mdb"
            SelectCommand="SELECT [hobby], [name] FROM
[introtable] WHERE ([hobby] = ?) ORDER BY [name]">
            <SelectParameters>
                <asp:ControlParameter ControlID="TextBox1"
Name="hobby" PropertyName="Text" Type="String" />
            </SelectParameters>
        </asp:AccessDataSource>
        <asp:GridView ID="GridView1" runat="server"
AutoGenerateColumns="False" DataSourceID="AccessDataSource1">
            <Columns>
                <asp:BoundField DataField="hobby"
HeaderText="hobby" SortExpression="hobby" />
                <asp:BoundField DataField="name"
HeaderText="name" SortExpression="name" />
            </Columns>
```

```
    </asp:GridView>
</div>
</form>
</body>
</html>
– Default.aspx.vb –
Partial Class _Default
Inherits System.Web.UI.Page
End Class
– Web.config –
<?xml version="1.0"?>
<!–
Note: As an alternative to hand editing this file you can use
the web admin tool to configure settings for your application.
Use the Website->Asp.Net Configuration option in Visual Studio.
A full list of settings and comments can be found in
machine.config.comments usually located in
\Windows\Microsoft.Net\Framework\v2.x\Config
–>
<configuration>
<appSettings/>
<connectionStrings/>
<system.web>
<!–
Set compilation debug="true" to insert debugging symbols into
the compiled page. Because this affects performance, set this
value to true only during development.
    Visual Basic options:
      et strict="true" to disallow all data type conversions
      where data loss can occur.
     Set explicit="true" to force declaration of all variables.
    –>
<compilation debug="false" strict="false" explicit="true" />
    <pages>
        <namespaces>
      <clear />
```

```
<add namespace="System" />
<add namespace="System.Collections" />
<add namespace="System.Collections.Specialized" />
<add namespace="System.Configuration" />
<add namespace="System.Text" />
<add namespace="System.Text.RegularExpressions" />
<add namespace="System.Web" />
<add namespace="System.Web.Caching" />
<add namespace="System.Web.SessionState" />
<add namespace="System.Web.Security" />
<add namespace="System.Web.Profile" />
<add namespace="System.Web.UI" />
<add namespace="System.Web.UI.WebControls" />
<add namespace="System.Web.UI.WebControls.WebParts" />
<add namespace="System.Web.UI.HtmlControls" />
</namespaces>
</pages>
<!–
The <authentication> section enables configuration of the security authentication mode used by ASP.NET to identify an incoming user.
->
<authentication mode="Windows" />
<!–
The <customErrors> section enables configuration of what to do if/when an unhandled error occurs during the execution of a request. Specifically, it enables developers to configure html error pages to be displayed in place of a error stack trace.
<customErrors mode="RemoteOnly"
defaultRedirect="GenericErrorPage.htm">
<error statusCode="403" redirect="NoAccess.htm" />
<error statusCode="404" redirect="FileNotFound.htm" />
</customErrors>
->
</system.web>
</configuration>
```

3 Database Connectivity with Visual Basic 2005

INTRODUCTION

In the previous chapter you have seen the database connectivity and filtering using ASP.Net 2.0. In this chapter you will see how you can make the connection with Visual Basic 2005. This will help you in understanding Windows programming.

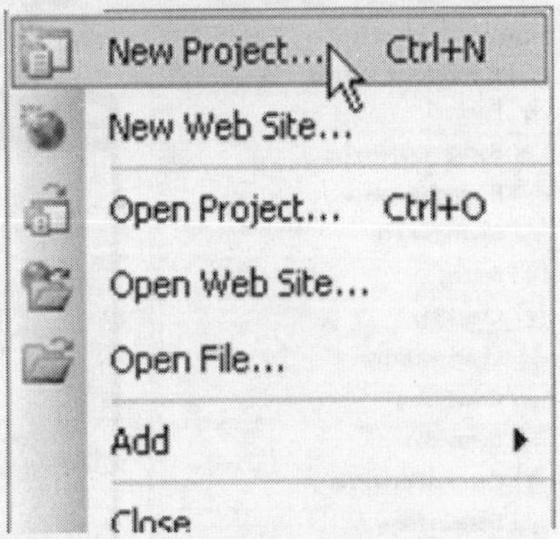

First of all we have to create a dataset. In the last chapter we had explained what is dataset?

Perform the following steps to do this:

1. Start Visual Studio 2005
2. On menu bar click File
3. Click New Project
4. You will get following window

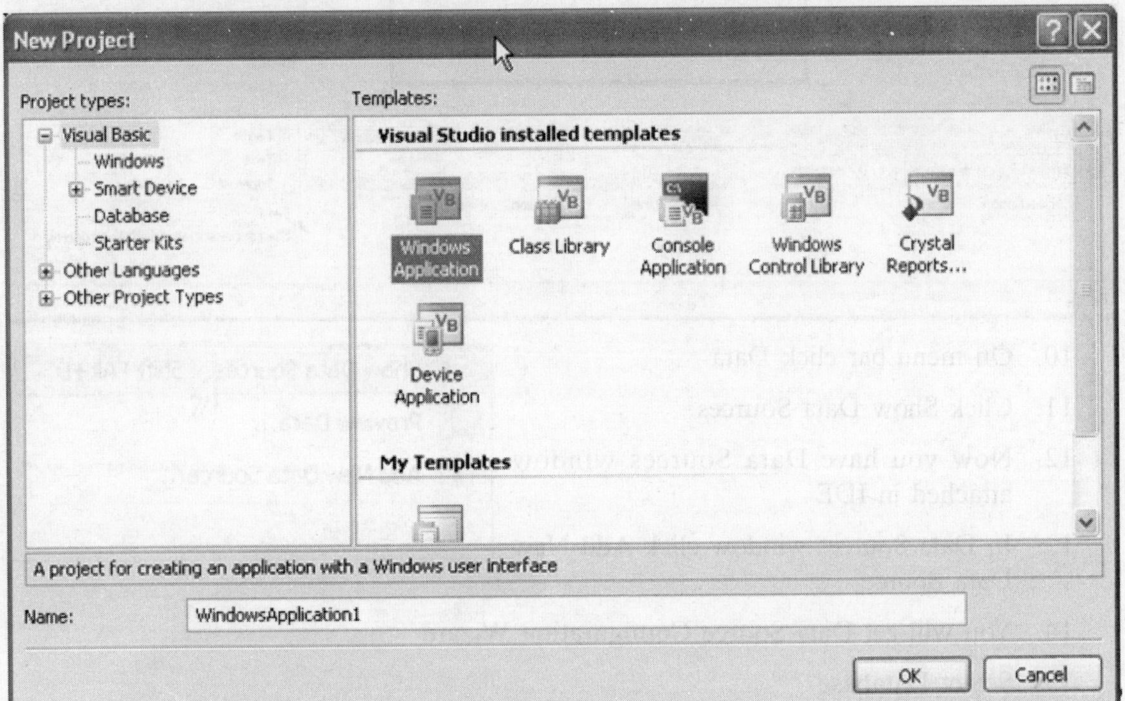

5. In Project types: select Visual Basic.
6. Under Templates select Windows Application
7. Keep default name.
8. Click OK
9. At present we have following scenario

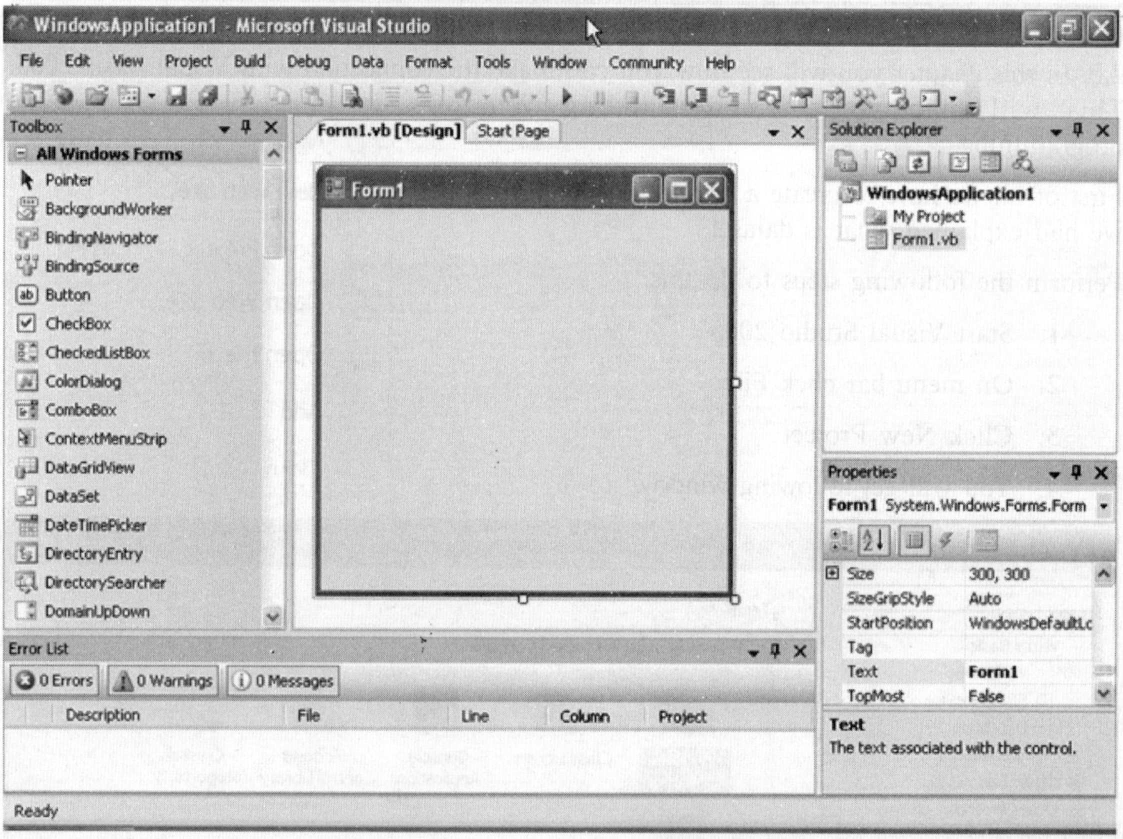

10. On menu bar click Data
11. Click Show Data Sources
12. Now you have Data Sources window attached in IDE
13. In Data Sources window click Add New Data Source

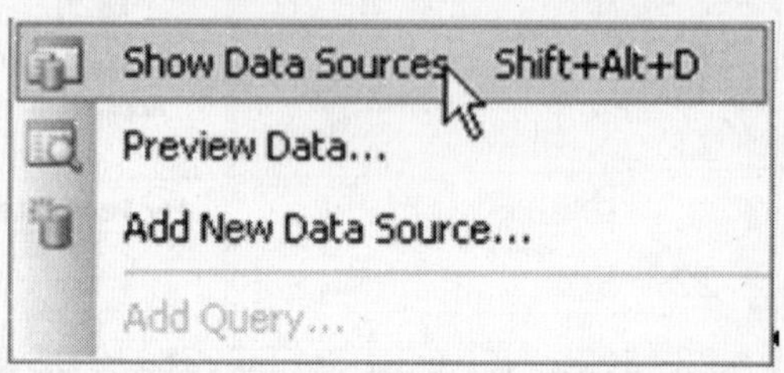

14. You will get Data Source Configuration Wizard
15. Select Database
16. Click Next

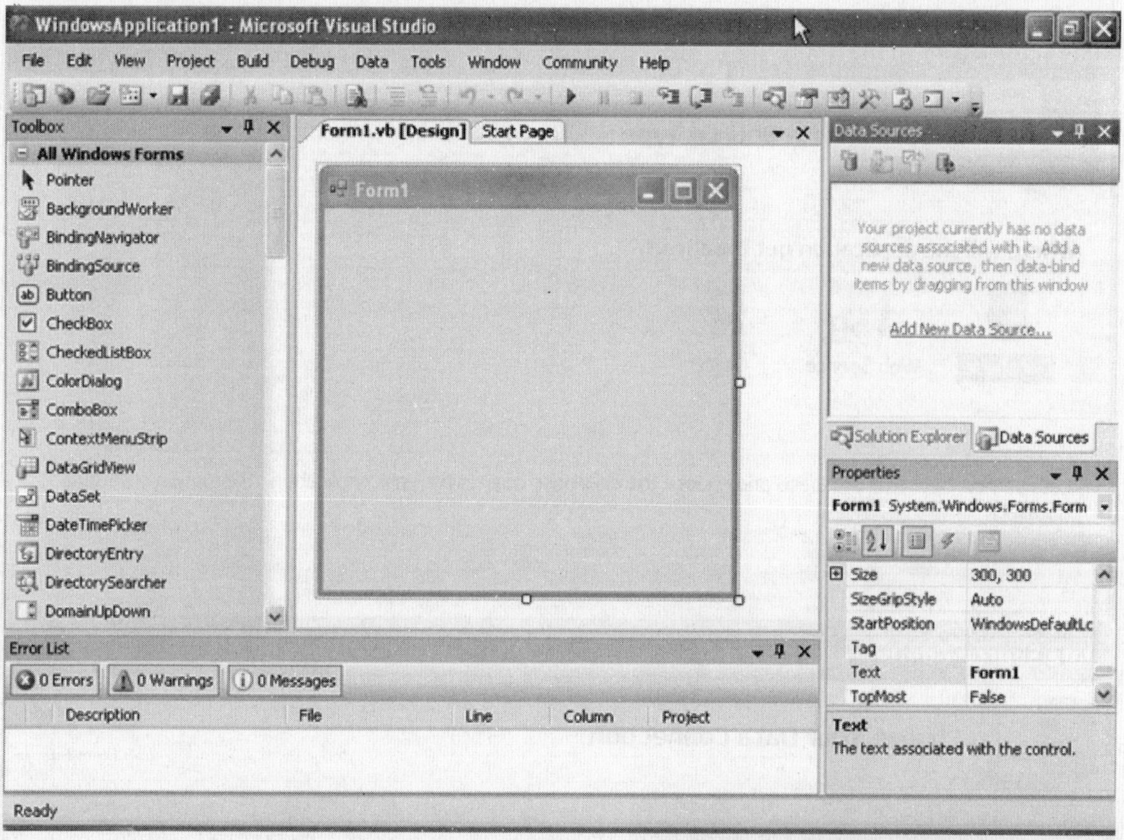

17. Now you will get following window

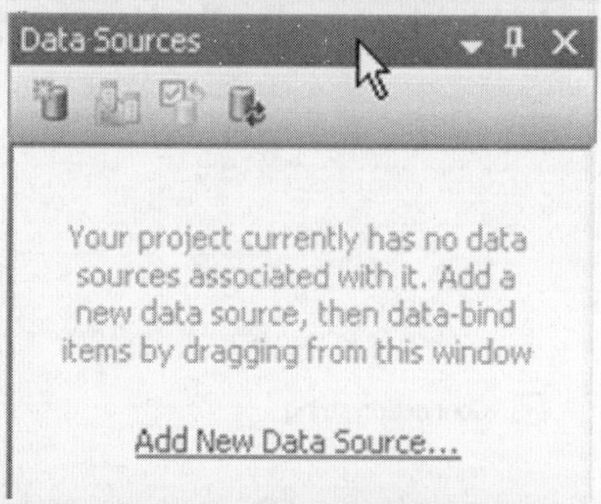

18. Click New Connection…
19. You will get Add Connection dialog box.
20. Be sure that in Data source you have selected Microsoft Access Database File (OLE DB), if not then click on Change button and do the selection from here
21. Now in Add Connection dialog box, click Browse button
22. Select the introdatabase
23. Click Open
24. Click Test Connection
25. You will get following confirmation
26. Click OK

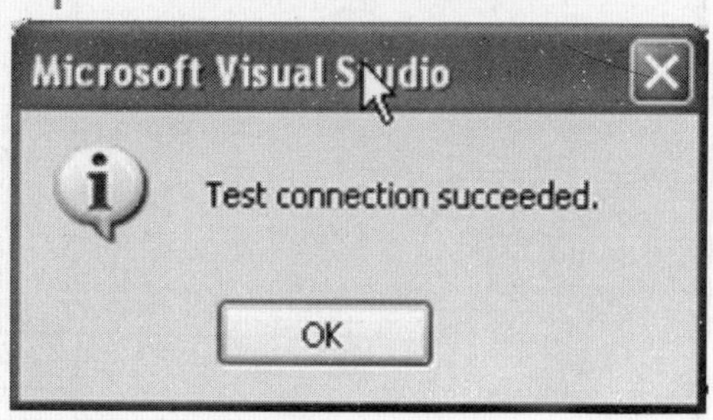

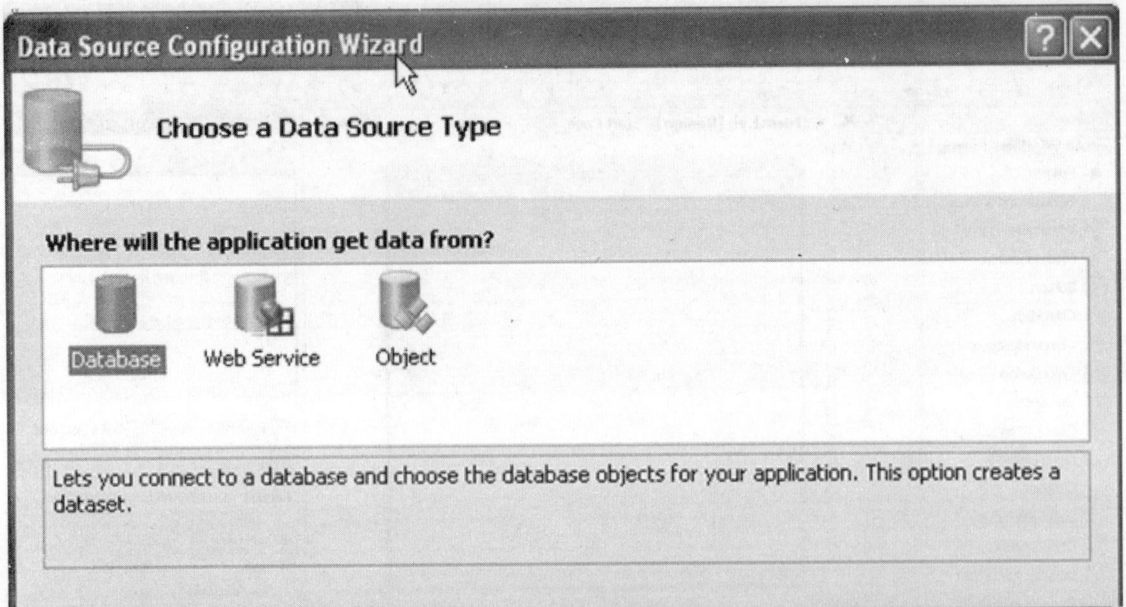
Data Source Configuration Wizard
Choose a Data Source Type
Where will the application get data from?
Database
Web Service
Object
Lets you connect to a database and choose the database objects for your application. This option creates a dataset.

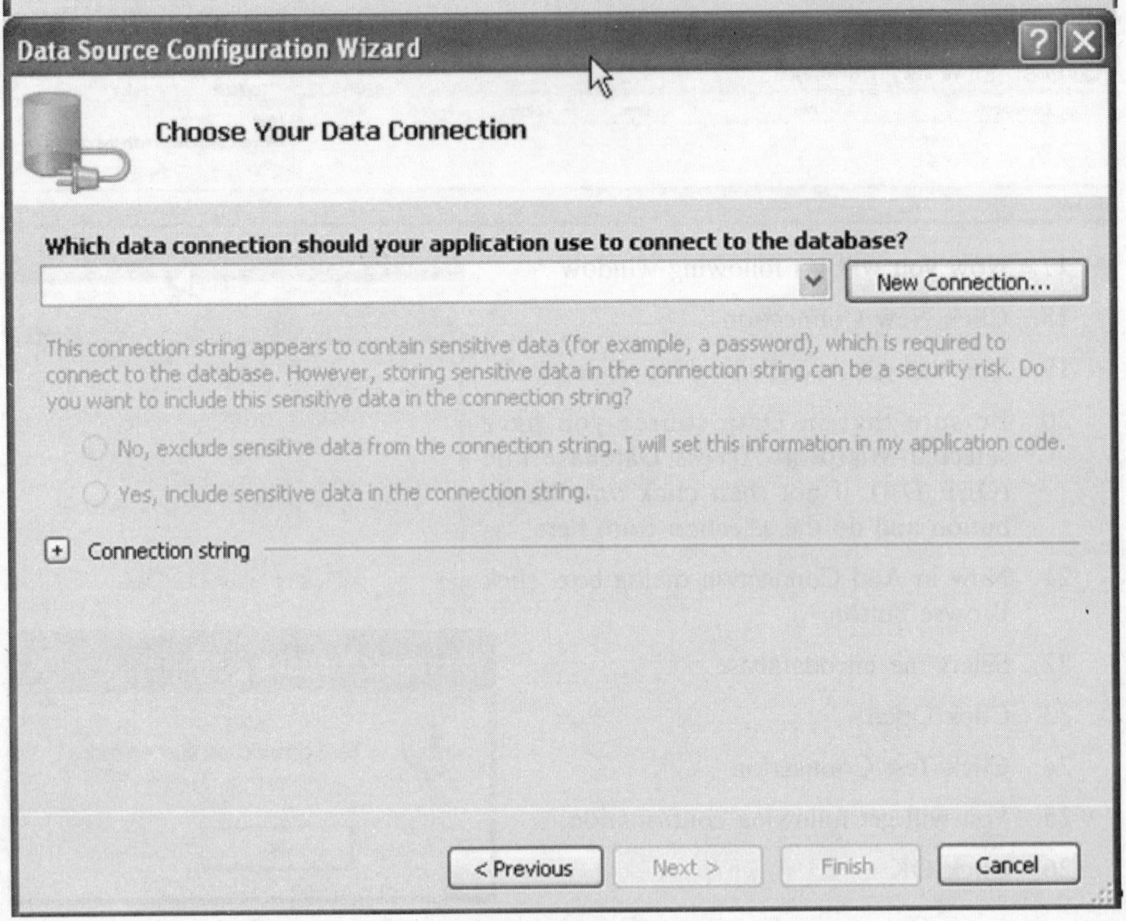
Data Source Configuration Wizard
Choose Your Data Connection
Which data connection should your application use to connect to the database?
New Connection...
This connection string appears to contain sensitive data (for example, a password), which is required to connect to the database. However, storing sensitive data in the connection string can be a security risk. Do you want to include this sensitive data in the connection string?
No, exclude sensitive data from the connection string. I will set this information in my application code.
Yes, include sensitive data in the connection string.
Connection string
< Previous
Next >
Finish
Cancel

Add Connection
Enter information to connect to the selected data source or click "Change" to choose a different data source and/or provider.
Data source:
Microsoft Access Database File (OLE DB)
Change...
Database file name:
Browse...
Log on to the database
User name:
Admin
Password:
Save my password
Advanced...
Test Connection
OK
Cancel

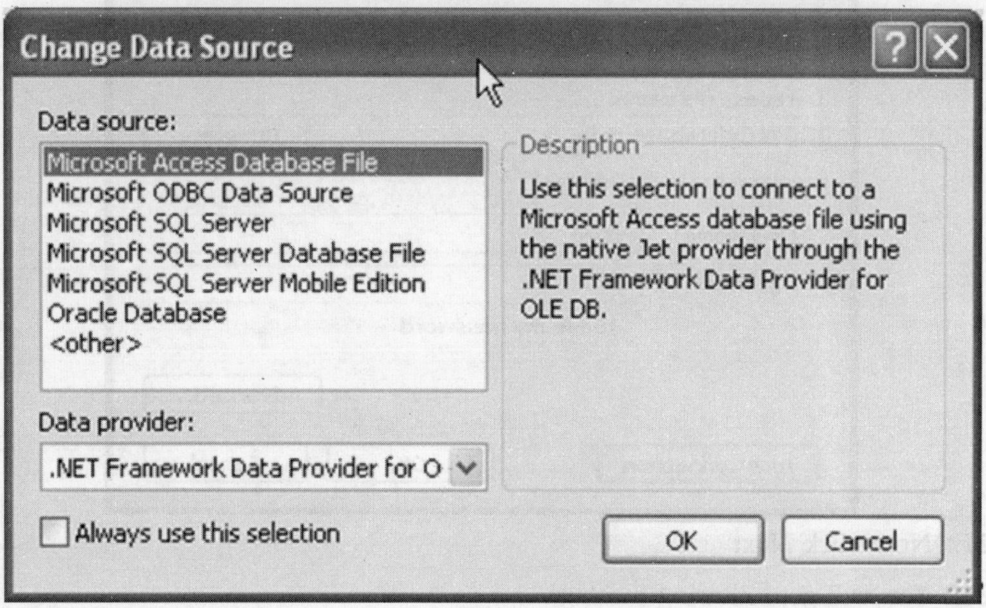
Change Data Source
Data source:
Microsoft Access Database File
Microsoft ODBC Data Source
Microsoft SQL Server
Microsoft SQL Server Database File
Microsoft SQL Server Mobile Edition
Oracle Database
<other>
Description
Use this selection to connect to a Microsoft Access database file using the native Jet provider through the .NET Framework Data Provider for OLE DB.
Data provider:
.NET Framework Data Provider for O
Always use this selection
OK
Cancel

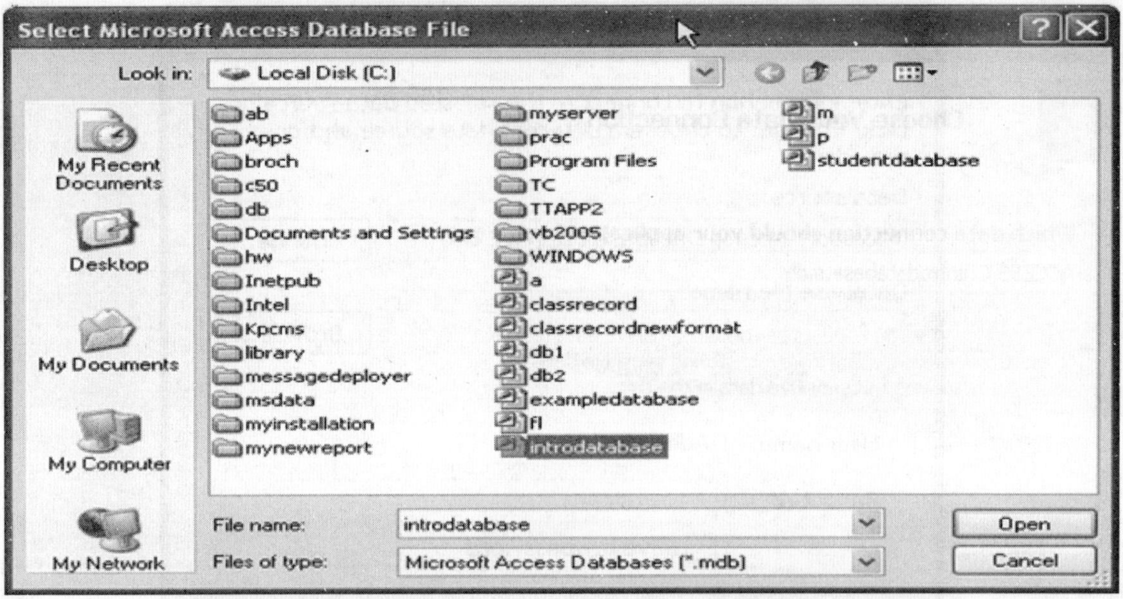

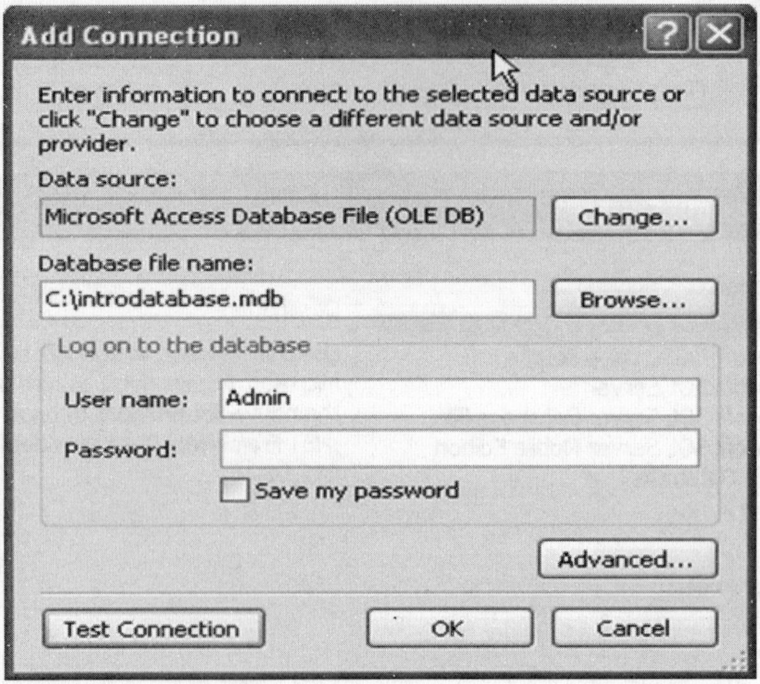

27. Now click Next
28. You will get following message
29. Click Yes
30. Keep default name as introdatabaseConnectionString

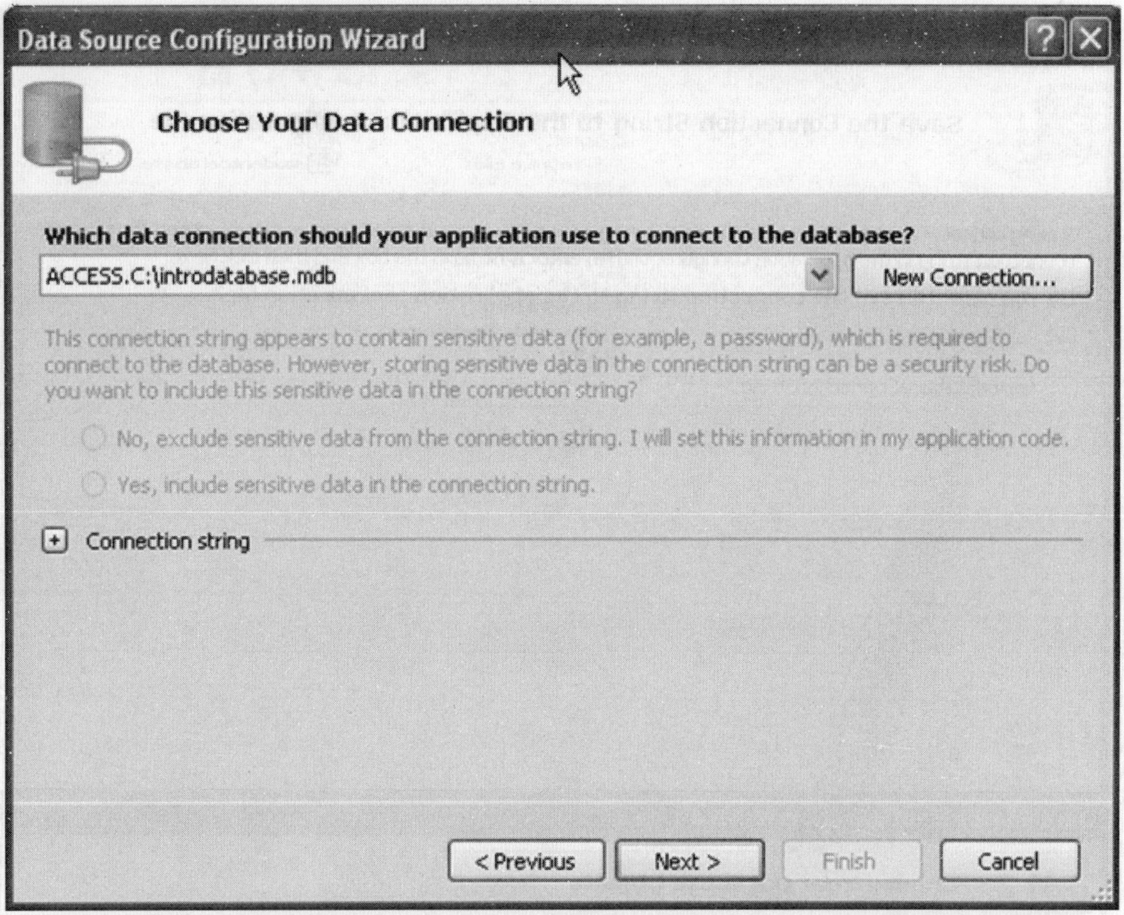

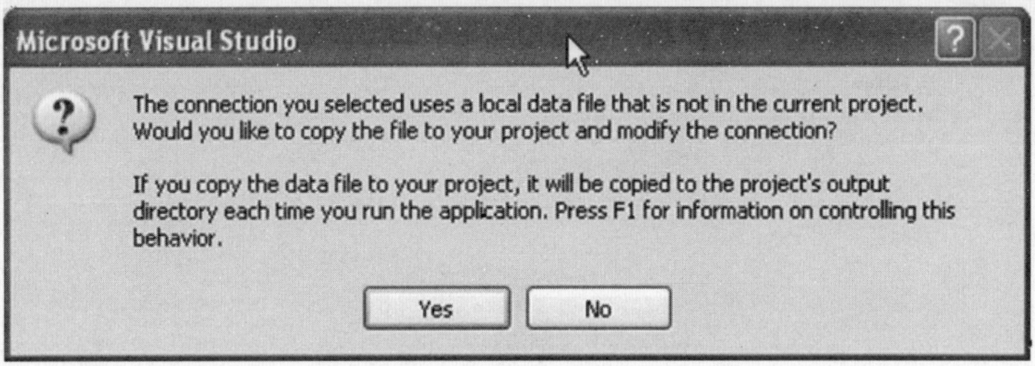

31. Click Next
32. Click + sign of Tables
33. At present you have one Table
34. Now click on + sign of introtable

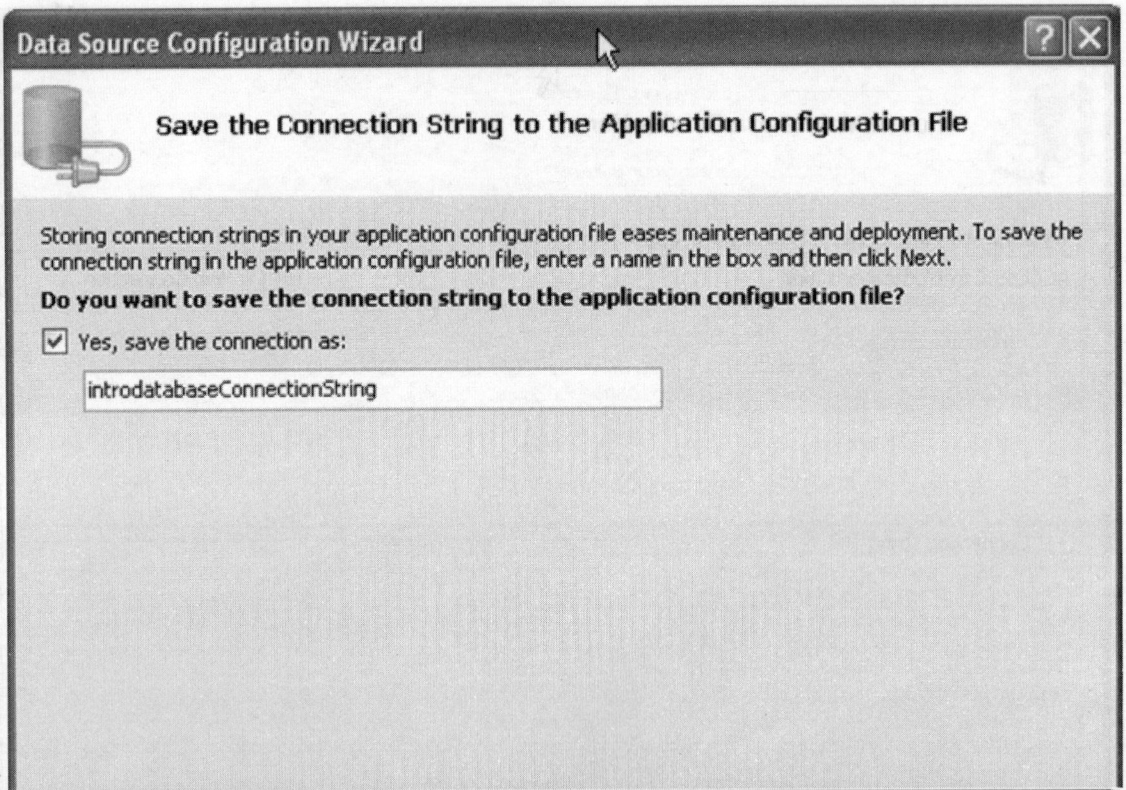
Data Source Configuration Wizard
Save the Connection String to the Application Configuration File
Storing connection strings in your application configuration file eases maintenance and deployment. To save the connection string in the application configuration file, enter a name in the box and then click Next.
Do you want to save the connection string to the application configuration file?
Yes, save the connection as:
introdatabaseConnectionString

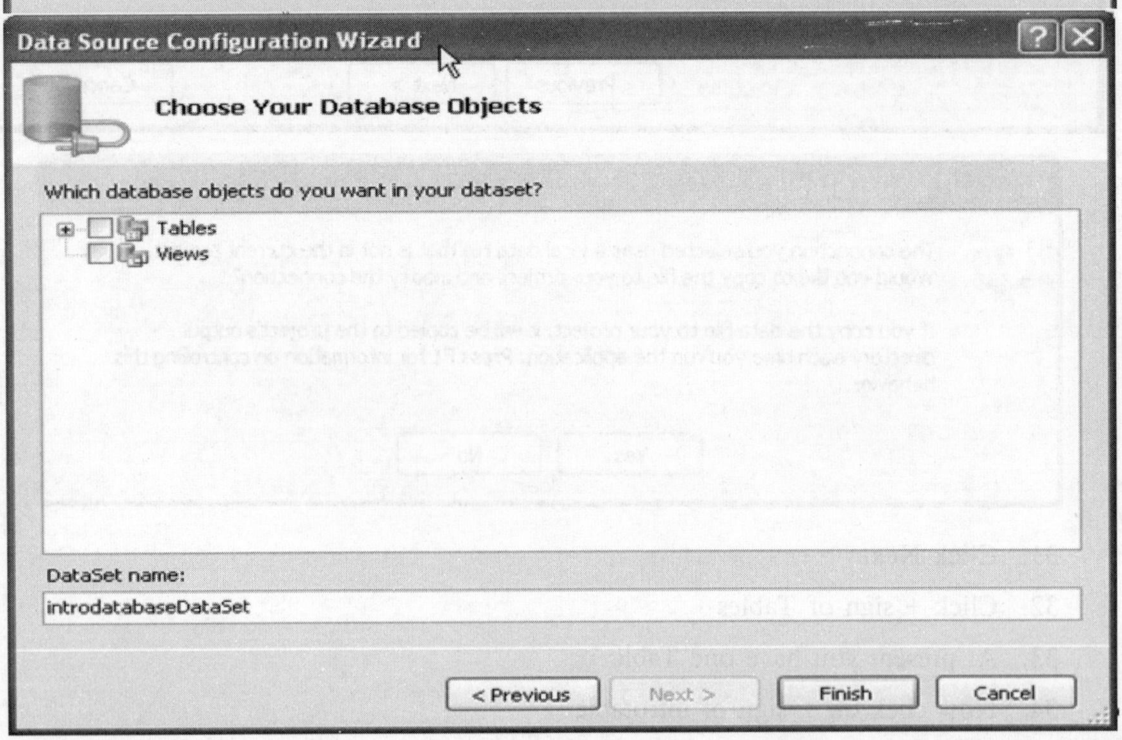
Data Source Configuration Wizard
Choose Your Database Objects
Which database objects do you want in your dataset?
Tables
Views
DataSet name:
introdatabaseDataSet
< Previous
Next >
Finish
Cancel

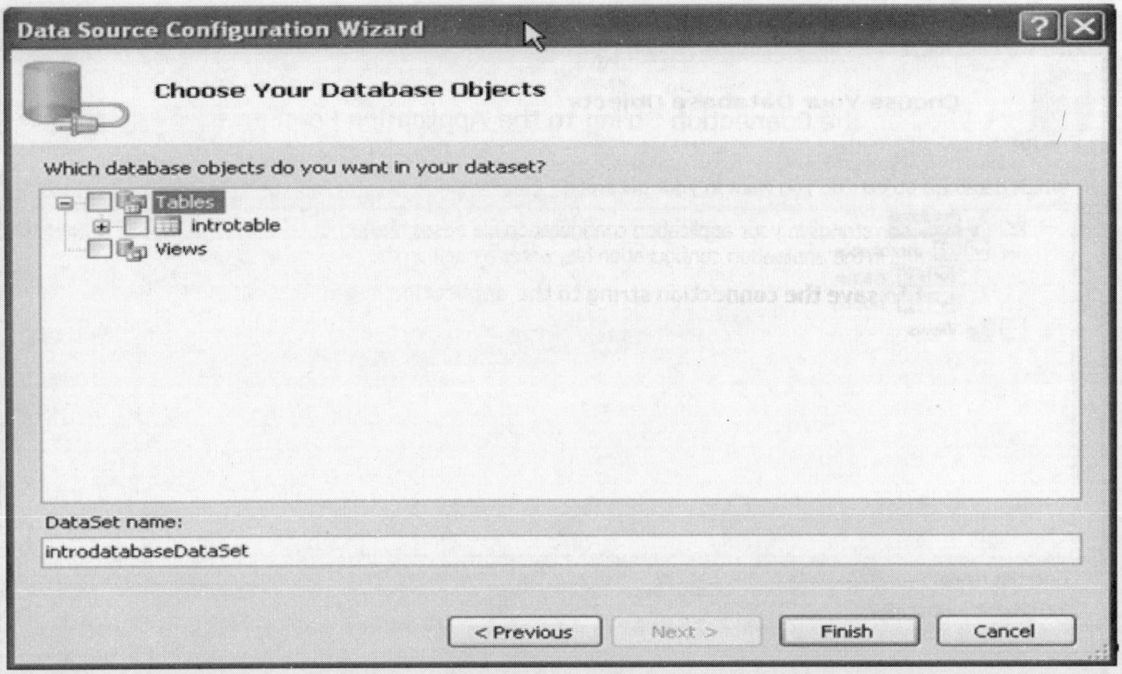

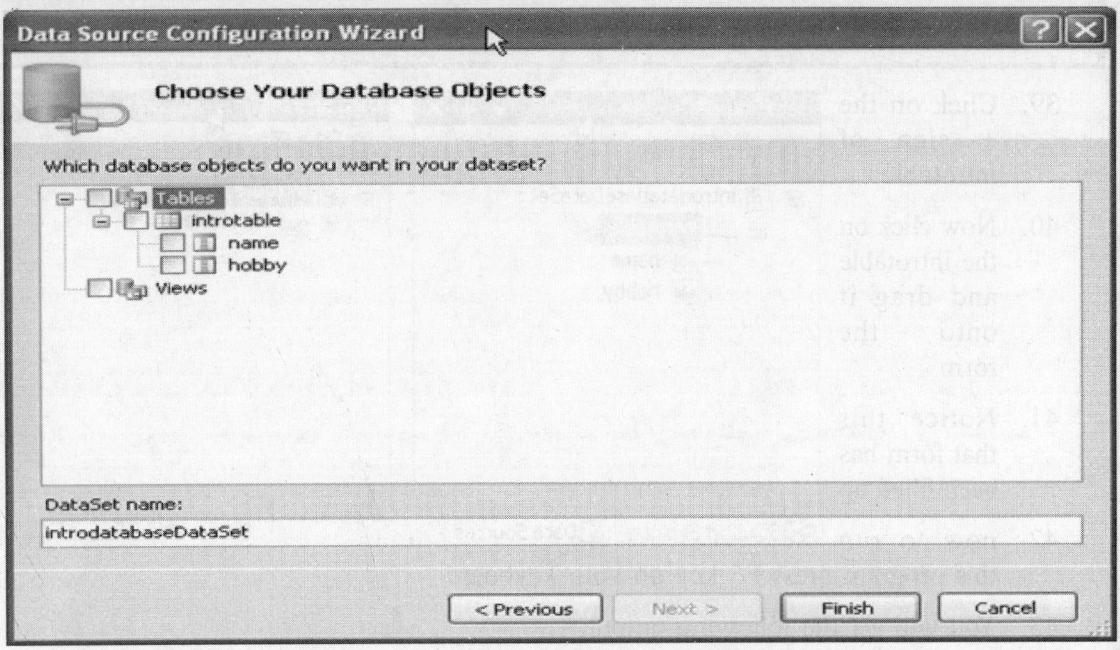

35. At present you have two fields, select both of them
36. Click Finish
37. Now notice the Data Sources window
38. The table has been added here.

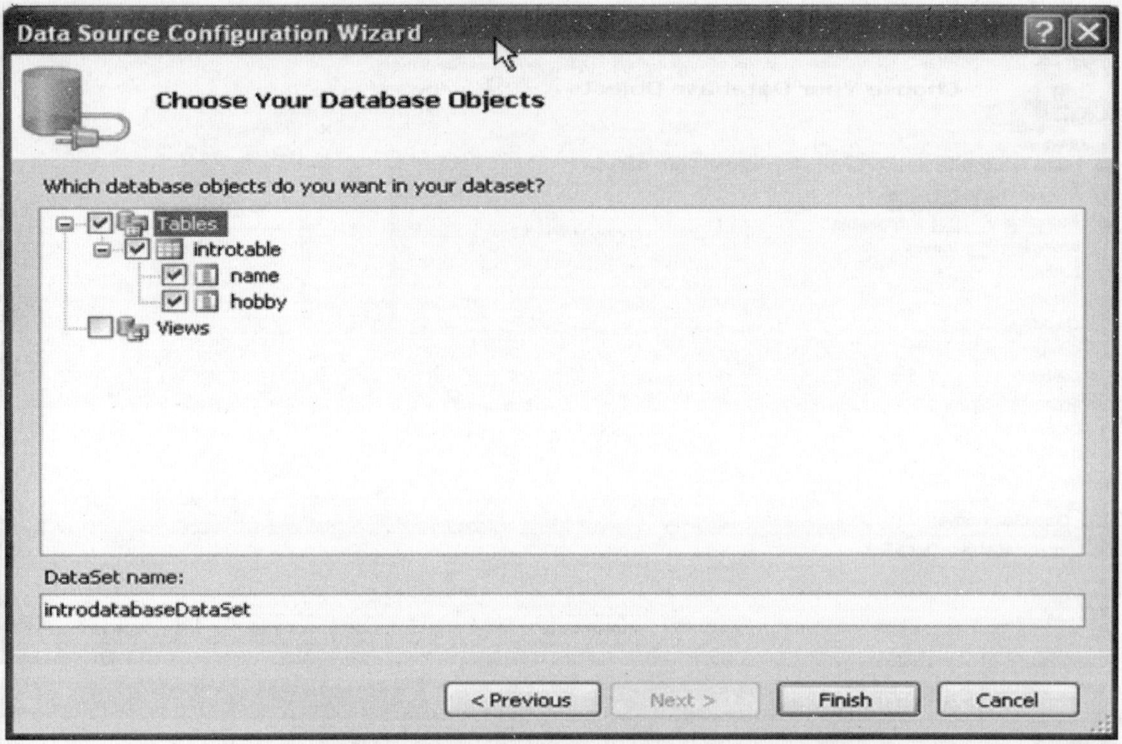

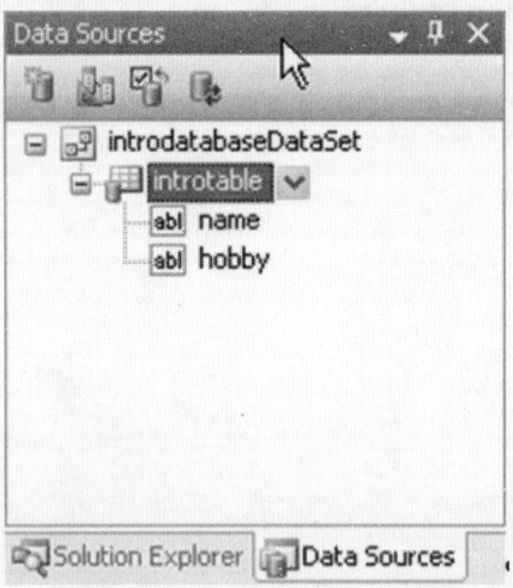

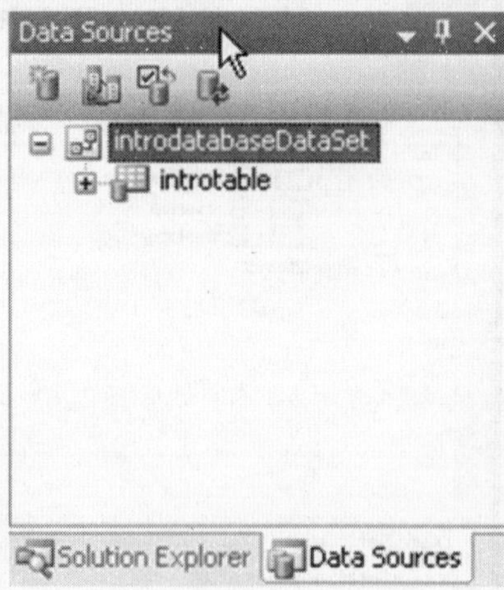

39. Click on the + sign of introtable
40. Now click on the introtable and drag it onto the form
41. Notice this that form has been filled up
42. now to run this program press F5 key on your keyboard
43. You will get the following output:
44. Now you can also navigate between records by clicking < > signs.

— code Form1.vb —

```
Public Class Form1
    Private Sub IntrotableBindingNavigatorSaveItem_Click(ByVal
```

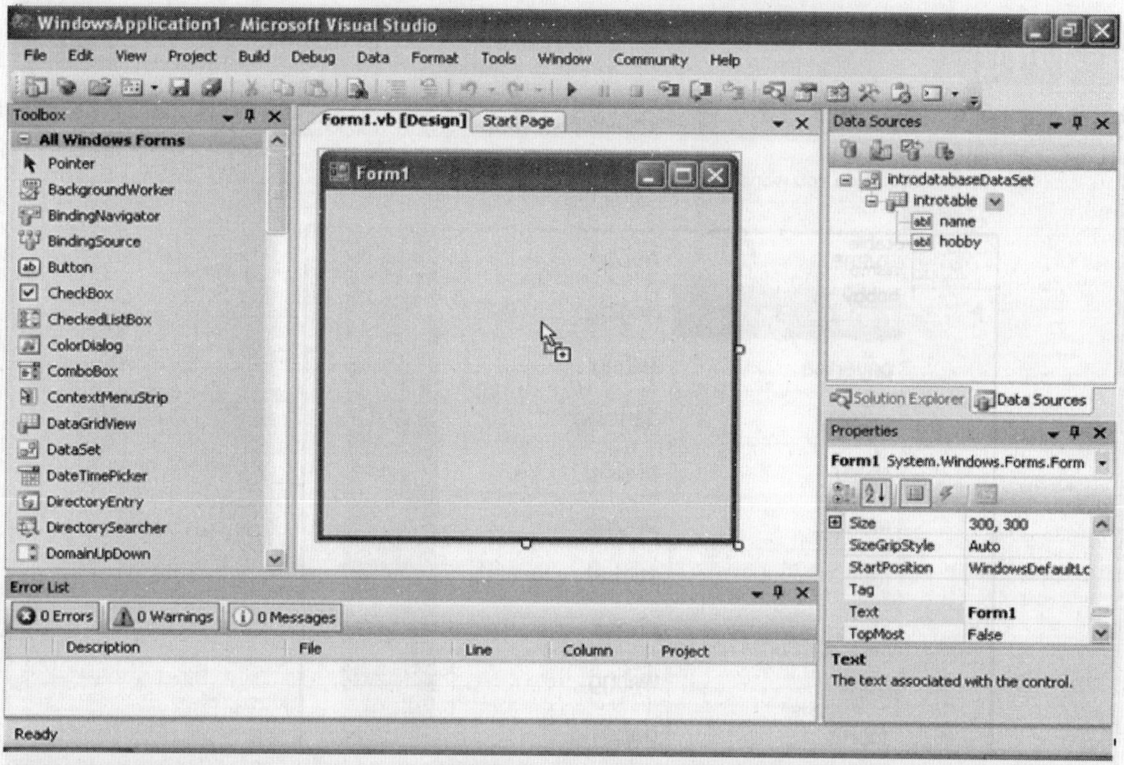
WindowsApplication1 - Microsoft Visual Studio
File Edit View Project Build Debug Data Format Tools Window Community Help
Toolbox
All Windows Forms
Pointer
BackgroundWorker
BindingNavigator
BindingSource
Button
CheckBox
CheckedListBox
ColorDialog
ComboBox
ContextMenuStrip
DataGridView
DataSet
DateTimePicker
DirectoryEntry
DirectorySearcher
DomainUpDown
Form1.vb [Design]
Start Page
Form1
Data Sources
introdatabaseDataSet
introtable
name
hobby
Solution Explorer
Data Sources
Properties
Form1 System.Windows.Forms.Form
Size 300, 300
SizeGripStyle Auto
StartPosition WindowsDefaultLc
Tag
Text Form1
TopMost False
Text
The text associated with the control.
Error List
0 Errors
0 Warnings
0 Messages
Description
File
Line
Column
Project
Ready

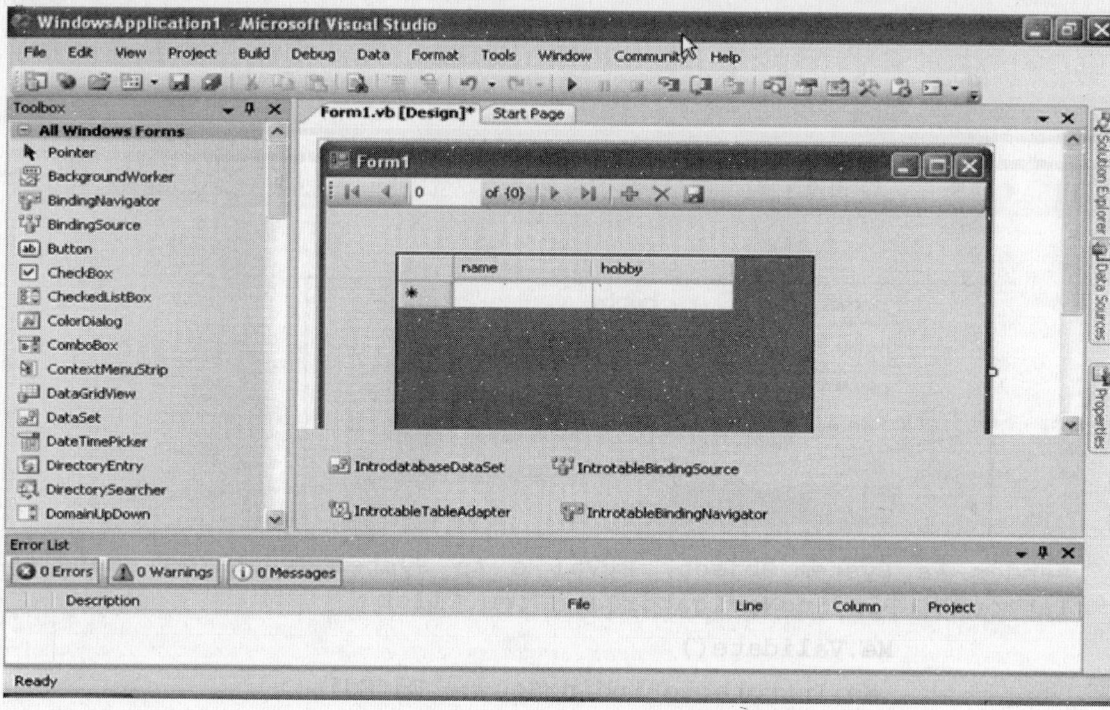
WindowsApplication1 - Microsoft Visual Studio
File Edit View Project Build Debug Data Format Tools Window Community Help
Toolbox
All Windows Forms
Pointer
BackgroundWorker
BindingNavigator
BindingSource
Button
CheckBox
CheckedListBox
ColorDialog
ComboBox
ContextMenuStrip
DataGridView
DataSet
DateTimePicker
DirectoryEntry
DirectorySearcher
DomainUpDown
Form1.vb [Design]*
Start Page
Form1
of {0}
name
hobby
IntrodatabaseDataSet
IntrotableBindingSource
IntrotableTableAdapter
IntrotableBindingNavigator
Solution Explorer
Data Sources
Properties
Error List
0 Errors
0 Warnings
0 Messages
Description
File
Line
Column
Project
Ready

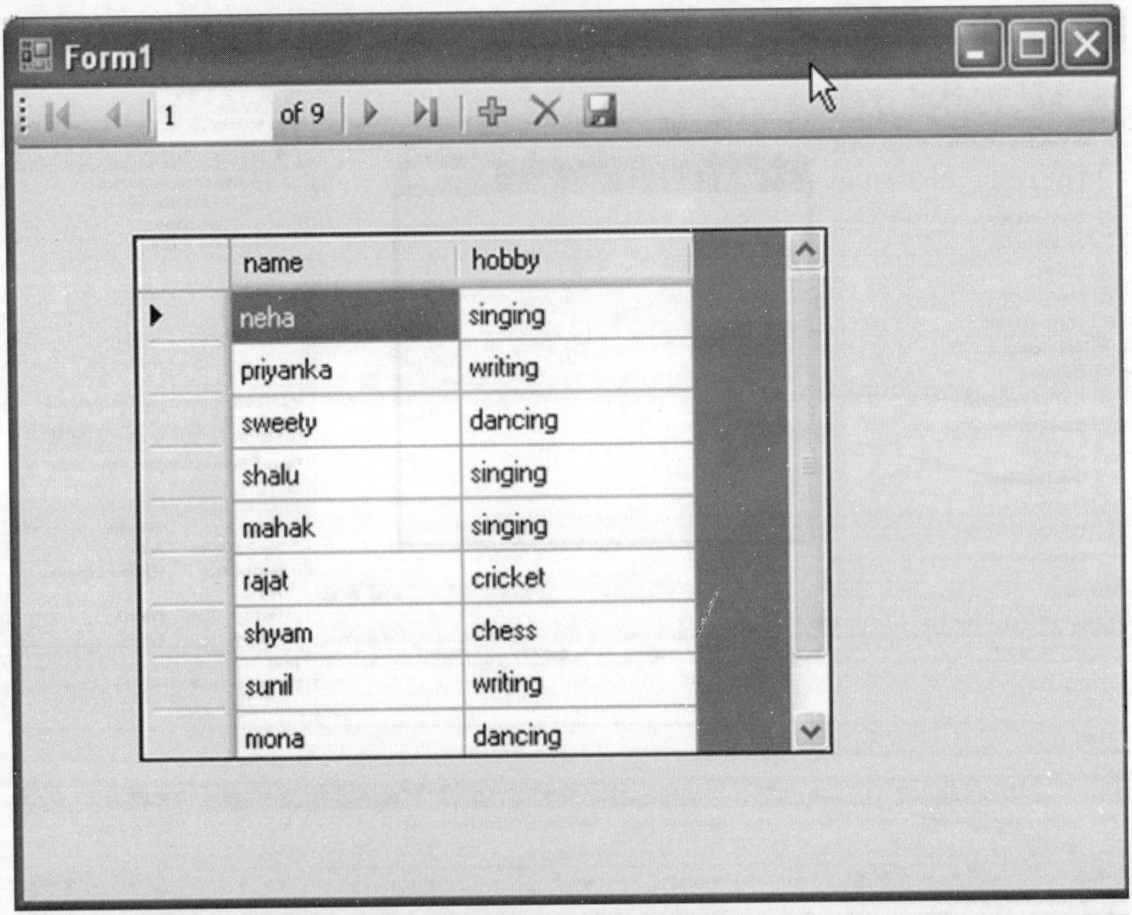

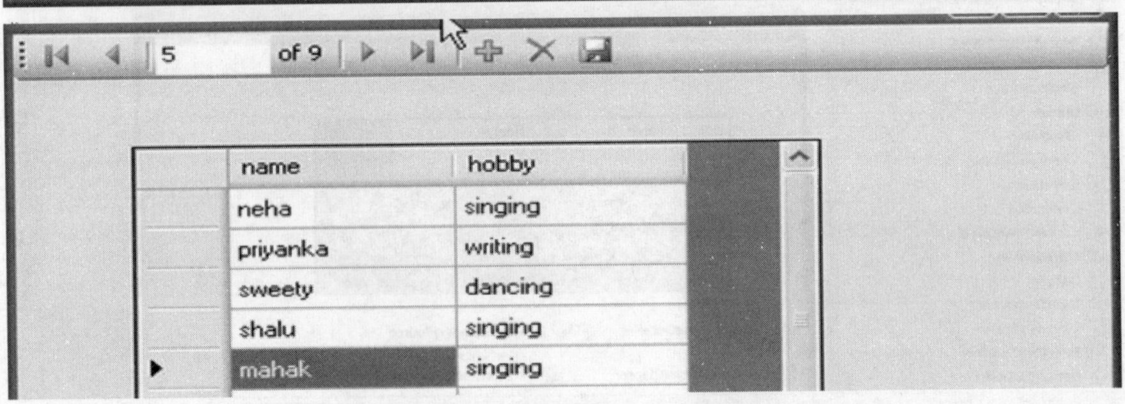


```
sender As System.Object, ByVal e As System.EventArgs) Handles
IntrotableBindingNavigatorSaveItem.Click
        Me.Validate()
         Me.IntrotableBindingSource.EndEdit()
    Me.IntrotableTableAdapter.Update(Me.IntrodatabaseDataSet.introtable)
```

```
    End Sub
      Private Sub Form1_Load(ByVal sender As System.Object, ByVal
  e As System.EventArgs) Handles MyBase.Load
            'TODO: This line of code loads data into the
  'IntrodatabaseDataSet.introtable' table. You can move, or remove
  it, as needed.
      Me.IntrotableTableAdapter.Fill(Me.IntrodatabaseDataSet.introtable)
    End Sub
  End Class
  — code app.config —
  <?xml version="1.0" encoding="utf-8" ?>
  <configuration>
      <configSections>
      </configSections>
      <connectionStrings>
                                                              <add
  name="WindowsApplication1.My.MySettings.introdatabaseConnectionString"
            connectionString="Provider=Microsoft.Jet.OLEDB.4.0;Data
  Source=|DataDirectory|\introdatabase.mdb"
                  providerName="System.Data.OleDb" />
      </connectionStrings>
      <system.diagnostics>
          <sources>
                  <!— This section defines the logging
  configuration for My.Application.Log —>
                      <source name="DefaultSource"
  switchName="DefaultSwitch">
                  <listeners>
                      <add name="FileLog"/>
                      <!— Uncomment the below section to
  write to the Application Event Log —>
                      <!—<add name="EventLog"/>—>
                  </listeners>
              </source>
          </sources>
          <switches>
```

```
                <add name="DefaultSwitch" value="Information" /
>
            </switches>
            <sharedListeners>
                <add name="FileLog"
                type="Microsoft.VisualBasic.Logging.FileLogTraceListener,
Microsoft.VisualBasic, Version=8.0.0.0, Culture=neutral,
PublicKeyToken=b03f5f7f11d50a3a, processorArchitecture=MSIL"
                    initializeData="FileLogWriter"/>
                <!— Uncomment the below section and replace
APPLICATION_NAME with the name of your application to write
to the Application Event Log —>
                        <!—<add name="EventLog"
type="System.Diagnostics.EventLogTraceListener"
initializeData="APPLICATION_NAME"/> —>
            </sharedListeners>
        </system.diagnostics>
</configuration>
```

If you wish you can also modify the above program. The way you want to change the look and appearance of data you can do that. For this first remove everything from the form. Make it plane.

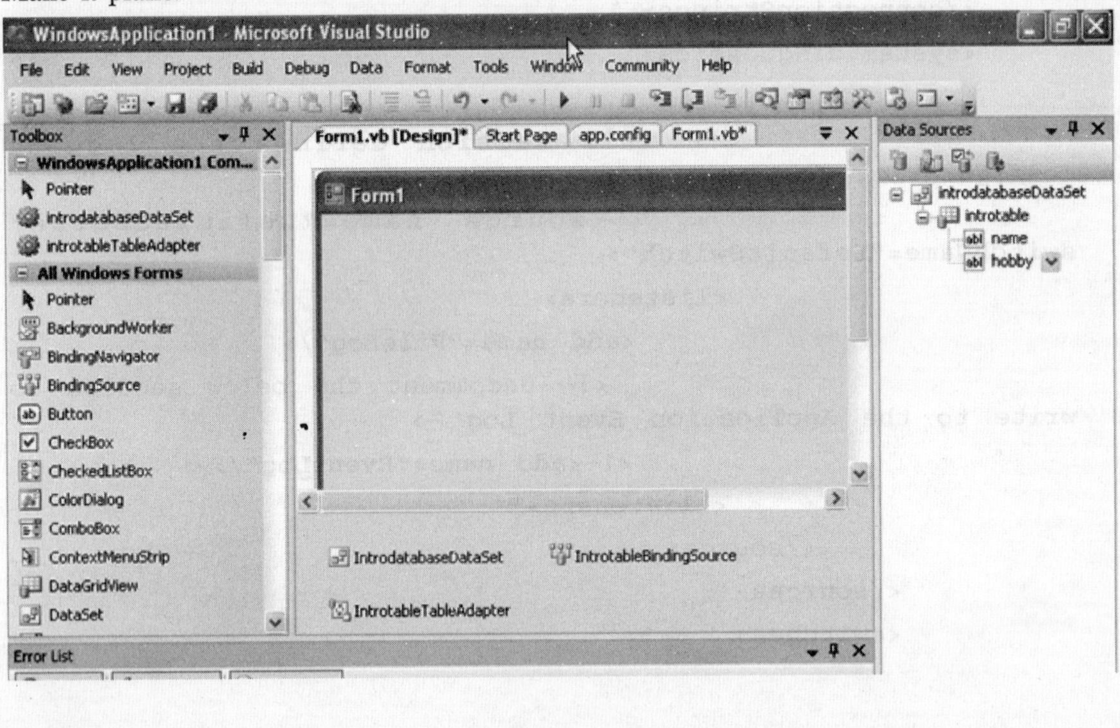

45. Now in Data Sources window click the name field and drag it onto the form.

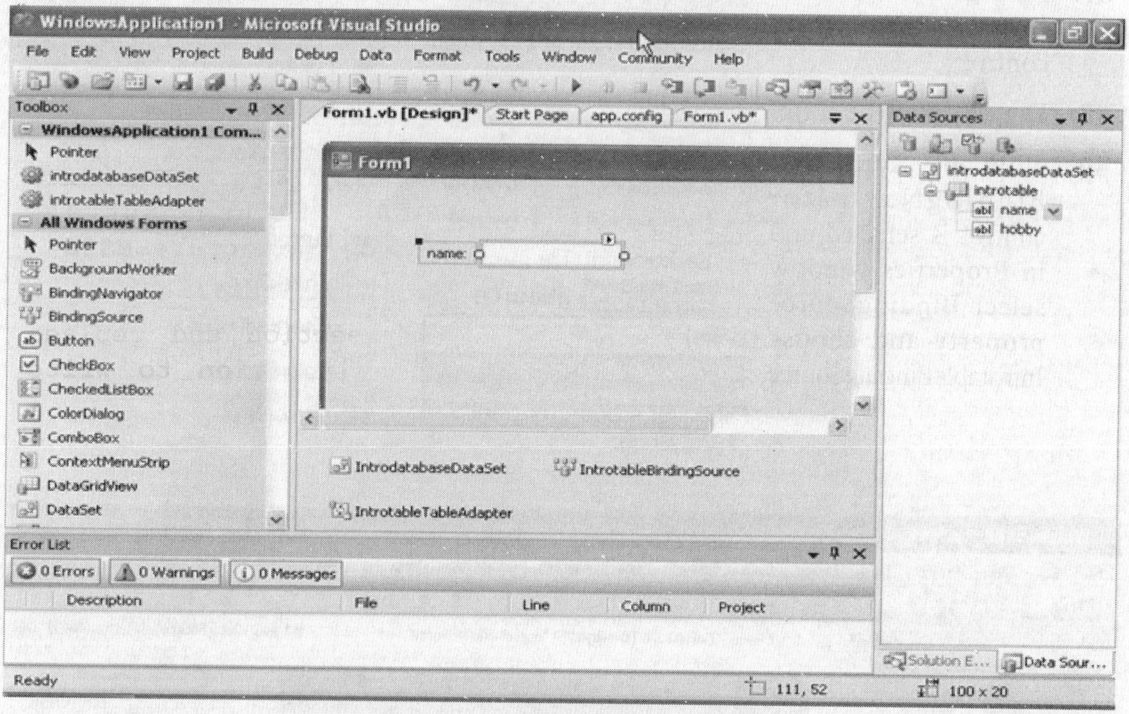

46. Now click the hobby field and drag it onto the form

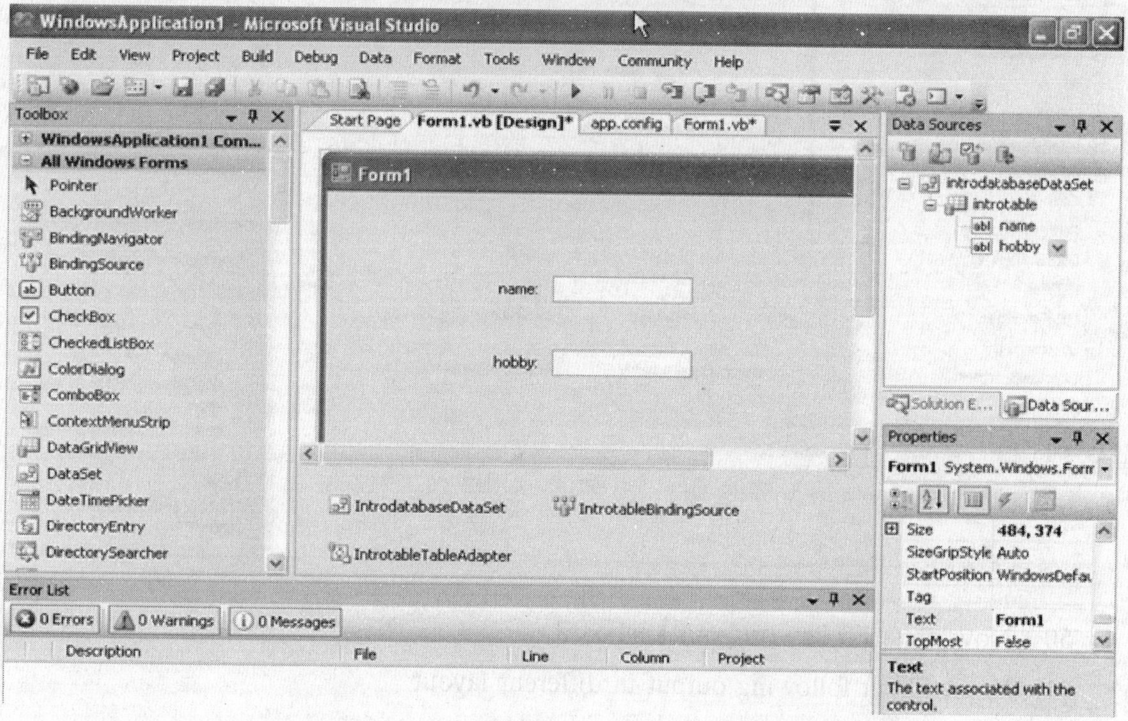

47. Now in Toolbox click BindingNaviagtor control
48. Drag it onto the form
49. Now be sure that BindingNavigator control is selected and in Properties window select BindingSource property and choose IntrotableBindingSource

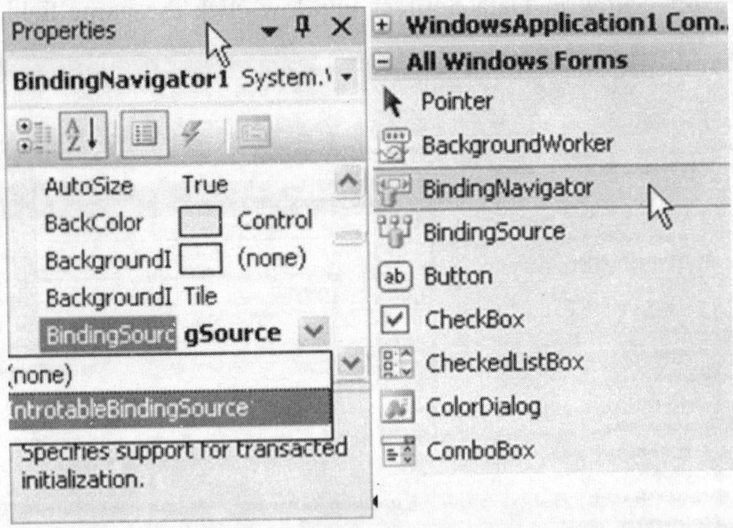

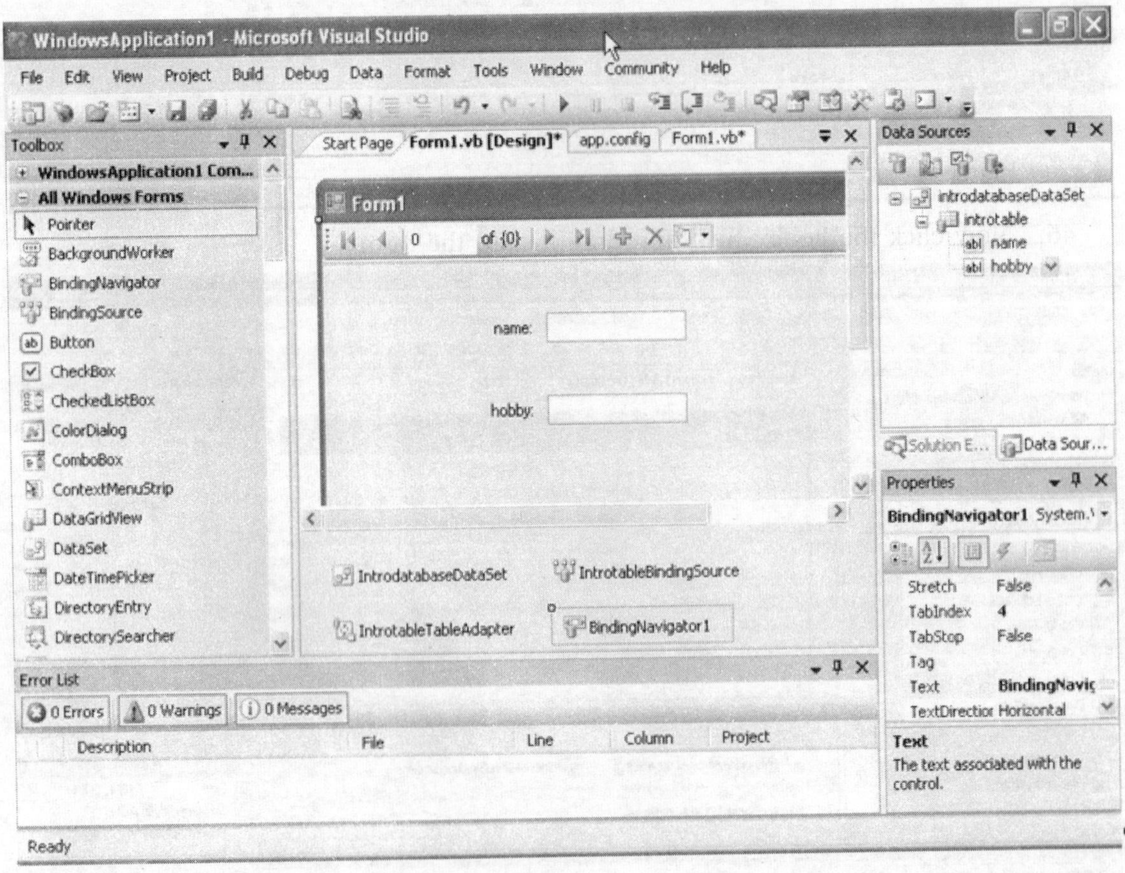

50. Now press F5 key on your keyboard
51. You will get following output in different layout:

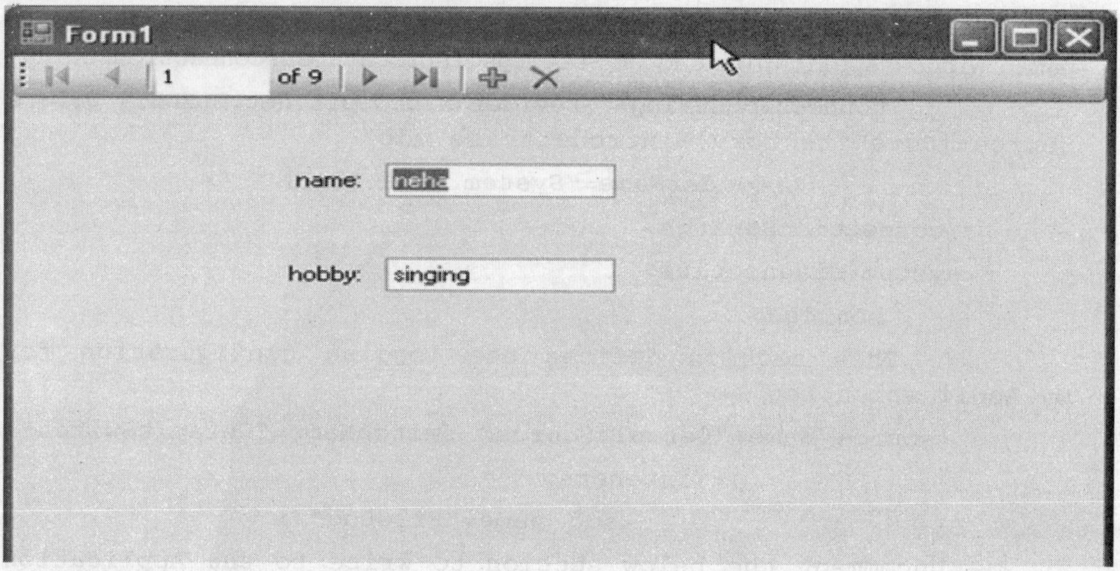

— code Form1.VB —

```
Public Class Form1
     Private Sub IntrotableBindingNavigatorSaveItem_Click(ByVal
sender As System.Object, ByVal e As System.EventArgs)
          Me.Validate()
           Me.IntrotableBindingSource.EndEdit()
                          Me.IntrotableTableAdapter.
Update(Me.IntrodatabaseDataSet.introtable)
     End Sub
    Private Sub Form1_Load(ByVal sender As System.Object, ByVal
e As System.EventArgs) Handles MyBase.Load
          'TODO: This line of code loads data into the
'IntrodatabaseDataSet.introtable' table. You can move, or remove
it, as needed.
       Me.IntrotableTableAdapter.Fill(Me.IntrodatabaseDataSet.introtable)
     End Sub
End Class
```

— app.config —

```
<?xml version="1.0" encoding="utf-8" ?>
<configuration>
     <configSections>
     </configSections>
     <connectionStrings>
```

```
                                                    <add
name="WindowsApplication1.My.MySettings.introdatabaseConnectionString"
        connectionString="Provider=Microsoft.Jet.OLEDB.4.0;Data
Source=|DataDirectory|\introdatabase.mdb"
            providerName="System.Data.OleDb" />
    </connectionStrings>
    <system.diagnostics>
        <sources>
    <!— This section defines the logging configuration for
My.Application.Log —>
      <source name="DefaultSource" switchName="DefaultSwitch">
                <listeners>
                    <add name="FileLog"/>
   <!— Uncomment the below section to write to the Application
Event Log —>
                    <!—<add name="EventLog"/>—>
                </listeners>
            </source>
        </sources>
        <switches>
         <add name="DefaultSwitch" value="Information" />
        </switches>
        <sharedListeners>
            <add name="FileLog"
           type="Microsoft.VisualBasic.Logging.FileLogTraceListener,
Microsoft.VisualBasic, Version=8.0.0.0, Culture=neutral,
PublicKeyToken=b03f5f7f11d50a3a, processorArchitecture=MSIL"
                initializeData="FileLogWriter"/>
             <!— Uncomment the below section and replace
APPLICATION_NAME with the name of your application to write
to the Application Event Log —>
                    <!—<add         name="EventLog"
type="System.Diagnostics.EventLogTraceListener"
initializeData="APPLICATION_NAME"/> —>
        </sharedListeners>
    </system.diagnostics>
</configuration>
```

4 Visual C# and ADO.Net

INTRODUCTION

In this chapter I'll show you how fast you can make make the database navigate with Visual C# 2005 and ADO.NET. The specialty of Visual Studio 2005 is such that you do not have to write a single code for this.

We will create the connection with our created MS Access database created in the last chapter. Then we will use simple techniques in Visual C# for data navigation form.

Perform the following steps:

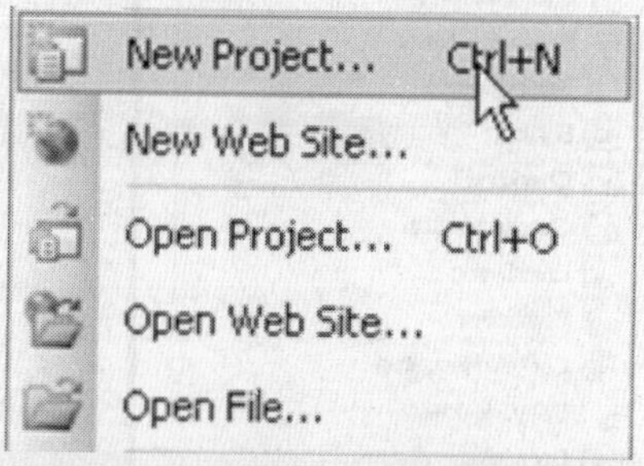

1. Start Visual Studio 2005
2. On menu bar click File
3. Click New Project
4. You will get New Project dialog box

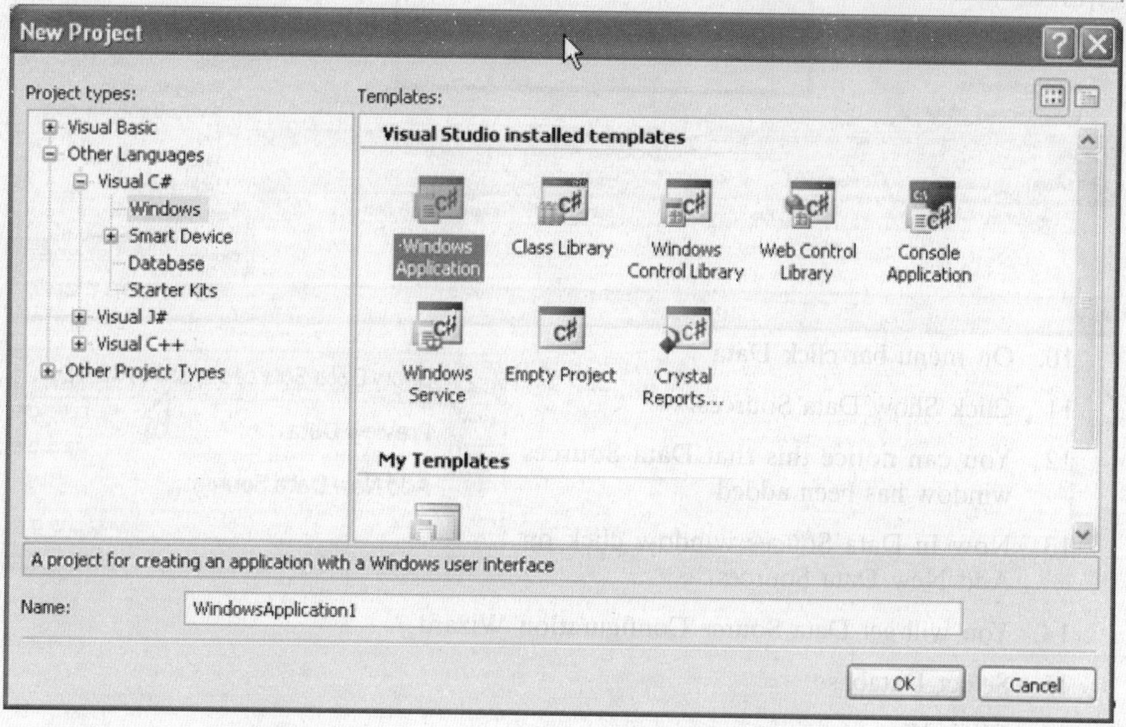

5. Under Project types select Visual C#
6. Under Templates select Windows Applications
7. Keep default name
8. Click OK
9. At present you have following scenario

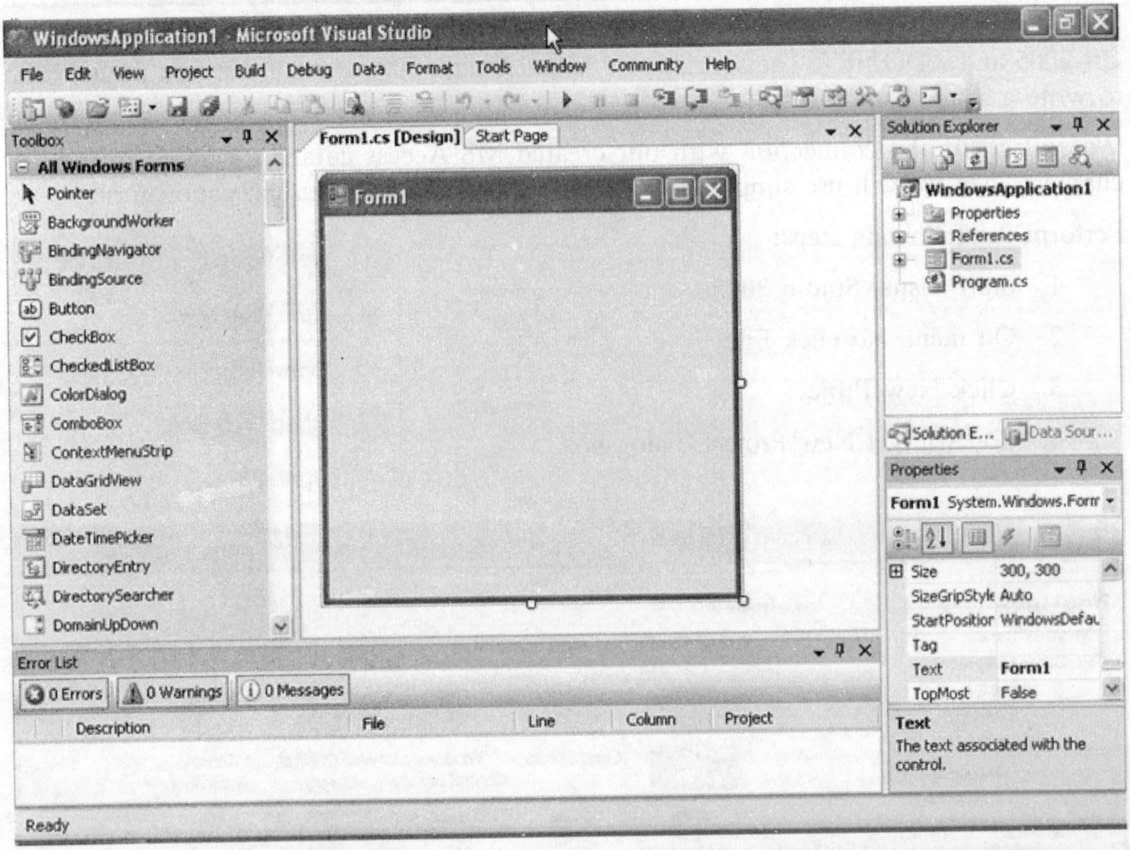

10. On menu bar click Data
11. Click Show Data Sources
12. You can notice this that Data Sources window has been added
13. Now in Data Souces window click on Add New Data Sources

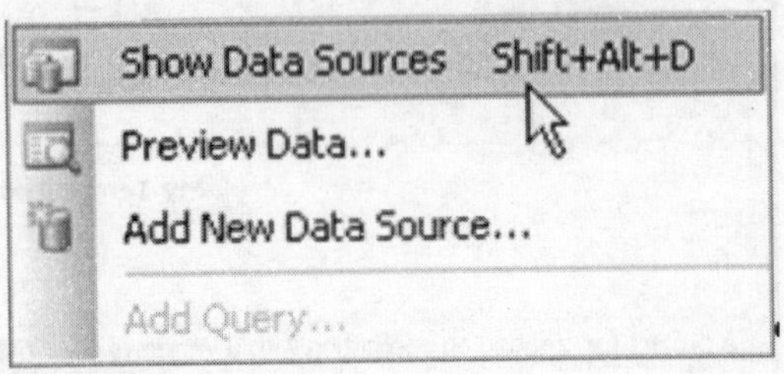

14. You will get Data Source Configuration Wizard
15. Select Database
16. Click Next

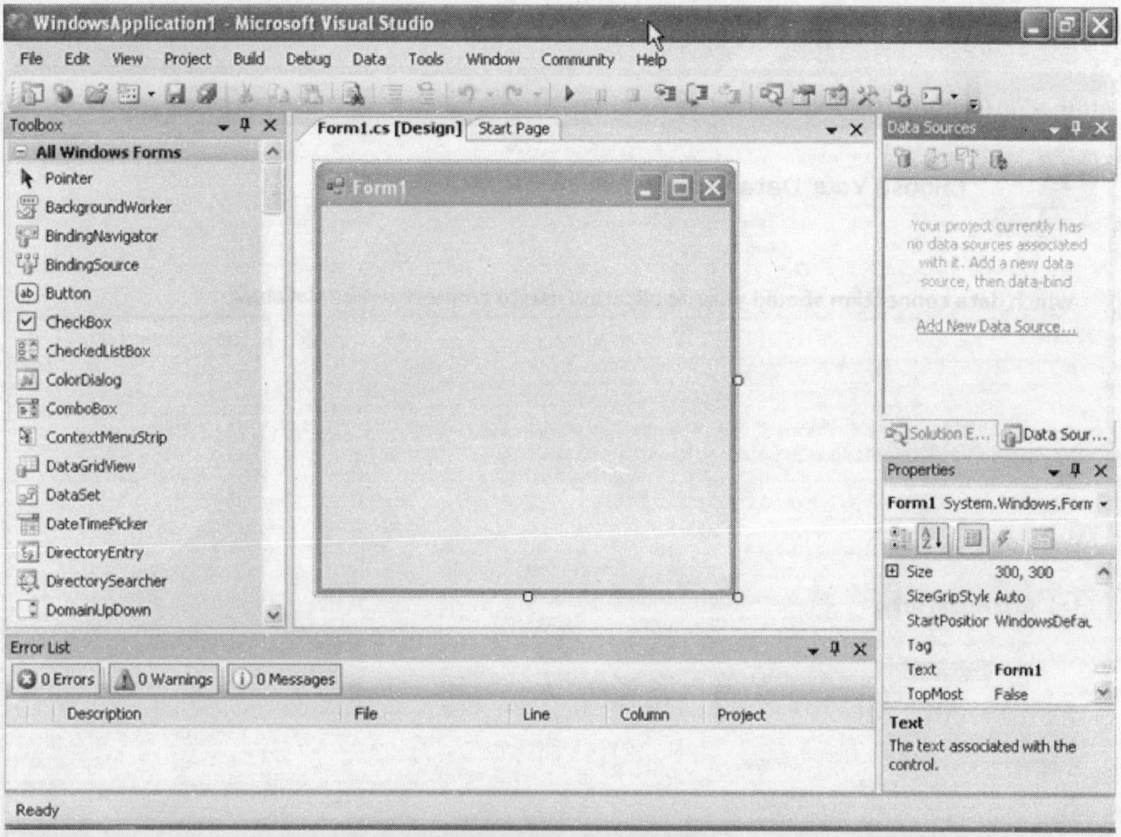
WindowsApplication1 - Microsoft Visual Studio
File Edit View Project Build Debug Data Tools Window Community Help
Toolbox
All Windows Forms
Pointer
BackgroundWorker
BindingNavigator
BindingSource
Button
CheckBox
CheckedListBox
ColorDialog
ComboBox
ContextMenuStrip
DataGridView
DataSet
DateTimePicker
DirectoryEntry
DirectorySearcher
DomainUpDown
Form1.cs [Design]
Start Page
Form1
Data Sources
Your project currently has no data sources associated with it. Add a new data source, then data-bind
Add New Data Source...
Solution E...
Data Sour...
Properties
Form1 System.Windows.Form
Size 300, 300
SizeGripStyle Auto
StartPosition WindowsDefau
Tag
Text Form1
TopMost False
Text
The text associated with the control.
Error List
0 Errors
0 Warnings
0 Messages
Description
File
Line
Column
Project
Ready

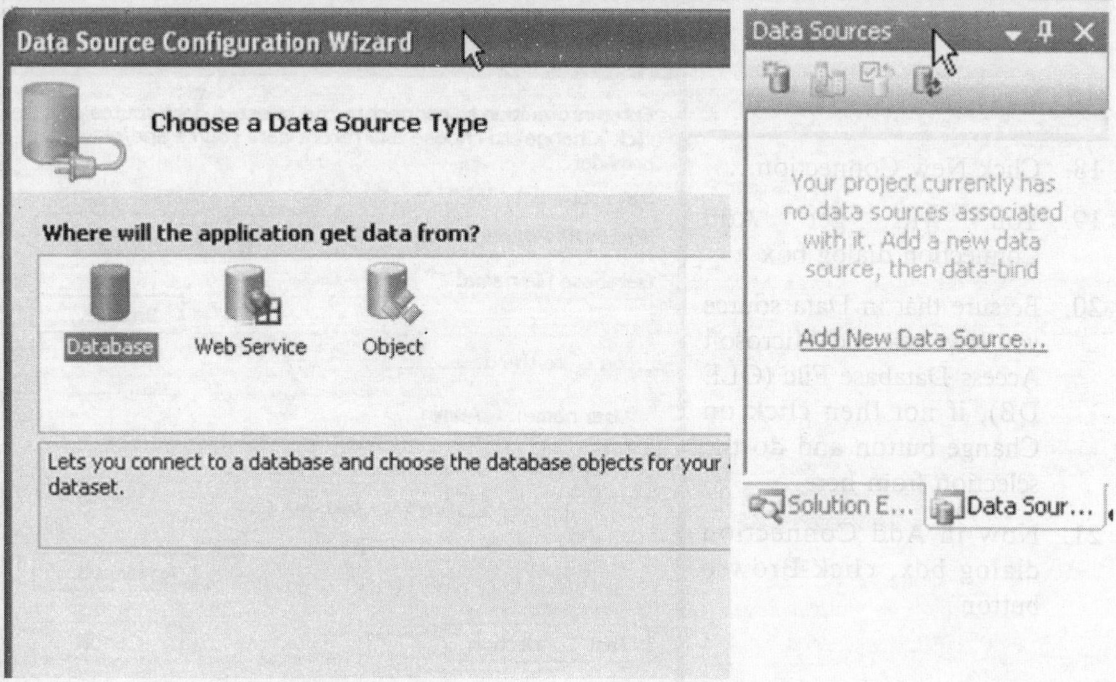
Data Source Configuration Wizard
Choose a Data Source Type
Where will the application get data from?
Database
Web Service
Object
Lets you connect to a database and choose the database objects for your dataset.
Data Sources
Your project currently has no data sources associated with it. Add a new data source, then data-bind
Add New Data Source...
Solution E...
Data Sour...

17. Now you will get following window

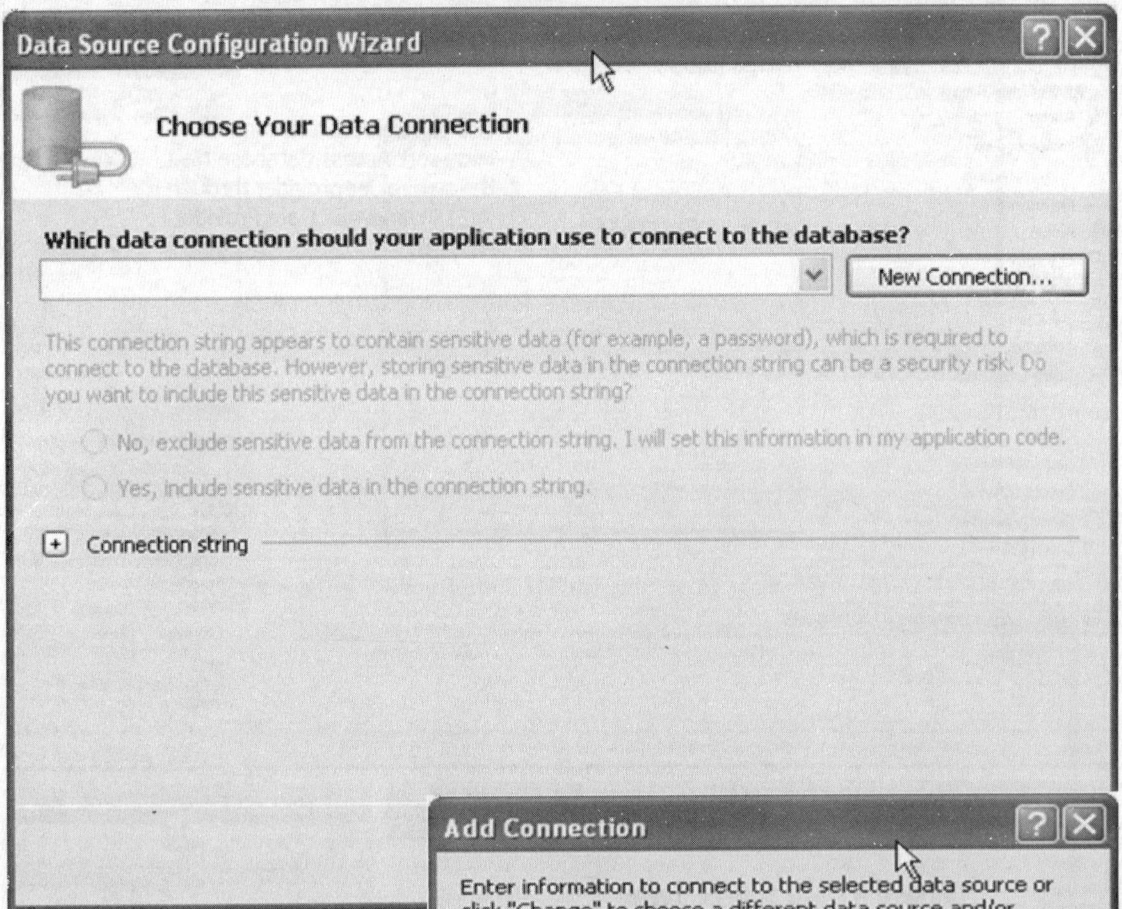

18. Click New Connection...
19. You will get Add Connection dialog box
20. Be sure that in Data source you have selected Microsoft Access Database File (OLE DB), if not then click on Change button and do the selection from here
21. Now in Add Connection dialog box, click Browse button

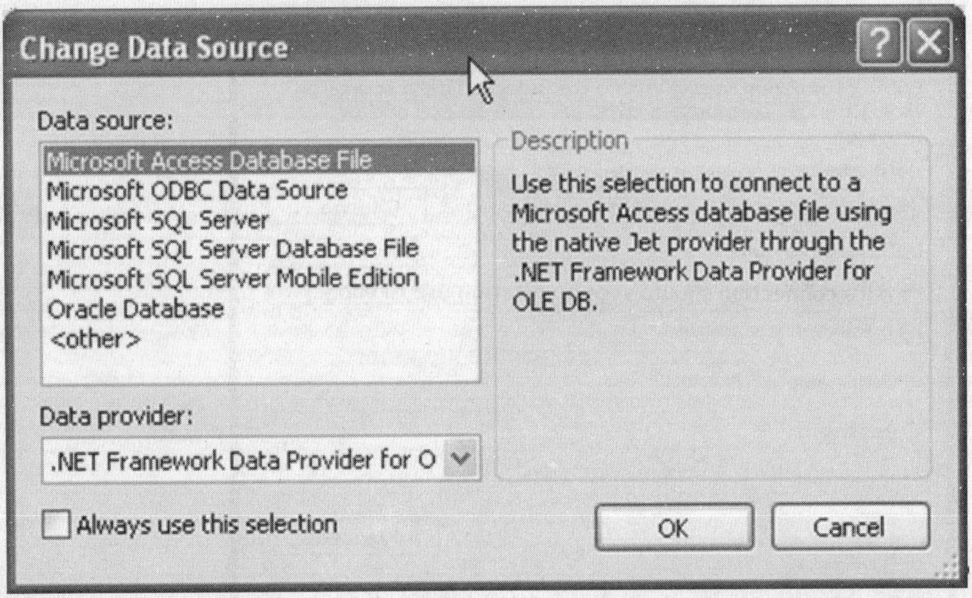

22. Select the introdatabase

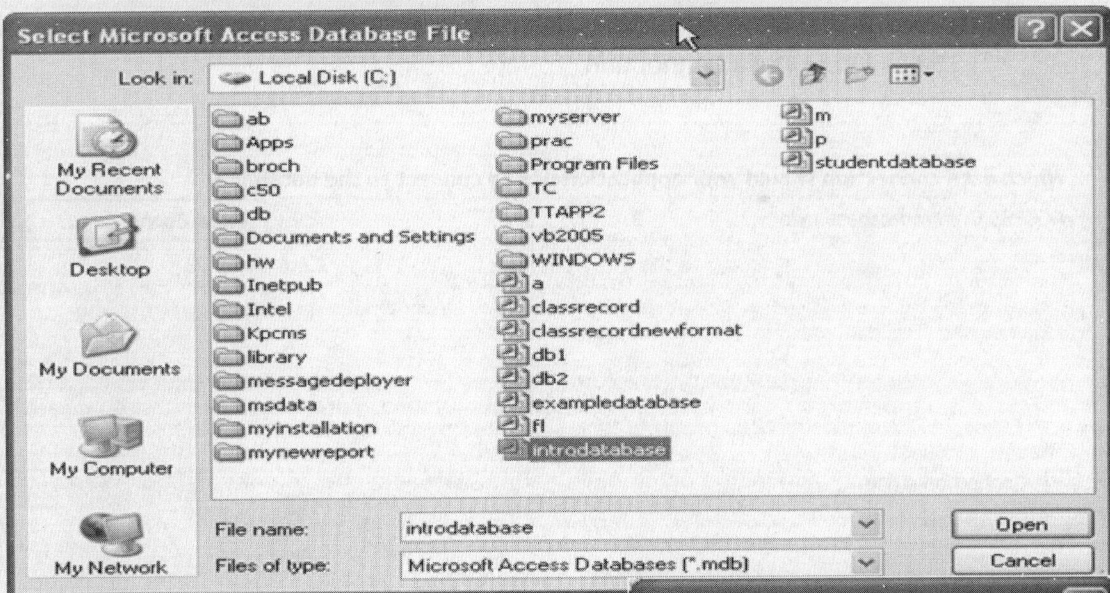

23. Click Open
24. Click Test Connection
25. You will get following confirmation
26. Click OK
27. Now click Next

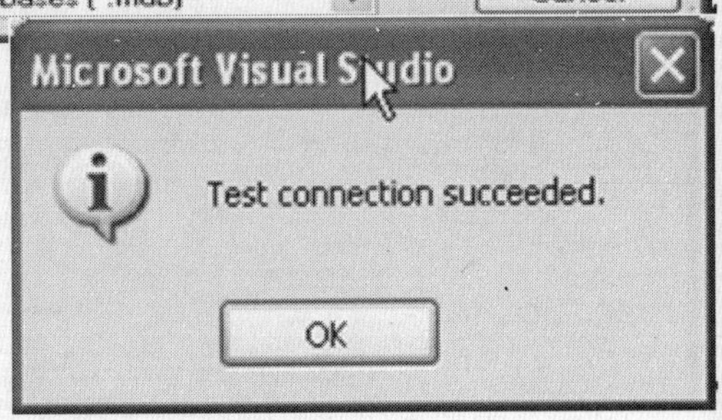

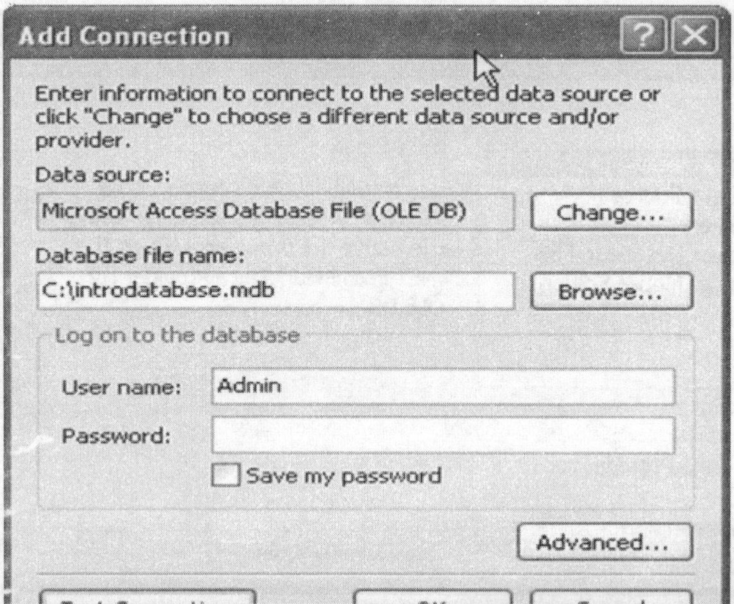
Add Connection
Enter information to connect to the selected data source or click "Change" to choose a different data source and/or provider.
Data source:
Microsoft Access Database File (OLE DB)
Change...
Database file name:
C:\introdatabase.mdb
Browse...
Log on to the database
User name:
Admin
Password:
Save my password
Advanced...

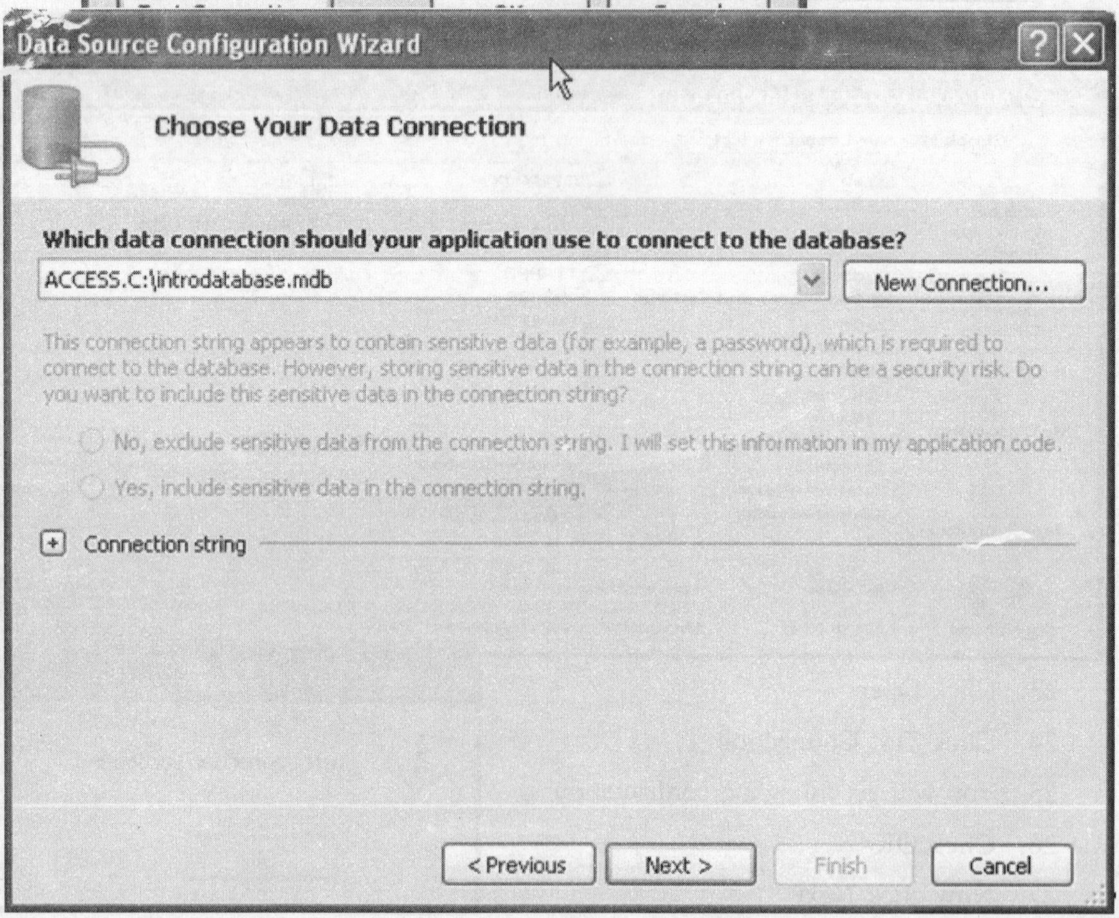
Data Source Configuration Wizard
Choose Your Data Connection
Which data connection should your application use to connect to the database?
ACCESS.C:\introdatabase.mdb
New Connection...
This connection string appears to contain sensitive data (for example, a password), which is required to connect to the database. However, storing sensitive data in the connection string can be a security risk. Do you want to include this sensitive data in the connection string?
No, exclude sensitive data from the connection string. I will set this information in my application code.
Yes, include sensitive data in the connection string.
Connection string
< Previous
Next >
Finish
Cancel

28. You will get following message

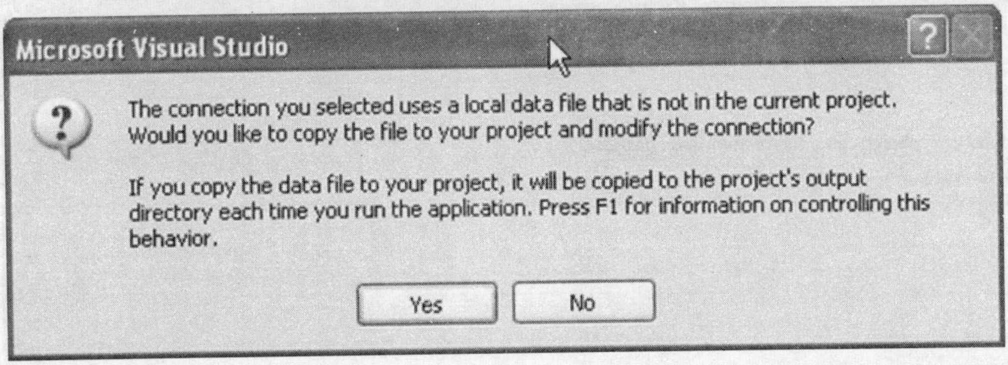

29. Click Yes

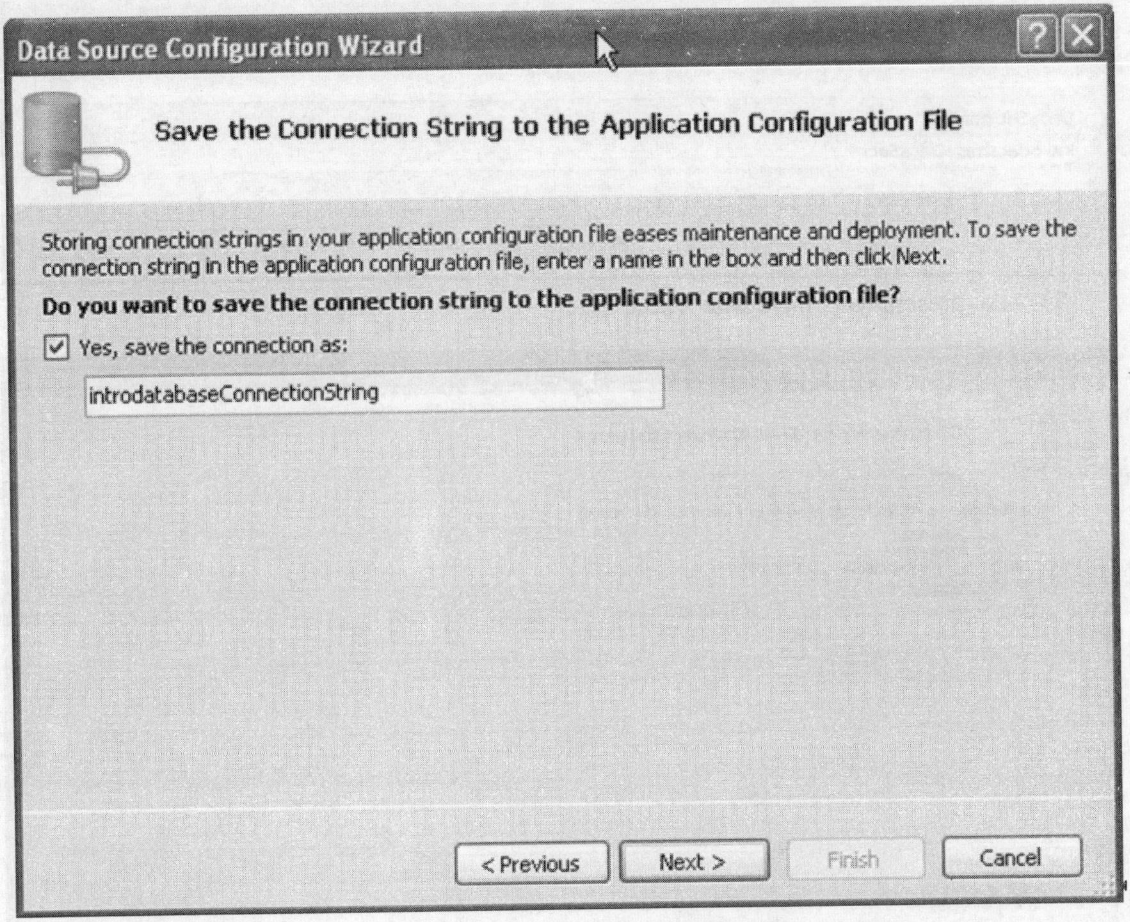

30. Keep default name as introdatabaseConnectionString
31. Click Next
32. Click + sign of Tables

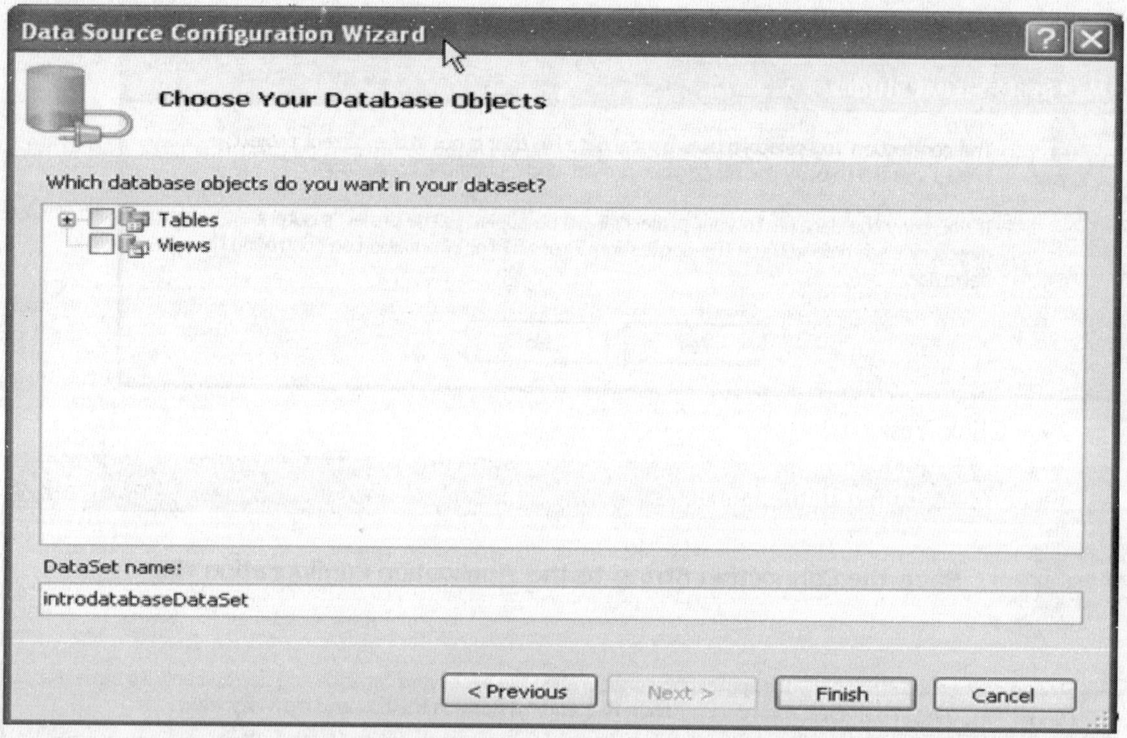

33. At present you have one Table

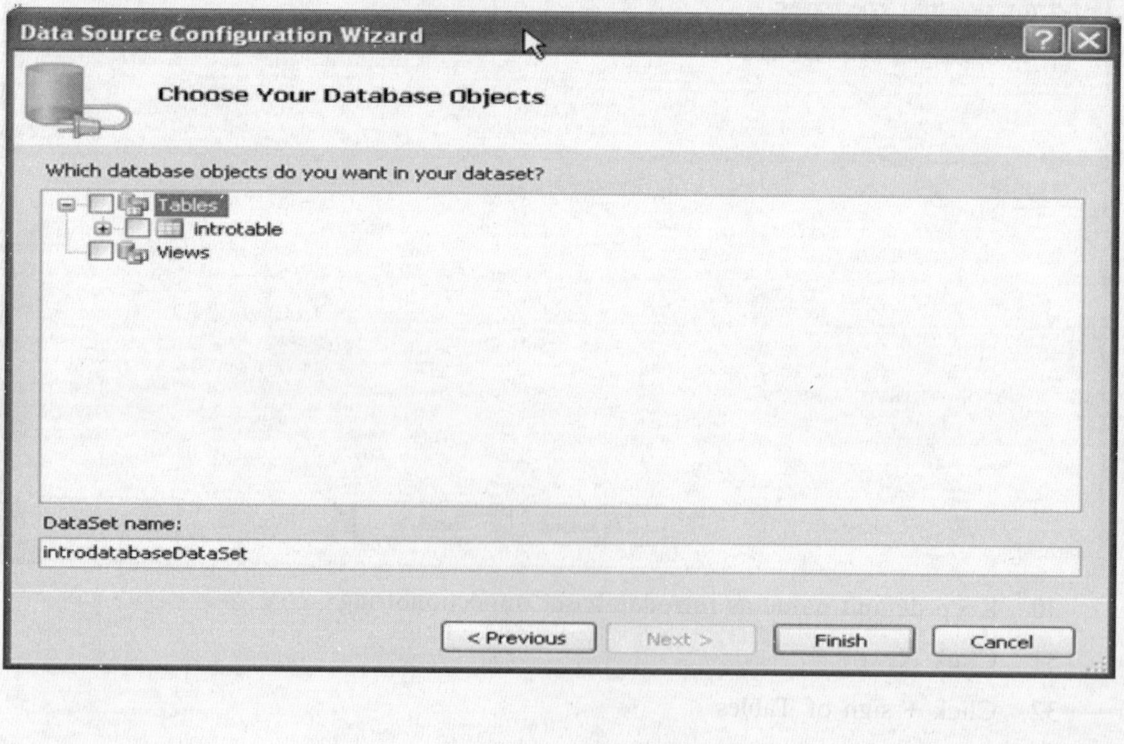

34. Now click on + sign of introtable

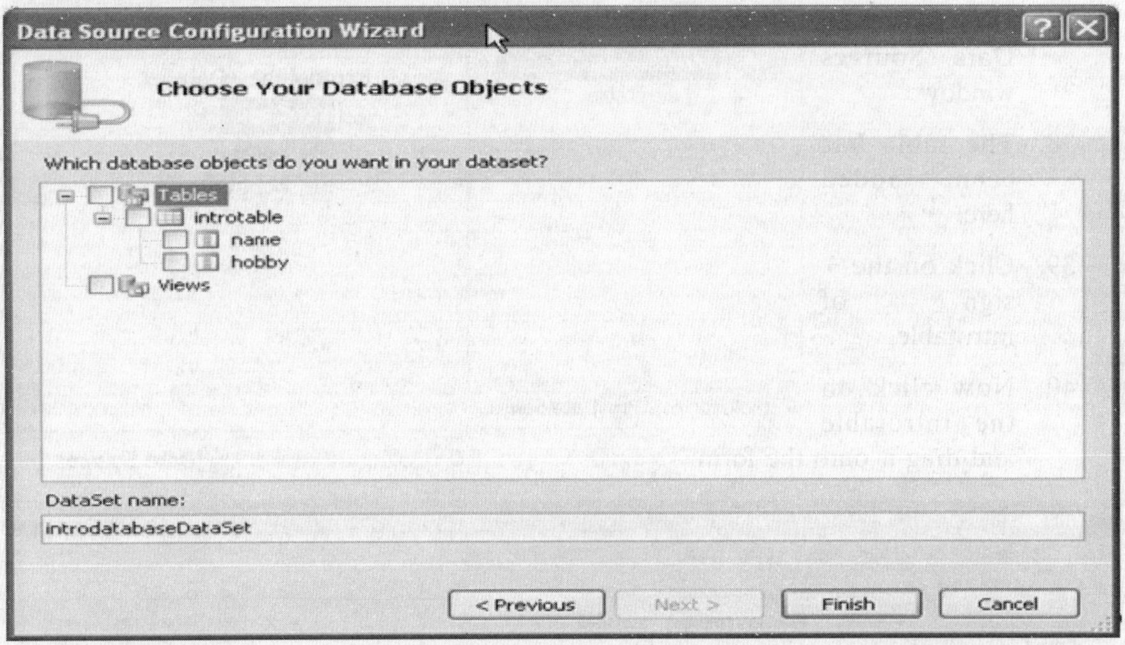

35. At present you have two fields, select both of them

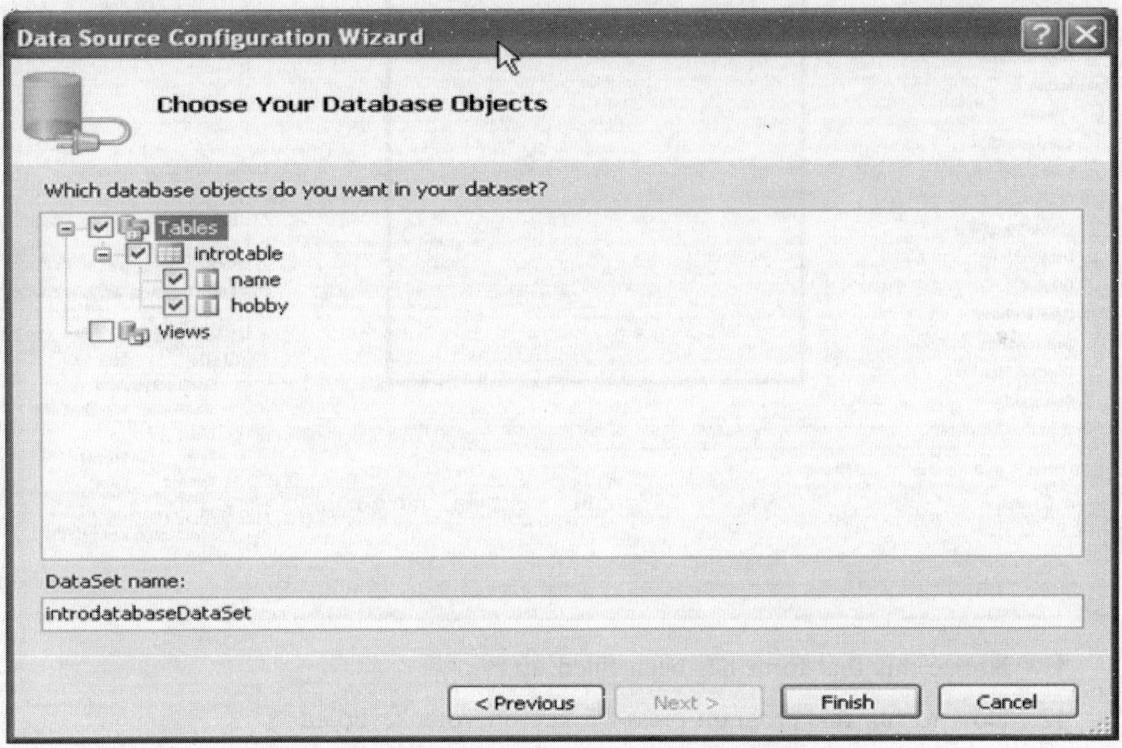

36. Click Finish
37. Now notice the Data Sources window
38. The table has been added here.
39. Click on the + sign of introtable
40. Now click on the introtable and drag it onto the form

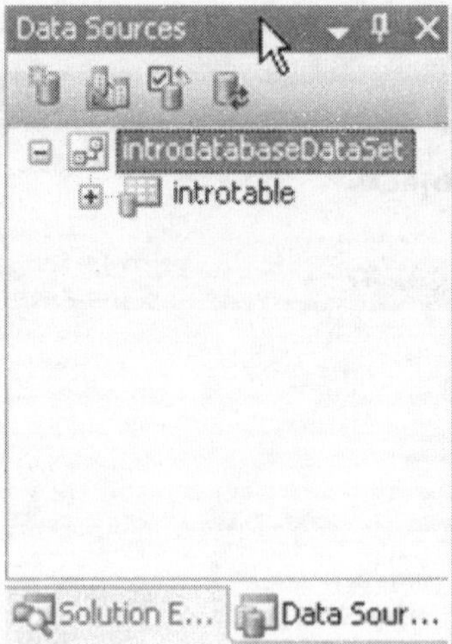

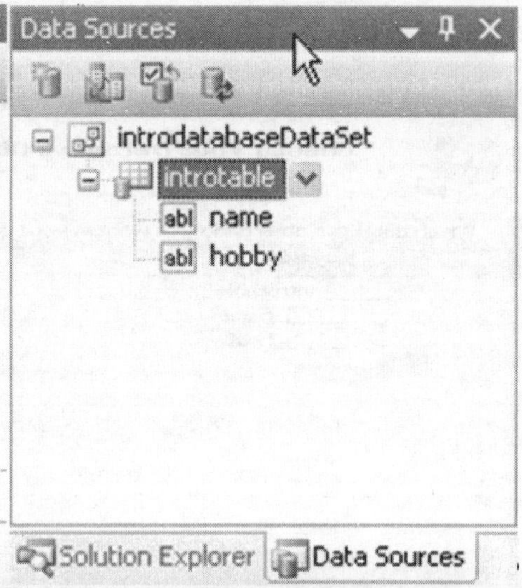

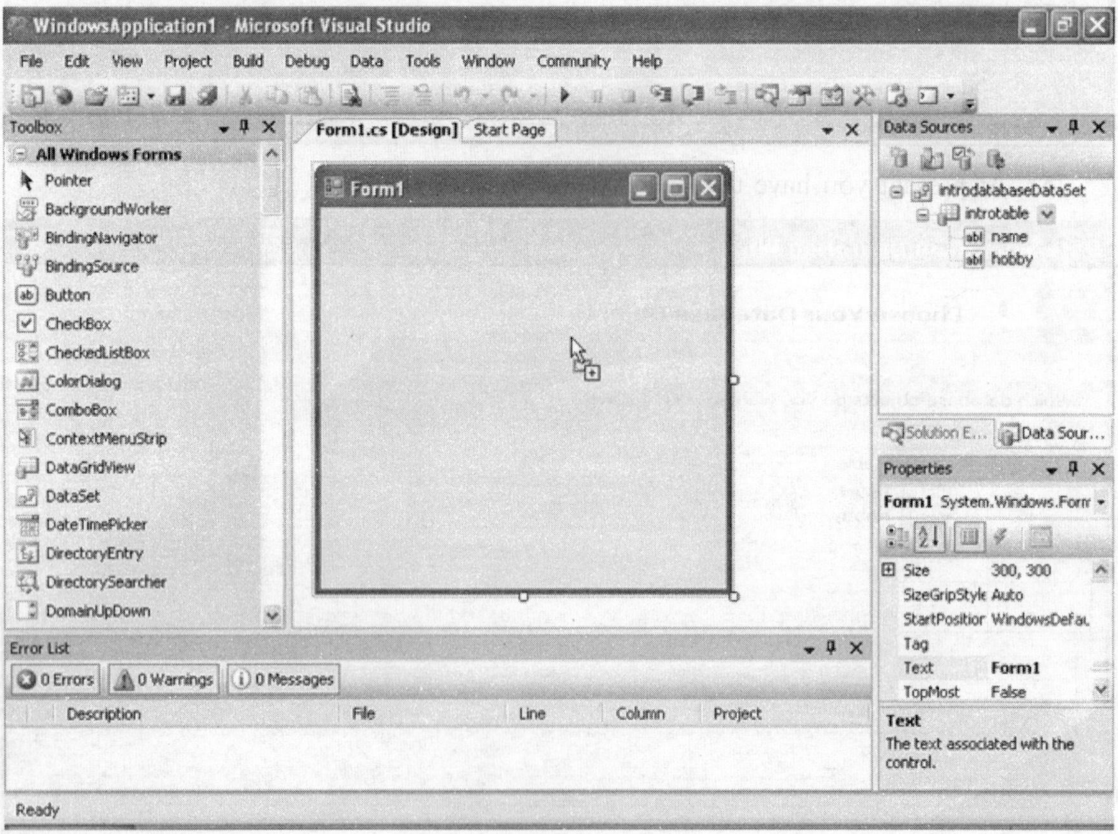

41. Notice this that form has been filled up
42. Now to run this program press F5 key on your keyboard

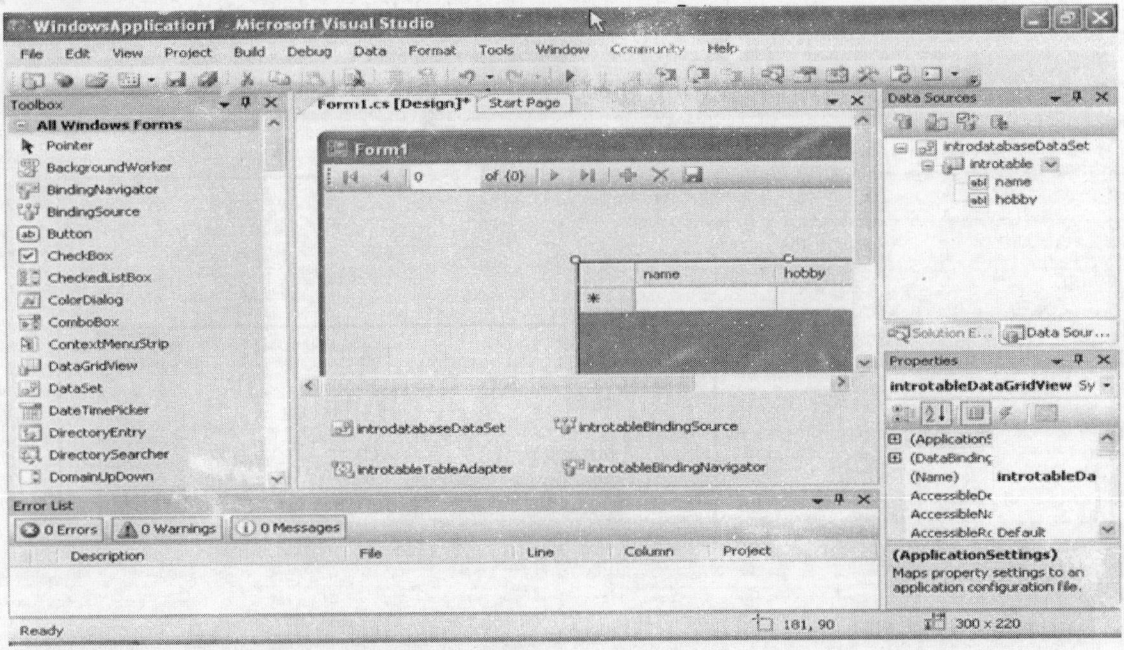

43. You will get the following output:

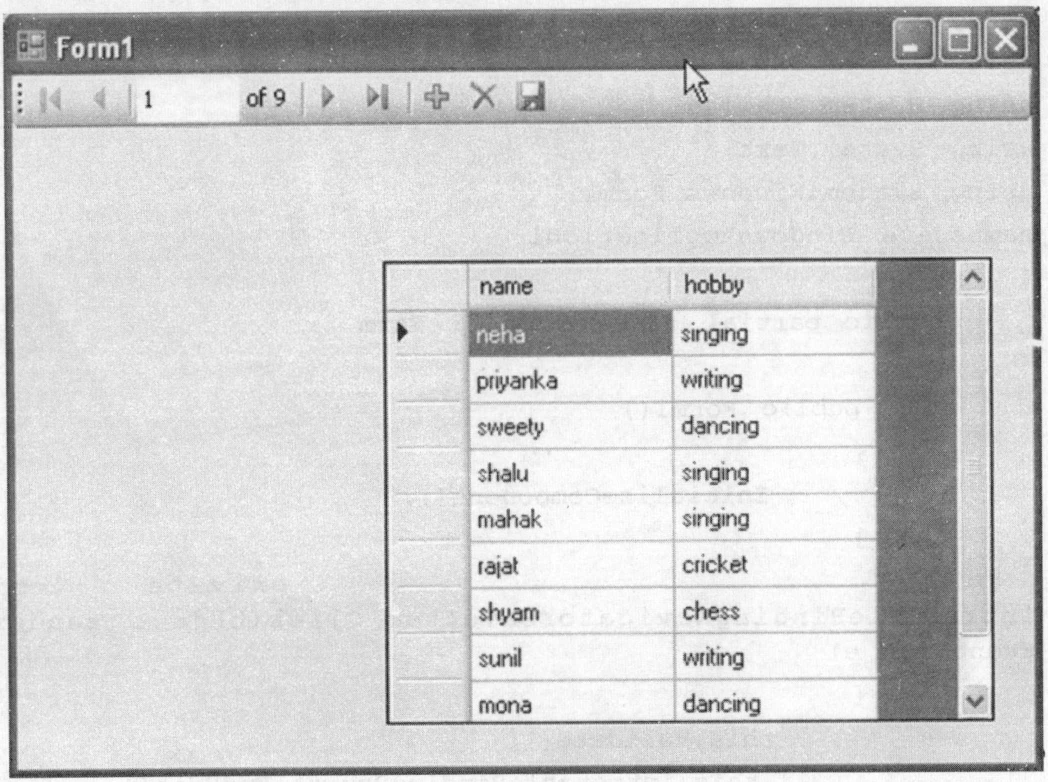

44. Now you can also navigate between records by clicking < > signs.

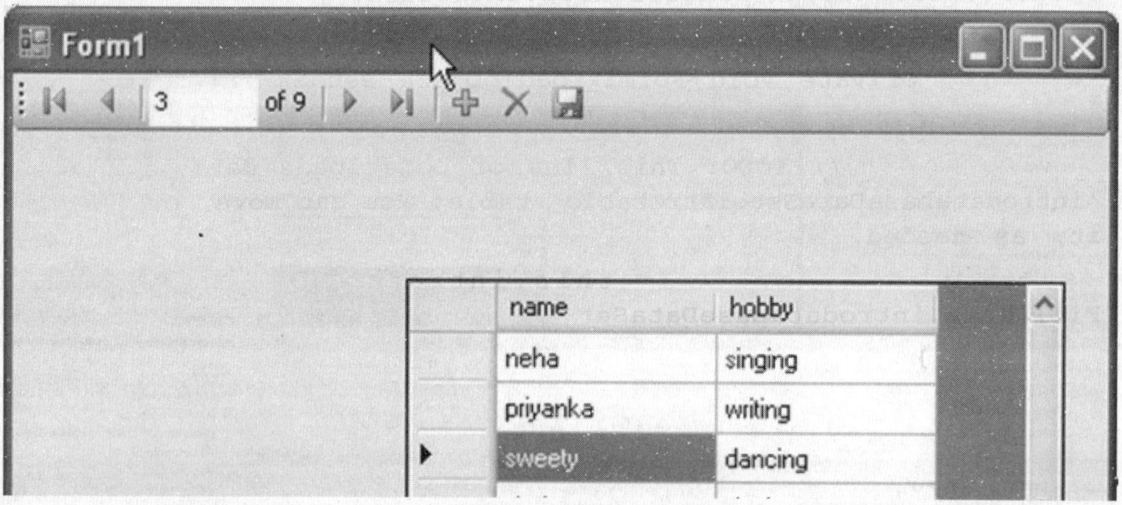

— Code Form1.cs —

```
using System;
using System.Collections.Generic;
using System.ComponentModel;
using System.Data;
using System.Drawing;
using System.Text;
using System.Windows.Forms;
namespace WindowsApplication1
{
    public partial class Form1 : Form
    {
        public Form1()
        {
            InitializeComponent();
        }
                                            private    void
introtableBindingNavigatorSaveItem_Click(object sender,
EventArgs e)
        {
            this.Validate();
             this.introtableBindingSource.EndEdit();
```

```
                        this.introtableTableAdapter.
Update(this.introdatabaseDataSet.introtable);
            }
            private void Form1_Load(object sender, EventArgs e)
            {
                // TODO: This line of code loads data into the
'introdatabaseDataSet.introtable' table. You can move, or remove
it, as needed.
                        this.introtableTableAdapter.
Fill(this.introdatabaseDataSet.introtable);
            }
        }
}
```

— code Form1.Designer.cs —

```
namespace WindowsApplication1
{
    partial class Form1
    {
        /// <summary>
        /// Required designer variable.
        /// </summary>
        private System.ComponentModel.IContainer components
= null;
        /// <summary>
        /// Clean up any resources being used.
        /// </summary>
        /// <param name="disposing">true if managed resources
should be disposed; otherwise, false.</param>
        protected override void Dispose(bool disposing)
        {
            if (disposing && (components != null))
            {
                components.Dispose();
            }
            base.Dispose(disposing);
        }
        #region Windows Form Designer generated code
```

```
        /// <summary>
        /// Required method for Designer support - do not
modify
        /// the contents of this method with the code editor.
        /// </summary>
        private void InitializeComponent()
        {
                                        this.components = new
System.ComponentModel.Container();
                    System.ComponentModel.ComponentResourceManager
resources                                         = new
System.ComponentModel.ComponentResourceManager(typeof(Form1));
                              this.introdatabaseDataSet = new
WindowsApplication1.introdatabaseDataSet();
                           this.introtableBindingSource = new
System.Windows.Forms.BindingSource(this.components);
                            this.introtableTableAdapter = new
WindowsApplication1.introdatabaseDataSetTableAdapters.
introtableTableAdapter();
                         this.introtableBindingNavigator = new
System.Windows.Forms.BindingNavigator(this.components);
                      this.bindingNavigatorMoveFirstItem = new
System.Windows.Forms.ToolStripButton();
                   this.bindingNavigatorMovePreviousItem = new
System.Windows.Forms.ToolStripButton();
                        this.bindingNavigatorSeparator = new
System.Windows.Forms.ToolStripSeparator();
                      this.bindingNavigatorPositionItem = new
System.Windows.Forms.ToolStripTextBox();
                         this.bindingNavigatorCountItem = new
System.Windows.Forms.ToolStripLabel();
                        this.bindingNavigatorSeparator1 = new
System.Windows.Forms.ToolStripSeparator();
                       this.bindingNavigatorMoveNextItem = new
System.Windows.Forms.ToolStripButton();
                       this.bindingNavigatorMoveLastItem = new
System.Windows.Forms.ToolStripButton();
                        this.bindingNavigatorSeparator2 = new
System.Windows.Forms.ToolStripSeparator();
```

```
                this.bindingNavigatorAddNewItem = new
System.Windows.Forms.ToolStripButton();
                this.bindingNavigatorDeleteItem = new
System.Windows.Forms.ToolStripButton();
              this.introtableBindingNavigatorSaveItem = new
System.Windows.Forms.ToolStripButton();
                this.introtableDataGridView = new
System.Windows.Forms.DataGridView();
                this.dataGridViewTextBoxColumn1 = new
System.Windows.Forms.DataGridViewTextBoxColumn();
                this.dataGridViewTextBoxColumn2 = new
System.Windows.Forms.DataGridViewTextBoxColumn();
               ((System.ComponentModel.ISupportInitialize)
(this.introdatabaseDataSet)).BeginInit();
               ((System.ComponentModel.ISupportInitialize)
(this.introtableBindingSource)).BeginInit();
               ((System.ComponentModel.ISupportInitialize)
(this.introtableBindingNavigator)).BeginInit();
            this.introtableBindingNavigator.SuspendLayout();
               ((System.ComponentModel.ISupportInitialize)
(this.introtableDataGridView)).BeginInit();
            this.SuspendLayout();
            //
            // introdatabaseDataSet
            //
               this.introdatabaseDataSet.DataSetName =
"introdatabaseDataSet";
            this.introdatabaseDataSet.SchemaSerializationMode
= System.Data.SchemaSerializationMode.IncludeSchema;
            //
            // introtableBindingSource
            //
               this.introtableBindingSource.DataMember =
"introtable";
               this.introtableBindingSource.DataSource =
this.introdatabaseDataSet;
            //
            // introtableTableAdapter
            //
              this.introtableTableAdapter.ClearBeforeFill =
true;
```

```
            //
            // introtableBindingNavigator
            //
            this.introtableBindingNavigator.AddNewItem =
this.bindingNavigatorAddNewItem;
            this.introtableBindingNavigator.BindingSource =
this.introtableBindingSource;
            this.introtableBindingNavigator.CountItem =
this.bindingNavigatorCountItem;
            this.introtableBindingNavigator.DeleteItem =
this.bindingNavigatorDeleteItem;
            this.introtableBindingNavigator.Items.AddRange(new
System.Windows.Forms.ToolStripItem[] {
            this.bindingNavigatorMoveFirstItem,
            this.bindingNavigatorMovePreviousItem,
            this.bindingNavigatorSeparator,
            this.bindingNavigatorPositionItem,
            this.bindingNavigatorCountItem,
            this.bindingNavigatorSeparator1,
            this.bindingNavigatorMoveNextItem,
            this.bindingNavigatorMoveLastItem,
            this.bindingNavigatorSeparator2,
            this.bindingNavigatorAddNewItem,
            this.bindingNavigatorDeleteItem,
            this.introtableBindingNavigatorSaveItem});
            this.introtableBindingNavigator.Location = new
System.Drawing.Point(0, 0);
            this.introtableBindingNavigator.MoveFirstItem =
this.bindingNavigatorMoveFirstItem;
            this.introtableBindingNavigator.MoveLastItem =
this.bindingNavigatorMoveLastItem;
            this.introtableBindingNavigator.MoveNextItem =
this.bindingNavigatorMoveNextItem;
            this.introtableBindingNavigator.MovePreviousItem
= this.bindingNavigatorMovePreviousItem;
            this.introtableBindingNavigator.Name =
"introtableBindingNavigator";
```

```
                this.introtableBindingNavigator.PositionItem =
this.bindingNavigatorPositionItem;
                this.introtableBindingNavigator.Size = new
System.Drawing.Size(501, 25);
                this.introtableBindingNavigator.TabIndex = 0;
                this.introtableBindingNavigator.Text =
"bindingNavigator1";
                //
                // bindingNavigatorMoveFirstItem
                //
                this.bindingNavigatorMoveFirstItem.DisplayStyle
= System.Windows.Forms.ToolStripItemDisplayStyle.Image;
                this.bindingNavigatorMoveFirstItem.Image =
((System.Drawing.Image)(resources.GetObject
("bindingNavigatorMoveFirstItem.Image")));
                this.bindingNavigatorMoveFirstItem.Name =
"bindingNavigatorMoveFirstItem";
                this.bindingNavigatorMoveFirstItem.
RightToLeftAutoMirrorImage = true;
                this.bindingNavigatorMoveFirstItem.Size = new
System.Drawing.Size(23, 22);
                this.bindingNavigatorMoveFirstItem.Text = "Move
first";
                //
                // bindingNavigatorMovePreviousItem
                //
                this.bindingNavigatorMovePreviousItem.DisplayStyle
= System.Windows.Forms.ToolStripItemDisplayStyle.Image;
                this.bindingNavigatorMovePreviousItem.Image =
((System.Drawing.Image)(resources.GetObject
("bindingNavigatorMovePreviousItem.Image")));
                this.bindingNavigatorMovePreviousItem.Name =
"bindingNavigatorMovePreviousItem";
                this.bindingNavigatorMovePreviousItem.
RightToLeftAutoMirrorImage = true;
                this.bindingNavigatorMovePreviousItem.Size = new
System.Drawing.Size(23, 22);
                this.bindingNavigatorMovePreviousItem.Text =
"Move previous";
```

```
            //
            // bindingNavigatorSeparator
            //
                this.bindingNavigatorSeparator.Name =
"bindingNavigatorSeparator";
                this.bindingNavigatorSeparator.Size = new
System.Drawing.Size(6, 25);
            //
            // bindingNavigatorPositionItem
            //
            this.bindingNavigatorPositionItem.AccessibleName
= "Position";
                this.bindingNavigatorPositionItem.AutoSize =
false;
                this.bindingNavigatorPositionItem.Name =
"bindingNavigatorPositionItem";
                this.bindingNavigatorPositionItem.Size = new
System.Drawing.Size(50, 21);
            this.bindingNavigatorPositionItem.Text = "0";
            this.bindingNavigatorPositionItem.ToolTipText =
"Current position";
            //
            // bindingNavigatorCountItem
            //
                this.bindingNavigatorCountItem.Name =
"bindingNavigatorCountItem";
                this.bindingNavigatorCountItem.Size = new
System.Drawing.Size(36, 13);
            this.bindingNavigatorCountItem.Text = "of {0}";
                this.bindingNavigatorCountItem.ToolTipText =
"Total number of items";
            //
            // bindingNavigatorSeparator1
            //
                this.bindingNavigatorSeparator1.Name =
"bindingNavigatorSeparator";
                this.bindingNavigatorSeparator1.Size = new
```

```
System.Drawing.Size(6, 6);
            //
            // bindingNavigatorMoveNextItem
            //
            this.bindingNavigatorMoveNextItem.DisplayStyle =
System.Windows.Forms.ToolStripItemDisplayStyle.Image;
            this.bindingNavigatorMoveNextItem.Image =
((System.Drawing.Image)(resources.GetObject
("bindingNavigatorMoveNextItem.Image")));
            this.bindingNavigatorMoveNextItem.Name =
"bindingNavigatorMoveNextItem";
            this.bindingNavigatorMoveNextItem.
RightToLeftAutoMirrorImage = true;
            this.bindingNavigatorMoveNextItem.Size = new
System.Drawing.Size(23, 20);
            this.bindingNavigatorMoveNextItem.Text = "Move
next";
            //
            // bindingNavigatorMoveLastItem
            //
            this.bindingNavigatorMoveLastItem.DisplayStyle =
System.Windows.Forms.ToolStripItemDisplayStyle.Image;
            this.bindingNavigatorMoveLastItem.Image =
((System.Drawing.Image)(resources.GetObject
("bindingNavigatorMoveLastItem.Image")));
            this.bindingNavigatorMoveLastItem.Name =
"bindingNavigatorMoveLastItem";
            this.bindingNavigatorMoveLastItem.
RightToLeftAutoMirrorImage = true;
            this.bindingNavigatorMoveLastItem.Size = new
System.Drawing.Size(23, 20);
            this.bindingNavigatorMoveLastItem.Text = "Move
last";
            //
            // bindingNavigatorSeparator2
            //
            this.bindingNavigatorSeparator2.Name =
```

```
"bindingNavigatorSeparator";
                this.bindingNavigatorSeparator2.Size = new
System.Drawing.Size(6, 6);
            //
            // bindingNavigatorAddNewItem
            //
            this.bindingNavigatorAddNewItem.DisplayStyle =
System.Windows.Forms.ToolStripItemDisplayStyle.Image;
            this.bindingNavigatorAddNewItem.Image =
((System.Drawing.Image)(resources.GetObject
("bindingNavigatorAddNewItem.Image")));
            this.bindingNavigatorAddNewItem.Name =
"bindingNavigatorAddNewItem";
            this.bindingNavigatorAddNewItem.
RightToLeftAutoMirrorImage = true;
            this.bindingNavigatorAddNewItem.Size = new
System.Drawing.Size(23, 22);
        this.bindingNavigatorAddNewItem.Text = "Add new";
            //
            // bindingNavigatorDeleteItem
            //
            this.bindingNavigatorDeleteItem.DisplayStyle =
System.Windows.Forms.ToolStripItemDisplayStyle.Image;
            this.bindingNavigatorDeleteItem.Image =
((System.Drawing.Image)(resources.GetObject
("bindingNavigatorDeleteItem.Image")));
            this.bindingNavigatorDeleteItem.Name =
"bindingNavigatorDeleteItem";
        this.bindingNavigatorDeleteItem.RightToLeftAutoMirrorImage
= true;
            this.bindingNavigatorDeleteItem.Size = new
System.Drawing.Size(23, 20);
        this.bindingNavigatorDeleteItem.Text = "Delete";
            //
            // introtableBindingNavigatorSaveItem
            //
        this.introtableBindingNavigatorSaveItem.DisplayStyle
= System.Windows.Forms.ToolStripItemDisplayStyle.Image;
            this.introtableBindingNavigatorSaveItem.Image =
((System.Drawing.Image)(resources.GetObject
("introtableBindingNavigatorSaveItem.Image")));
```

```
            this.introtableBindingNavigatorSaveItem.Name =
"introtableBindingNavigatorSaveItem";
            this.introtableBindingNavigatorSaveItem.Size =
new System.Drawing.Size(23, 23);
            this.introtableBindingNavigatorSaveItem.Text =
"Save Data";
            this.introtableBindingNavigatorSaveItem.Click +=
new System.EventHandler (this.introtableBindingNavigator
SaveItem_Click);
            //
            // introtableDataGridView
            //
            this.introtableDataGridView.AutoGenerateColumns
= false;
            this.introtableDataGridView.Columns.AddRange(new
System.Windows.Forms.DataGridViewColumn[] {
            this.dataGridViewTextBoxColumn1,
            this.dataGridViewTextBoxColumn2});
            this.introtableDataGridView.DataSource =
this.introtableBindingSource;
            this.introtableDataGridView.Location = new
System.Drawing.Point(181, 90);
            this.introtableDataGridView.Name =
"introtableDataGridView";
            this.introtableDataGridView.Size = new
System.Drawing.Size(300, 220);
            this.introtableDataGridView.TabIndex = 1;
            //
            // dataGridViewTextBoxColumn1
            //
            this.dataGridViewTextBoxColumn1.DataPropertyName
= "name";
            this.dataGridViewTextBoxColumn1.HeaderText =
"name";
            this.dataGridViewTextBoxColumn1.Name =
"dataGridViewTextBoxColumn1";
            //
            // dataGridViewTextBoxColumn2
```

```
            //
            this.dataGridViewTextBoxColumn2.DataPropertyName
= "hobby";
              this.dataGridViewTextBoxColumn2.HeaderText =
"hobby";
               this.dataGridViewTextBoxColumn2.Name =
"dataGridViewTextBoxColumn2";
            //
            // Form1
            //
                  this.AutoScaleDimensions = new
System.Drawing.SizeF(6F, 13F);
                         this.AutoScaleMode =
System.Windows.Forms.AutoScaleMode.Font;
            this.ClientSize = new System.Drawing.Size(501,
330);
            this.Controls.Add(this.introtableDataGridView);
         this.Controls.Add(this.introtableBindingNavigator);
            this.Name = "Form1";
            this.Text = "Form1";
                           this.Load += new
System.EventHandler(this.Form1_Load);
              ((System.ComponentModel.ISupportInitialize)
(this.introdatabaseDataSet)).EndInit();
              ((System.ComponentModel.ISupportInitialize)
(this.introtableBindingSource)).EndInit();
              ((System.ComponentModel.ISupportInitialize)
(this.introtableBindingNavigator)).EndInit();
        this.introtableBindingNavigator.ResumeLayout(false);
           this.introtableBindingNavigator.PerformLayout();
              ((System.ComponentModel.ISupportInitialize)
(this.introtableDataGridView)).EndInit();
            this.ResumeLayout(false);
            this.PerformLayout();
        }
        #endregion
        private introdatabaseDataSet introdatabaseDataSet;
```

```
        private System.Windows.Forms.BindingSource
introtableBindingSource;
        private WindowsApplication1.introdatabaseDataSetTable
Adapters.introtableTableAdapter introtableTableAdapter;
        private System.Windows.Forms.BindingNavigator
introtableBindingNavigator;
        private System.Windows.Forms.ToolStripButton
bindingNavigatorAddNewItem;
        private System.Windows.Forms.ToolStripLabel
bindingNavigatorCountItem;
        private System.Windows.Forms.ToolStripButton
bindingNavigatorDeleteItem;
        private System.Windows.Forms.ToolStripButton
bindingNavigatorMoveFirstItem;
        private System.Windows.Forms.ToolStripButton
bindingNavigatorMovePreviousItem;
        private System.Windows.Forms.ToolStripSeparator
bindingNavigatorSeparator;
        private System.Windows.Forms.ToolStripTextBox
bindingNavigatorPositionItem;
        private System.Windows.Forms.ToolStripSeparator
bindingNavigatorSeparator1;
        private System.Windows.Forms.ToolStripButton
bindingNavigatorMoveNextItem;
        private System.Windows.Forms.ToolStripButton
bindingNavigatorMoveLastItem;
        private System.Windows.Forms.ToolStripSeparator
bindingNavigatorSeparator2;
        private System.Windows.Forms.ToolStripButton
introtableBindingNavigatorSaveItem;
        private System.Windows.Forms.DataGridView
introtableDataGridView;
        private System.Windows.Forms.DataGridViewTextBoxColumn
dataGridViewTextBoxColumn1;
        private System.Windows.Forms.DataGridViewTextBoxColumn
dataGridViewTextBoxColumn2;
    }
}
```

— code Program.cs —

```
using System;
using System.Collections.Generic;
using System.Windows.Forms;
namespace WindowsApplication1
{
      static class Program
      {
            /// <summary>
            /// The main entry point for the application.
            /// </summary>
            [STAThread]
            static void Main()
            {
                  Application.EnableVisualStyles();
             Application.SetCompatibleTextRenderingDefault(false);
                  Application.Run(new Form1());
            }
      }
}
```

— app.config —

```
<?xml version="1.0" encoding="utf-8" ?>
<configuration>
      <configSections>
      </configSections>
      <connectionStrings>
           <add   name="WindowsApplication1.Properties.
Settings.introdatabase ConnectionString"
           connectionString="Provider=Microsoft.Jet.OLEDB.4.0;Data
Source=|DataDirectory|\introdatabase.mdb"
                 providerName="System.Data.OleDb" />
      </connectionStrings>
</configuration>
```

If you wish you can also modify the above program. This way you can change the look and appearance. For this first take out everything from the form. Make it simple.

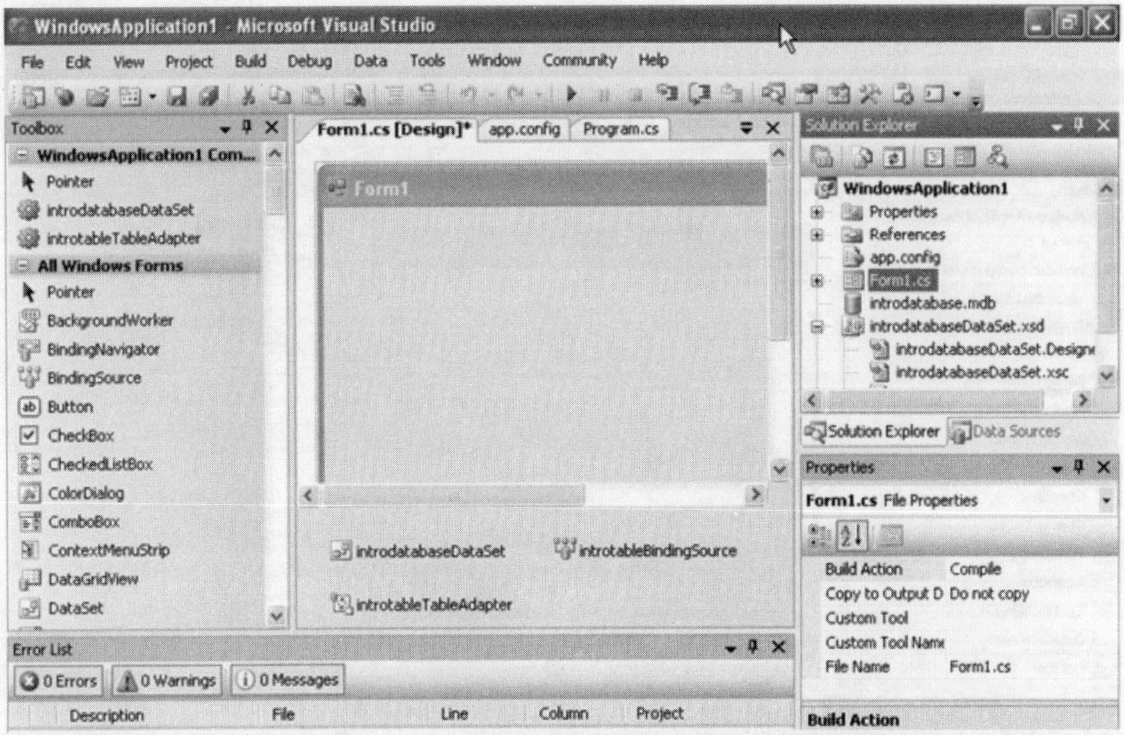

45. Now in Data Sources widow click the name field and drag it onto the form.

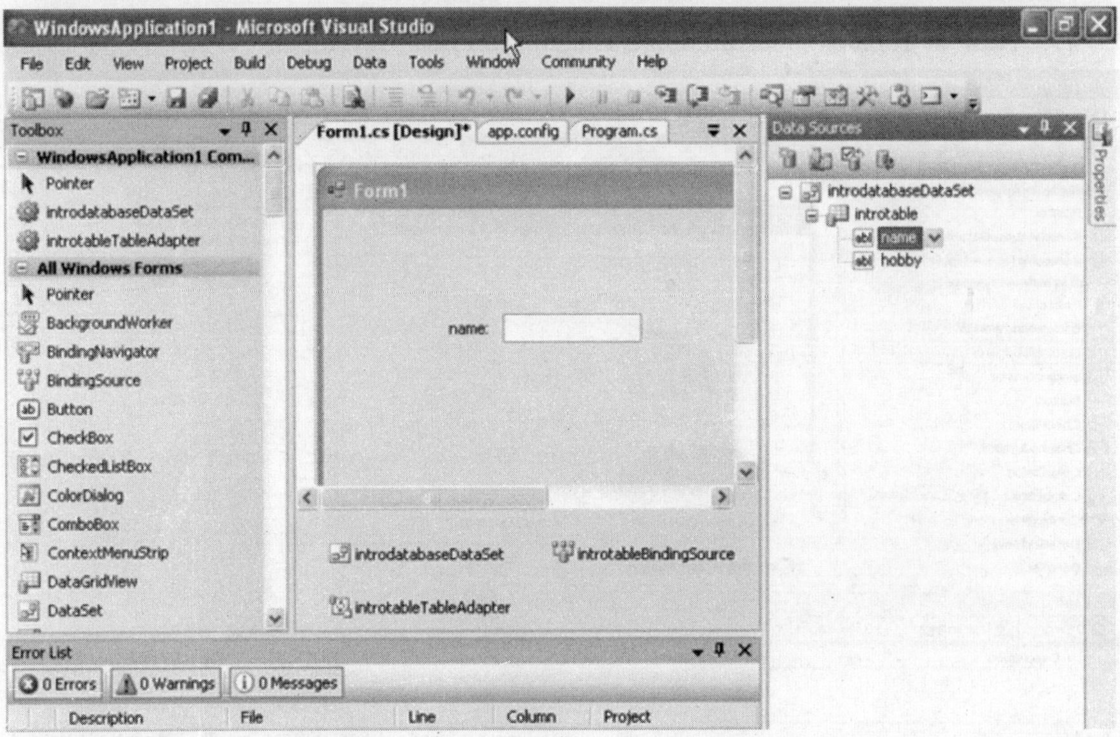

46. Now click the hobby field and drag it onto the form

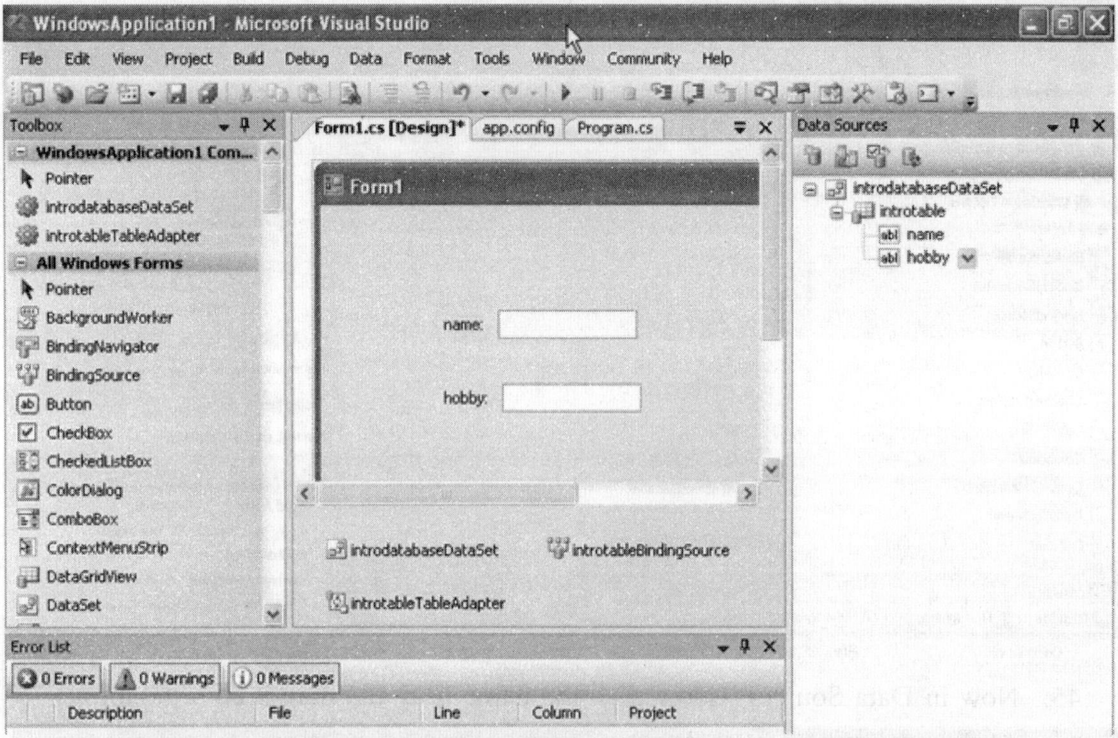

47. Now in Toolbox click BindingNaviagtor control

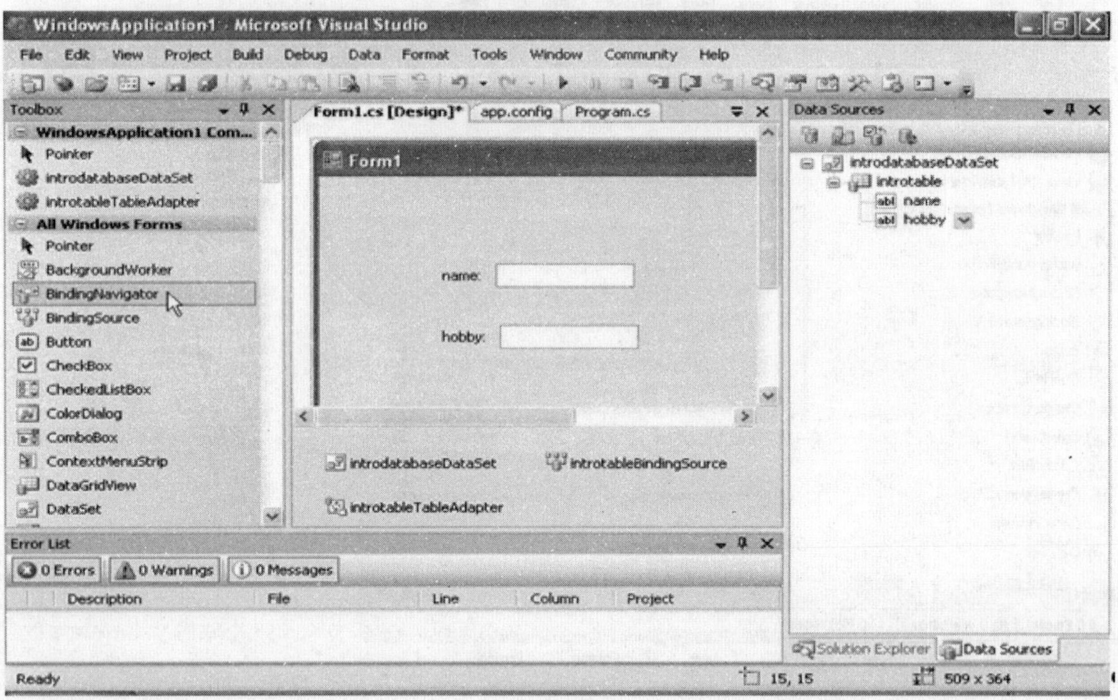

48. Drag it onto the form

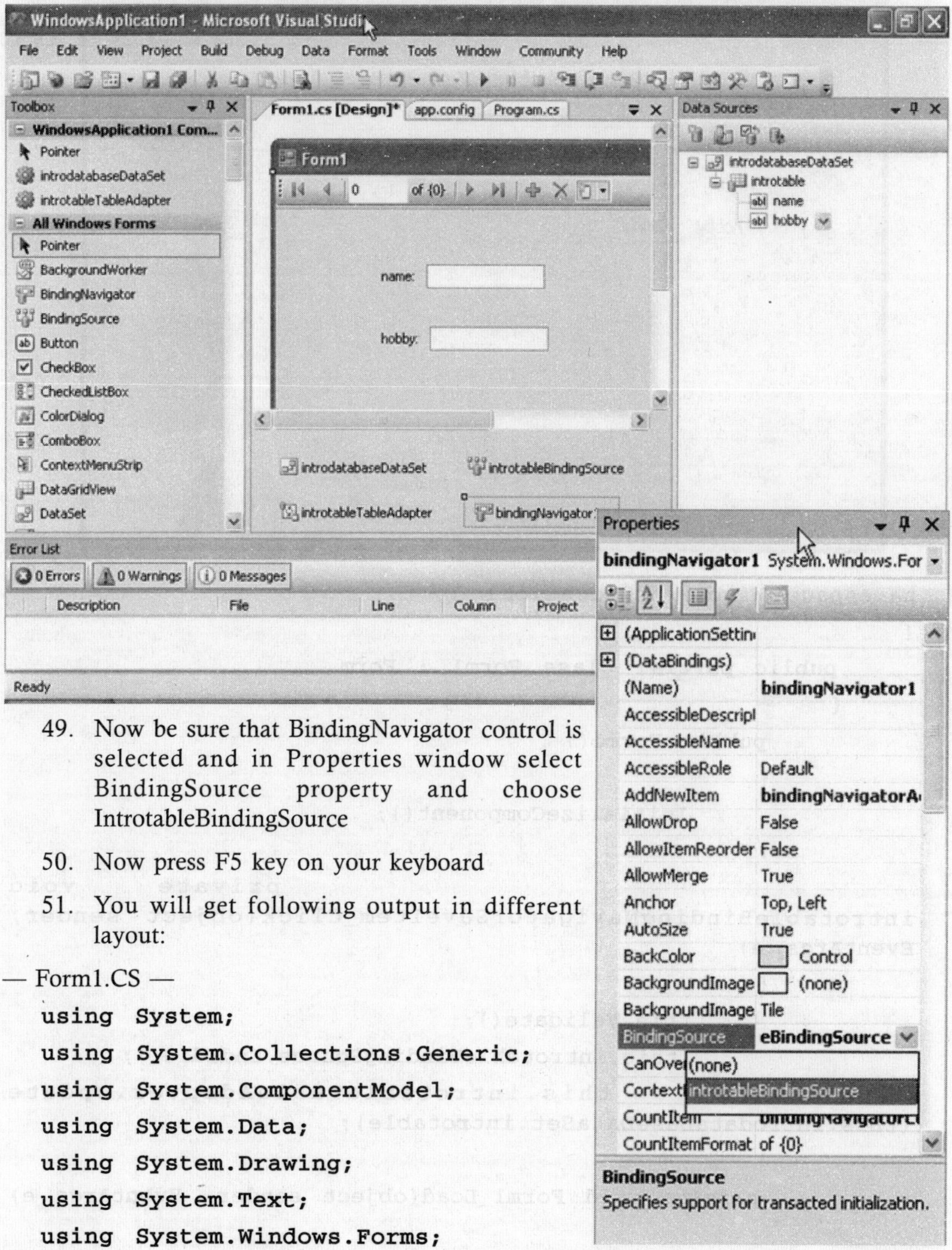

49. Now be sure that BindingNavigator control is selected and in Properties window select BindingSource property and choose IntrotableBindingSource

50. Now press F5 key on your keyboard

51. You will get following output in different layout:

— Form1.CS —

```
using System;
using System.Collections.Generic;
using System.ComponentModel;
using System.Data;
using System.Drawing;
using System.Text;
using System.Windows.Forms;
```

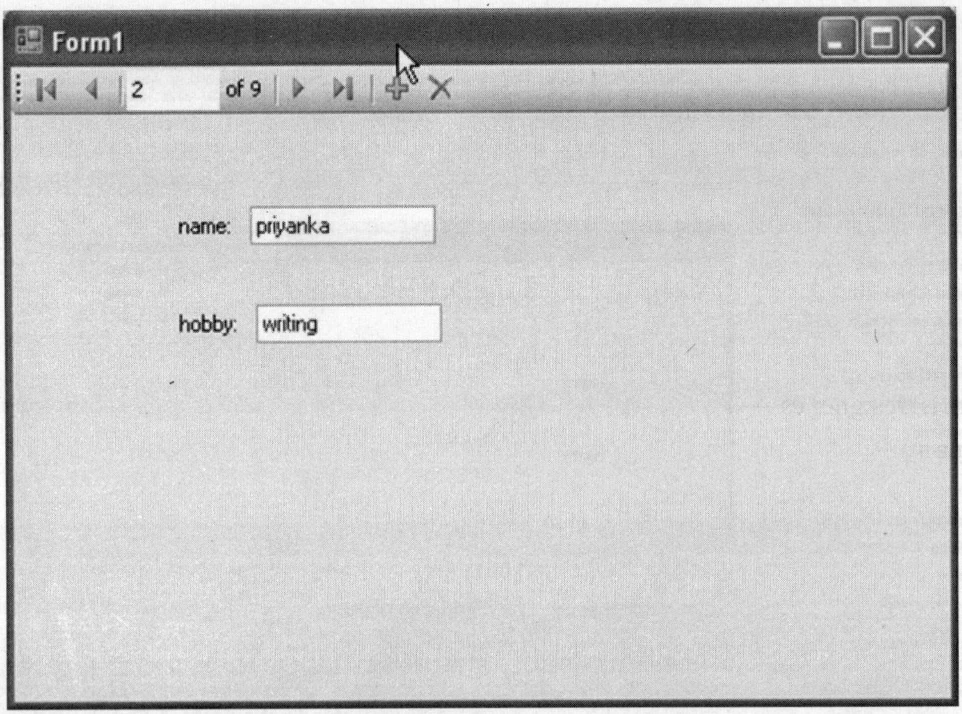


```
namespace WindowsApplication1
{
     public partial class Form1 : Form
     {
          public Form1()
          {
               InitializeComponent();
          }
                                        private void
introtableBindingNavigatorSaveItem_Click(object sender,
EventArgs e)
          {
               this.Validate();
                this.introtableBindingSource.EndEdit();
                    this.introtableTableAdapter.Update
(this.introdatabaseDataSet.introtable);
          }
          private void Form1_Load(object sender, EventArgs e)
```

```
            {
                // TODO: This line of code loads data into the
'introdatabaseDataSet.introtable' table. You can move, or remove
it, as needed.
                          this.introtableTableAdapter.
Fill(this.introdatabaseDataSet.introtable);
            }
        }
}
```

— Form1.Designer.cs —

```
namespace WindowsApplication1
{
    partial class Form1
    {
        /// <summary>
        /// Required designer variable.
        /// </summary>
        private System.ComponentModel.IContainer components
= null;
        /// <summary>
        /// Clean up any resources being used.
        /// </summary>
       /// <param name="disposing">true if managed resources
should be disposed; otherwise, false.</param>
        protected override void Dispose(bool disposing)
        {
            if (disposing && (components != null))
            {
                components.Dispose();
            }
            base.Dispose(disposing);
        }
        #region Windows Form Designer generated code
        /// <summary>
        /// Required method for Designer support - do not
modify
```

```
        /// the contents of this method with the code editor.
        /// </summary>
        private void InitializeComponent()
        {
                this.components = new System.ComponentModel.Container();
            System.Windows.Forms.Label nameLabel;
            System.Windows.Forms.Label hobbyLabel;
            System.ComponentModel.ComponentResourceManager resources = new System.ComponentModel.ComponentResourceManager(typeof(Form1));
            this.introdatabaseDataSet = new WindowsApplication1.introdatabaseDataSet();
            this.introtableBindingSource = new System.Windows.Forms.BindingSource(this.components);
            this.introtableTableAdapter = new WindowsApplication1.introdatabaseDataSetTable Adapters.introtableTableAdapter();
            this.nameTextBox = new System.Windows.Forms.TextBox();
            this.hobbyTextBox = new System.Windows.Forms.TextBox();
            this.bindingNavigator1 = new System.Windows.Forms.BindingNavigator(this.components);
            this.bindingNavigatorMoveFirstItem = new System.Windows.Forms.ToolStripButton();
            this.bindingNavigatorMovePreviousItem = new System.Windows.Forms.ToolStripButton();
            this.bindingNavigatorSeparator = new System.Windows.Forms.ToolStripSeparator();
            this.bindingNavigatorPositionItem = new System.Windows.Forms.ToolStripTextBox();
            this.bindingNavigatorCountItem = new System.Windows.Forms.ToolStripLabel();
            this.bindingNavigatorSeparator1 = new System.Windows.Forms.ToolStripSeparator();
            this.bindingNavigatorMoveNextItem = new System.Windows.Forms.ToolStripButton();
```

```
            this.bindingNavigatorMoveLastItem = new
System.Windows.Forms.ToolStripButton();
            this.bindingNavigatorSeparator2 = new
System.Windows.Forms.ToolStripSeparator();
            this.bindingNavigatorAddNewItem = new
System.Windows.Forms.ToolStripButton();
            this.bindingNavigatorDeleteItem = new
System.Windows.Forms.ToolStripButton();
        nameLabel = new System.Windows.Forms.Label();
        hobbyLabel = new System.Windows.Forms.Label();
            ((System.ComponentModel.ISupportInitialize)
(this.introdatabaseDataSet)).BeginInit();
            ((System.ComponentModel.ISupportInitialize)
(this.introtableBindingSource)).BeginInit();
            ((System.ComponentModel.ISupportInitialize)
(this.bindingNavigator1)).BeginInit();
        this.bindingNavigator1.SuspendLayout();
        this.SuspendLayout();
        //
        // introdatabaseDataSet
        //
            this.introdatabaseDataSet.DataSetName =
"introdatabaseDataSet";
        this.introdatabaseDataSet.SchemaSerializationMode
= System.Data.SchemaSerializationMode.IncludeSchema;
        //
        // introtableBindingSource
        //
            this.introtableBindingSource.DataMember =
"introtable";
            this.introtableBindingSource.DataSource =
this.introdatabaseDataSet;
        //
        // introtableTableAdapter
        //
            this.introtableTableAdapter.ClearBeforeFill =
true;
        //
        // nameLabel
```

```
            //
            nameLabel.AutoSize = true;
            nameLabel.Location = new System.Drawing.Point(86,
76);
            nameLabel.Name = "nameLabel";
            nameLabel.Size = new System.Drawing.Size(36, 13);
            nameLabel.TabIndex = 0;
            nameLabel.Text = "name:";
            //
            // nameTextBox
            //
            this.nameTextBox.DataBindings.Add(new
System.Windows.Forms.Binding("Text",
this.introtableBindingSource, "name", true));
            this.nameTextBox.Location = new
System.Drawing.Point(128, 73);
            this.nameTextBox.Name = "nameTextBox";
            this.nameTextBox.Size = new
System.Drawing.Size(100, 20);
            this.nameTextBox.TabIndex = 1;
            //
            // hobbyLabel
            //
            hobbyLabel.AutoSize = true;
            hobbyLabel.Location = new
System.Drawing.Point(86, 127);
            hobbyLabel.Name = "hobbyLabel";
            hobbyLabel.Size = new System.Drawing.Size(39,
13);
            hobbyLabel.TabIndex = 2;
            hobbyLabel.Text = "hobby:";
            //
            // hobbyTextBox
            //
            this.hobbyTextBox.DataBindings.Add(new
System.Windows.Forms.Binding("Text", this.introtableBinding
Source, "hobby", true));
```

```
                this.hobbyTextBox.Location = new
System.Drawing.Point(131, 124);
            this.hobbyTextBox.Name = "hobbyTextBox";
                this.hobbyTextBox.Size = new
System.Drawing.Size(100, 20);
            this.hobbyTextBox.TabIndex = 3;
            //
            // bindingNavigator1
            //
                this.bindingNavigator1.AddNewItem =
this.bindingNavigatorAddNewItem;
              this.bindingNavigator1.BindingSource =
this.introtableBindingSource;
                this.bindingNavigator1.CountItem =
this.bindingNavigatorCountItem;
                this.bindingNavigator1.DeleteItem =
this.bindingNavigatorDeleteItem;
              this.bindingNavigator1.Items.AddRange(new
System.Windows.Forms.ToolStripItem[] {
            this.bindingNavigatorMoveFirstItem,
            this.bindingNavigatorMovePreviousItem,
            this.bindingNavigatorSeparator,
            this.bindingNavigatorPositionItem,
            this.bindingNavigatorCountItem,
            this.bindingNavigatorSeparator1,
            this.bindingNavigatorMoveNextItem,
            this.bindingNavigatorMoveLastItem,
            this.bindingNavigatorSeparator2,
            this.bindingNavigatorAddNewItem,
            this.bindingNavigatorDeleteItem});
              this.bindingNavigator1.Location = new
System.Drawing.Point(0, 0);
              this.bindingNavigator1.MoveFirstItem =
this.bindingNavigatorMoveFirstItem;
              this.bindingNavigator1.MoveLastItem =
```

```
this.bindingNavigatorMoveLastItem;
            this.bindingNavigator1.MoveNextItem =
this.bindingNavigatorMoveNextItem;
            this.bindingNavigator1.MovePreviousItem =
this.bindingNavigatorMovePreviousItem;
            this.bindingNavigator1.Name =
"bindingNavigator1";
            this.bindingNavigator1.PositionItem =
this.bindingNavigatorPositionItem;
            this.bindingNavigator1.Size = new
System.Drawing.Size(501, 25);
            this.bindingNavigator1.TabIndex = 4;
            this.bindingNavigator1.Text =
"bindingNavigator1";
            //
            // bindingNavigatorMoveFirstItem
            //
            this.bindingNavigatorMoveFirstItem.DisplayStyle
= System.Windows.Forms.ToolStripItemDisplayStyle.Image;
            this.bindingNavigatorMoveFirstItem.Image =
((System.Drawing.Image)(resources.GetObject(
"bindingNavigatorMoveFirstItem.Image")));
            this.bindingNavigatorMoveFirstItem.Name =
"bindingNavigatorMoveFirstItem";
            this.bindingNavigatorMoveFirstItem.
RightToLeftAutoMirrorImage = true;
            this.bindingNavigatorMoveFirstItem.Size = new
System.Drawing.Size(23, 22);
            this.bindingNavigatorMoveFirstItem.Text = "Move
first";
            //
            // bindingNavigatorMovePreviousItem
            //
            this.bindingNavigatorMovePreviousItem.DisplayStyle
= System.Windows.Forms.ToolStripItemDisplayStyle.Image;
            this.bindingNavigatorMovePreviousItem.Image =
((System.Drawing.Image)(resources.GetObject ("bindingNavigator
MovePreviousItem.Image")));
```

```
this.bindingNavigatorMovePreviousItem.Name =
"bindingNavigatorMovePreviousItem";
this.bindingNavigatorMovePreviousItem.
RightToLeftAutoMirrorImage = true;
this.bindingNavigatorMovePreviousItem.Size = new
System.Drawing.Size(23, 22);
this.bindingNavigatorMovePreviousItem.Text =
"Move previous";
//
// bindingNavigatorSeparator
//
this.bindingNavigatorSeparator.Name =
"bindingNavigatorSeparator";
this.bindingNavigatorSeparator.Size = new
System.Drawing.Size(6, 25);
//
// bindingNavigatorPositionItem
//
this.bindingNavigatorPositionItem.AccessibleName
= "Position";
this.bindingNavigatorPositionItem.AutoSize =
false;
this.bindingNavigatorPositionItem.Name =
"bindingNavigatorPositionItem";
this.bindingNavigatorPositionItem.Size = new
System.Drawing.Size(50, 21);
this.bindingNavigatorPositionItem.Text = "0";
this.bindingNavigatorPositionItem.ToolTipText =
"Current position";
//
// bindingNavigatorCountItem
//
this.bindingNavigatorCountItem.Name =
"bindingNavigatorCountItem";
this.bindingNavigatorCountItem.Size = new
System.Drawing.Size(36, 22);
this.bindingNavigatorCountItem.Text = "of {0}";
this.bindingNavigatorCountItem.ToolTipText =
```

```
"Total number of items";
            //
            // bindingNavigatorSeparator1
            //
            this.bindingNavigatorSeparator1.Name =
"bindingNavigatorSeparator";
            this.bindingNavigatorSeparator1.Size = new
System.Drawing.Size(6, 25);
            //
            // bindingNavigatorMoveNextItem
            //
            this.bindingNavigatorMoveNextItem.DisplayStyle =
System.Windows.Forms.ToolStripItemDisplayStyle.Image;
            this.bindingNavigatorMoveNextItem.Image =
((System.Drawing.Image)(resources.GetObject
("bindingNavigatorMoveNextItem.Image")));
            this.bindingNavigatorMoveNextItem.Name =
"bindingNavigatorMoveNextItem";
            this.bindingNavigatorMoveNextItem.
RightToLeftAutoMirrorImage = true;
            this.bindingNavigatorMoveNextItem.Size = new
System.Drawing.Size(23, 22);
            this.bindingNavigatorMoveNextItem.Text = "Move
next";
            //
            // bindingNavigatorMoveLastItem
            //
            this.bindingNavigatorMoveLastItem.DisplayStyle =
System.Windows.Forms.ToolStripItemDisplayStyle.Image;
            this.bindingNavigatorMoveLastItem.Image =
((System.Drawing.Image)(resources.GetObject
("bindingNavigatorMoveLastItem.Image")));
            this.bindingNavigatorMoveLastItem.Name =
"bindingNavigatorMoveLastItem";
            this.bindingNavigatorMoveLastItem.
RightToLeftAutoMirrorImage = true;
            this.bindingNavigatorMoveLastItem.Size = new
System.Drawing.Size(23, 22);
```

```
this.bindingNavigatorMoveLastItem.Text = "Move last";
//
// bindingNavigatorSeparator2
//
this.bindingNavigatorSeparator2.Name =
"bindingNavigatorSeparator";
this.bindingNavigatorSeparator2.Size = new
System.Drawing.Size(6, 25);
//
// bindingNavigatorAddNewItem
//
this.bindingNavigatorAddNewItem.DisplayStyle =
System.Windows.Forms.ToolStripItemDisplayStyle.Image;
this.bindingNavigatorAddNewItem.Image =
((System.Drawing.Image)(resources.GetObject
("bindingNavigatorAddNewItem.Image")));
this.bindingNavigatorAddNewItem.Name =
"bindingNavigatorAddNewItem";
this.bindingNavigatorAddNewItem.
RightToLeftAutoMirrorImage = true;
this.bindingNavigatorAddNewItem.Size = new
System.Drawing.Size(23, 22);
this.bindingNavigatorAddNewItem.Text = "Add new";
//
// bindingNavigatorDeleteItem
//
this.bindingNavigatorDeleteItem.DisplayStyle =
System.Windows.Forms.ToolStripItemDisplayStyle.Image;
this.bindingNavigatorDeleteItem.Image =
((System.Drawing.Image)(resources.GetObject("binding
NavigatorDeleteItem.Image")));
this.bindingNavigatorDeleteItem.Name =
"bindingNavigatorDeleteItem";
this.bindingNavigatorDeleteItem.RightToLeftAutoMirrorImage
= true;
this.bindingNavigatorDeleteItem.Size = new
System.Drawing.Size(23, 22);
this.bindingNavigatorDeleteItem.Text = "Delete";
//
```

```
            // Form1
            //
                        this.AutoScaleDimensions = new
System.Drawing.SizeF(6F, 13F);
                        this.AutoScaleMode =
System.Windows.Forms.AutoScaleMode.Font;
            this.ClientSize = new System.Drawing.Size(501, 330);
            this.Controls.Add(this.bindingNavigator1);
            this.Controls.Add(hobbyLabel);
            this.Controls.Add(this.hobbyTextBox);
            this.Controls.Add(nameLabel);
            this.Controls.Add(this.nameTextBox);
            this.Name = "Form1";
            this.Text = "Form1";
            this.Load += new System.EventHandler(this.Form1_Load);
                ((System.ComponentModel.ISupportInitialize)
(this.introdatabaseDataSet)).EndInit();
                ((System.ComponentModel.ISupportInitialize)
(this.introtableBindingSource)).EndInit();
                ((System.ComponentModel.ISupportInitialize)
(this.bindingNavigator1)).EndInit();
            this.bindingNavigator1.ResumeLayout(false);
            this.bindingNavigator1.PerformLayout();
            this.ResumeLayout(false);
            this.PerformLayout();
        }
        #endregion
        private introdatabaseDataSet introdatabaseDataSet;
        private System.Windows.Forms.BindingSource
introtableBindingSource;
        private WindowsApplication1.introdatabaseDataSet
TableAdapters.introtableTableAdapter introtableTableAdapter;
        private System.Windows.Forms.TextBox nameTextBox;
        private System.Windows.Forms.TextBox hobbyTextBox;
        private System.Windows.Forms.BindingNavigator
bindingNavigator1;
```

```
            private  System.Windows.Forms.ToolStripButton
bindingNavigatorAddNewItem;
            private  System.Windows.Forms.ToolStripLabel
bindingNavigatorCountItem;
            private  System.Windows.Forms.ToolStripButton
bindingNavigatorDeleteItem;
            private  System.Windows.Forms.ToolStripButton
bindingNavigatorMoveFirstItem;
            private  System.Windows.Forms.ToolStripButton
bindingNavigatorMovePreviousItem;
            private  System.Windows.Forms.ToolStripSeparator
bindingNavigatorSeparator;
            private  System.Windows.Forms.ToolStripTextBox
bindingNavigatorPositionItem;
            private  System.Windows.Forms.ToolStripSeparator
bindingNavigatorSeparator1;
            private  System.Windows.Forms.ToolStripButton
bindingNavigatorMoveNextItem;
            private  System.Windows.Forms.ToolStripButton
bindingNavigatorMoveLastItem;
            private  System.Windows.Forms.ToolStripSeparator
bindingNavigatorSeparator2;
    }
}
```

— app.config —

```
<?xml version="1.0" encoding="utf-8" ?>
<configuration>
      <configSections>
      </configSections>
      <connectionStrings>
            <add name="WindowsApplication1.Properties.
Settings.introdatabaseConnectionString"
         connectionString="Provider=Microsoft.Jet.OLEDB.4.0;Data
Source=|DataDirectory|\introdatabase.mdb"
               providerName="System.Data.OleDb" />
      </connectionStrings>
</configuration>
```

— Program.cs —

```
using System;
using System.Collections.Generic;
using System.Windows.Forms;
namespace WindowsApplication1
{
      static class Program
      {
            /// <summary>
            /// The main entry point for the application.
            /// </summary>
            [STAThread]
            static void Main()
            {
                  Application.EnableVisualStyles();
             Application.SetCompatibleTextRenderingDefault(false);
                  Application.Run(new Form1());
            }
      }
}
```

5 Visual J# and ADO.Net

INTRODUCTION

In this chapter I'll show you how fast you can make make the database navigate with Visual J# 2005 and ADO.NET. The specialty of Visual Studio 2005 is such that you do not have to write a single code for this.

We will create the connection with our created MS Access database created in the last chapter. Then we will use simple techniques in Visual J# for data navigation form.

Let us perform the following steps:

1. Start Visual Studio 2005
2. On menu bar click File
3. Click New Project
4. You will get New Project dialog box

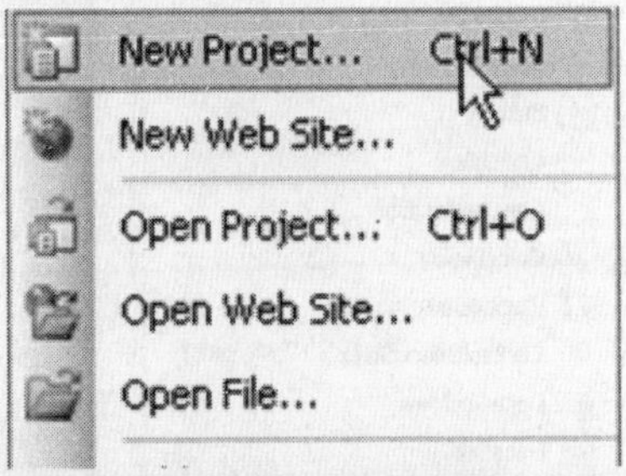

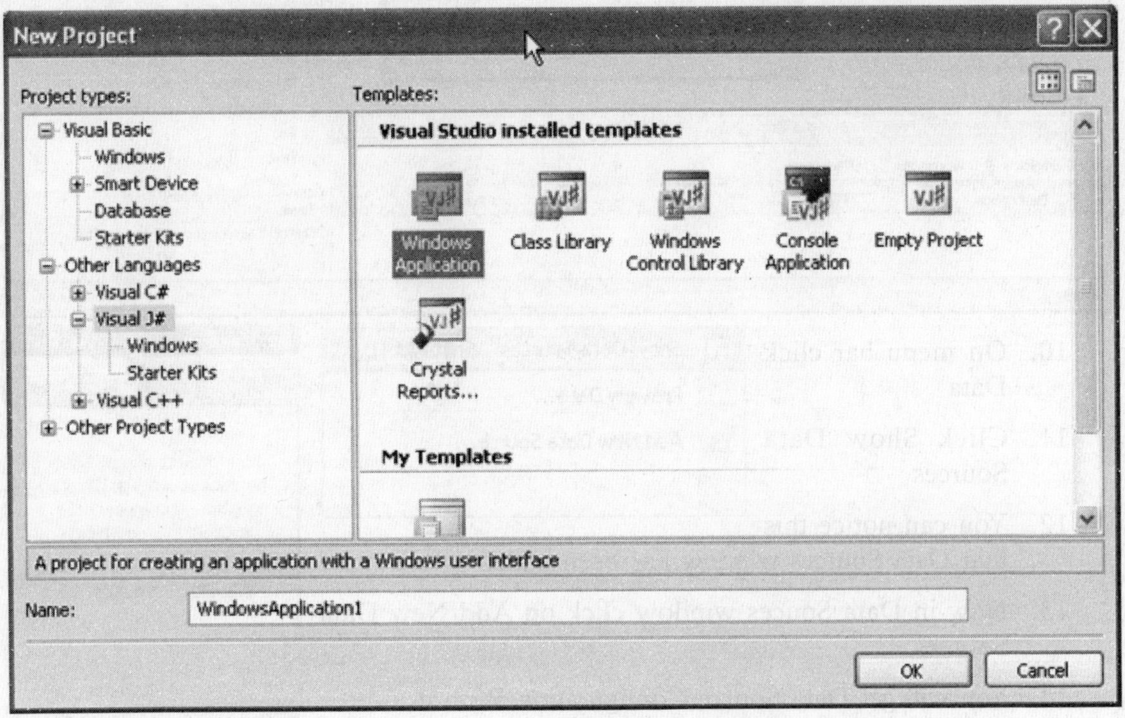

5. Under Project types select Visual J#
6. Under Templates select Windows Applications
7. Keep default name
8. Click OK
9. At present you have following scenario

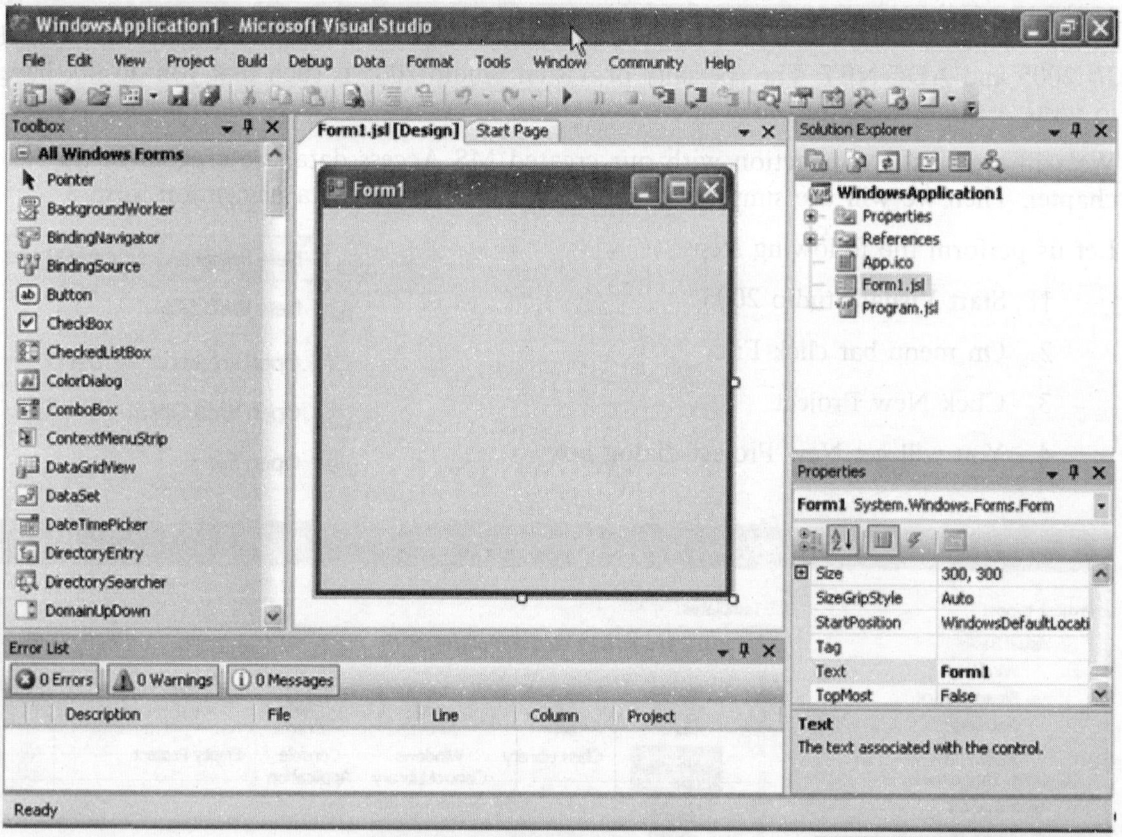

10. On menu bar click Data
11. Click Show Data Sources
12. You can notice this that Data Sources window has been added

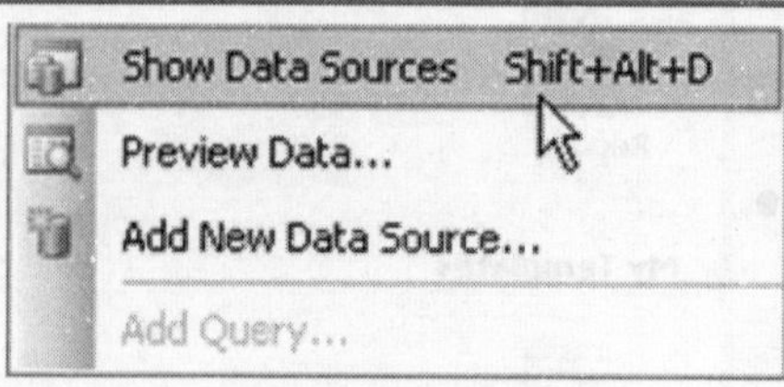

13. Now in Data Souces window click on Add New Data Sources
14. You will get Data Source Configuration Wizard

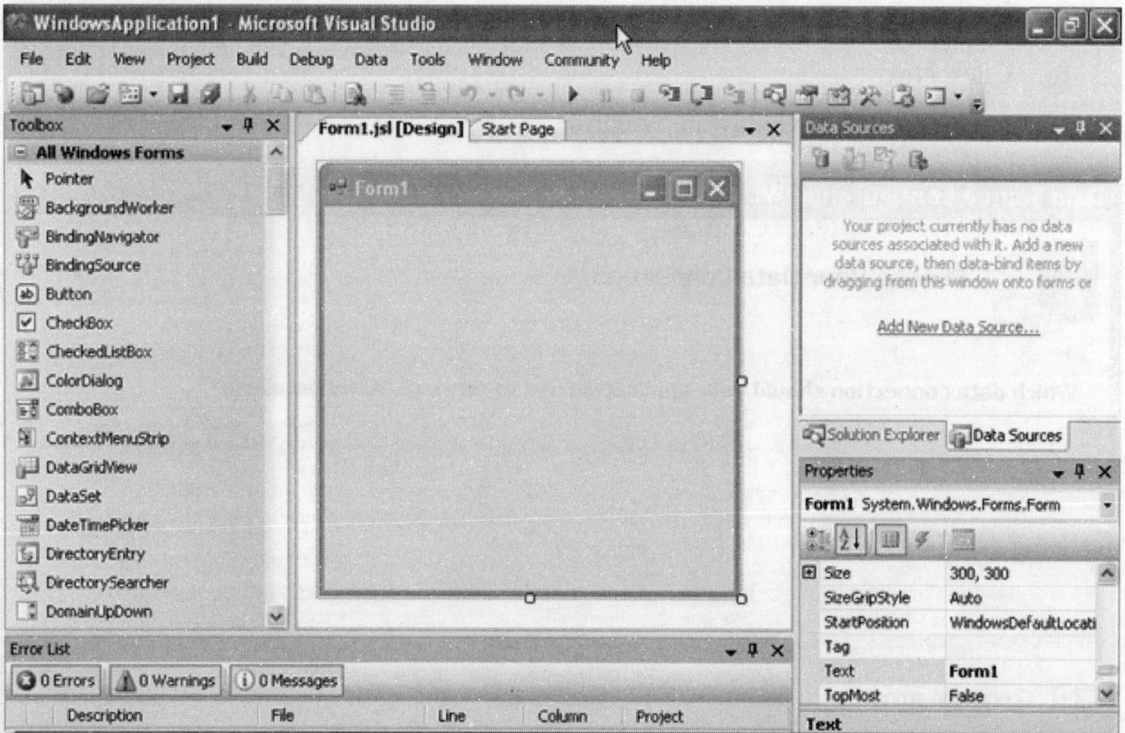
WindowsApplication1 - Microsoft Visual Studio
File Edit View Project Build Debug Data Tools Window Community Help
Toolbox
All Windows Forms
Pointer
BackgroundWorker
BindingNavigator
BindingSource
Button
CheckBox
CheckedListBox
ColorDialog
ComboBox
ContextMenuStrip
DataGridView
DataSet
DateTimePicker
DirectoryEntry
DirectorySearcher
DomainUpDown
Form1.jsl [Design]
Start Page
Form1
Data Sources
Your project currently has no data sources associated with it. Add a new data source, then data-bind items by dragging from this window onto forms or
Add New Data Source...
Solution Explorer
Data Sources
Properties
Form1 System.Windows.Forms.Form
Size 300, 300
SizeGripStyle Auto
StartPosition WindowsDefaultLocati
Tag
Text Form1
TopMost False
Text
Error List
0 Errors
0 Warnings
0 Messages
Description
File
Line
Column
Project

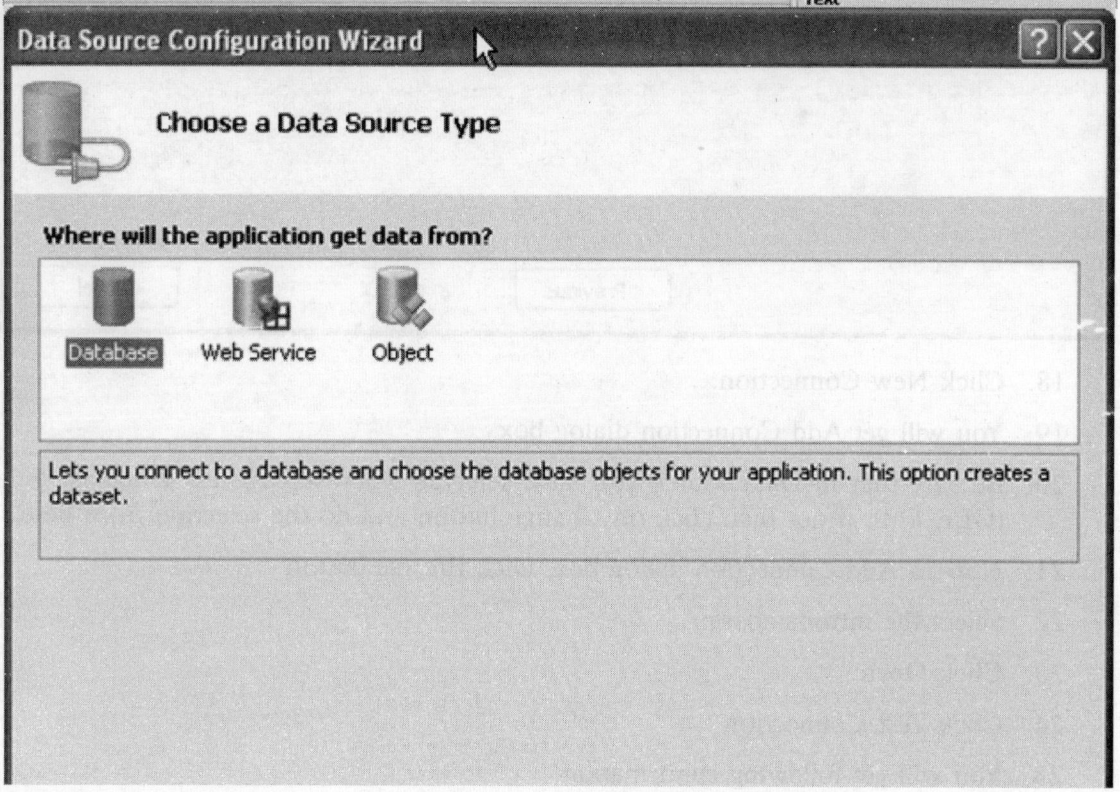
Data Source Configuration Wizard
Choose a Data Source Type
Where will the application get data from?
Database
Web Service
Object
Lets you connect to a database and choose the database objects for your application. This option creates a dataset.

15. Select Database
16. Click Next
17. Now you will get following window

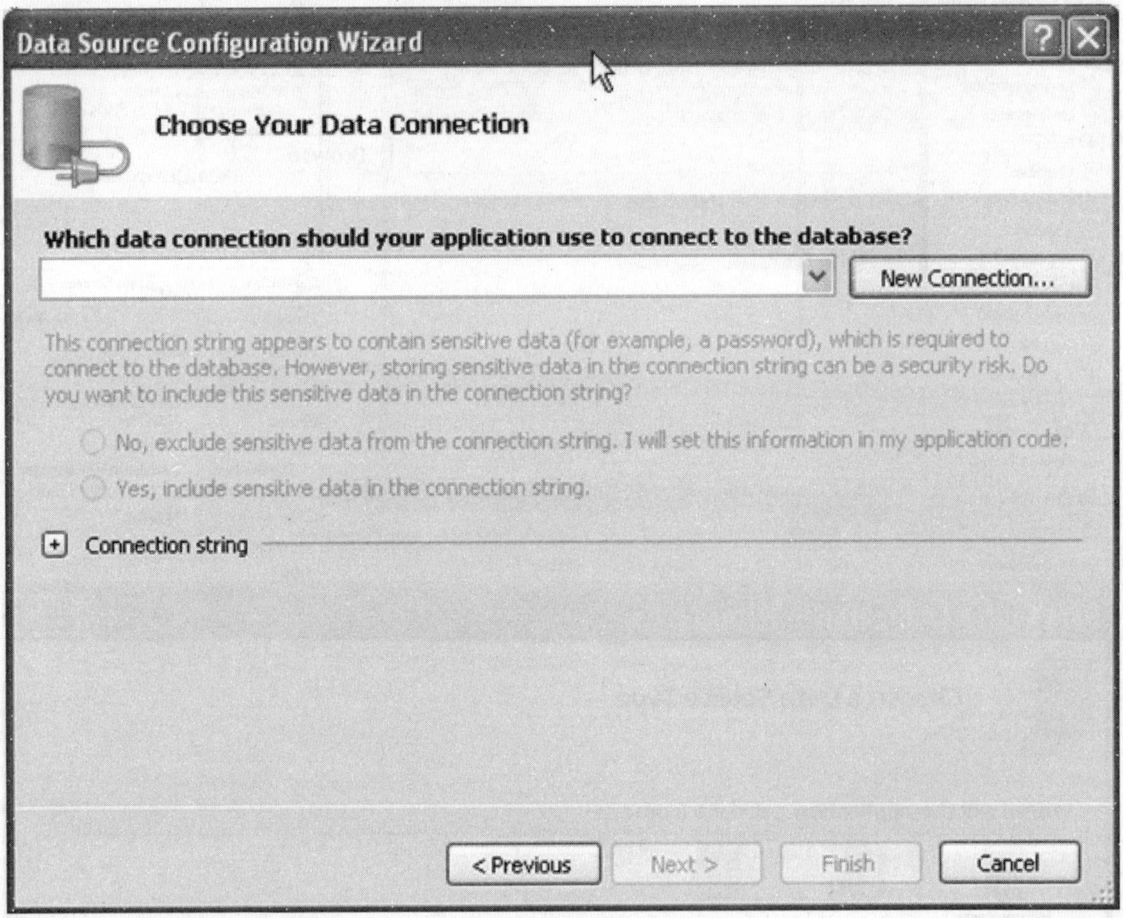

18. Click New Connection...
19. You will get Add Connection dialog box
20. Be sure that in Data source you have selected Microsoft Access Database File (OLE DB), if not then click on Change button and do the selection from here
21. Now in Add Connection dialog box, click Browse button
22. Select the introdatabase
23. Click Open
24. Click Test Connection
25. You will get following confirmation

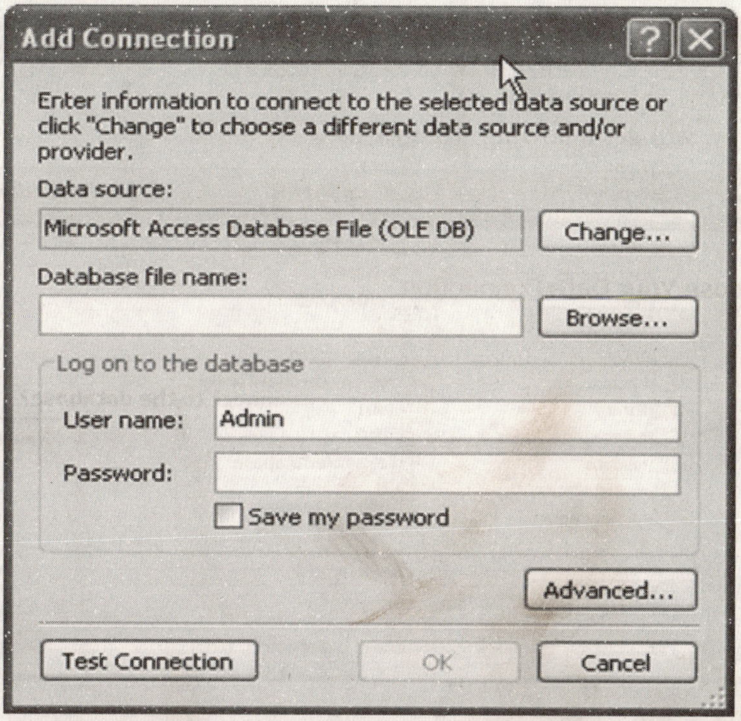

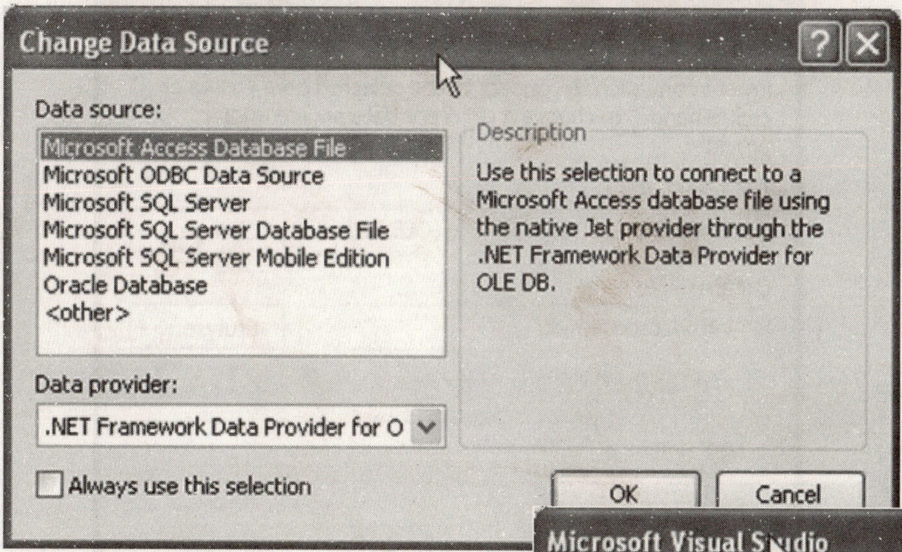

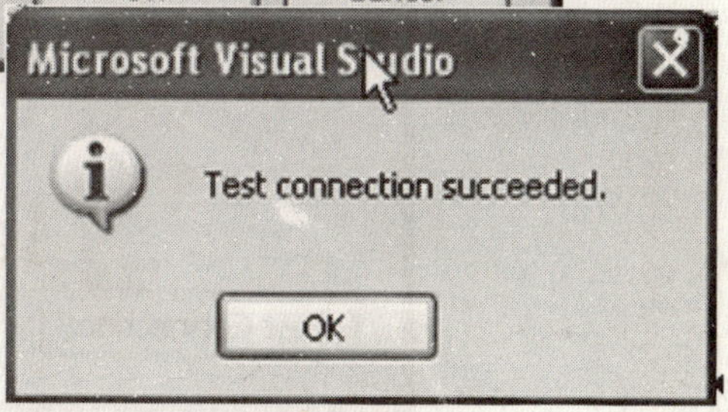

26. Click OK
27. Now click Next
28. You will get following message
29. Click Yes

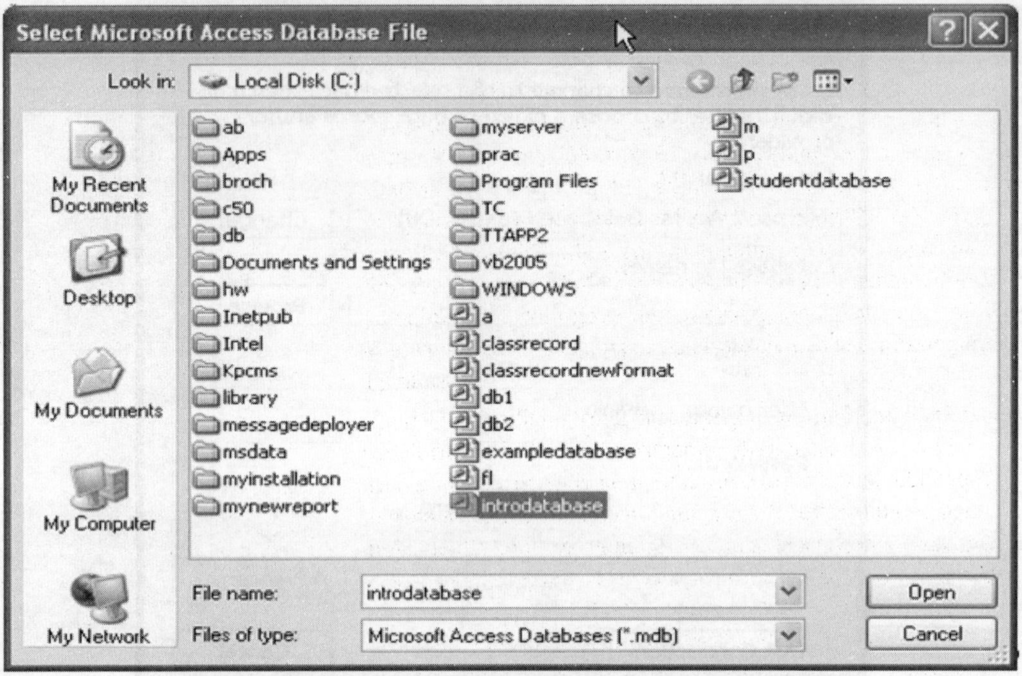
Select Microsoft Access Database File
Look in:
Local Disk (C:)
My Recent Documents
Desktop
My Documents
My Computer
My Network
ab
Apps
broch
c50
db
Documents and Settings
hw
Inetpub
Intel
Kpcms
library
messagedeployer
msdata
myinstallation
mynewreport
myserver
prac
Program Files
TC
TTAPP2
vb2005
WINDOWS
a
classrecord
classrecordnewformat
db1
db2
exampledatabase
fl
introdatabase
m
p
studentdatabase
File name:
introdatabase
Files of type:
Microsoft Access Databases (*.mdb)
Open
Cancel

Add Connection
Enter information to connect to the selected data source or click "Change" to choose a different data source and/or provider.
Data source:
Microsoft Access Database File (OLE DB)
Change...
Database file name:
C:\introdatabase.mdb
Browse...
Log on to the database
User name:
Admin
Password:
Save my password
Advanced...
Test Connection
OK
Cancel

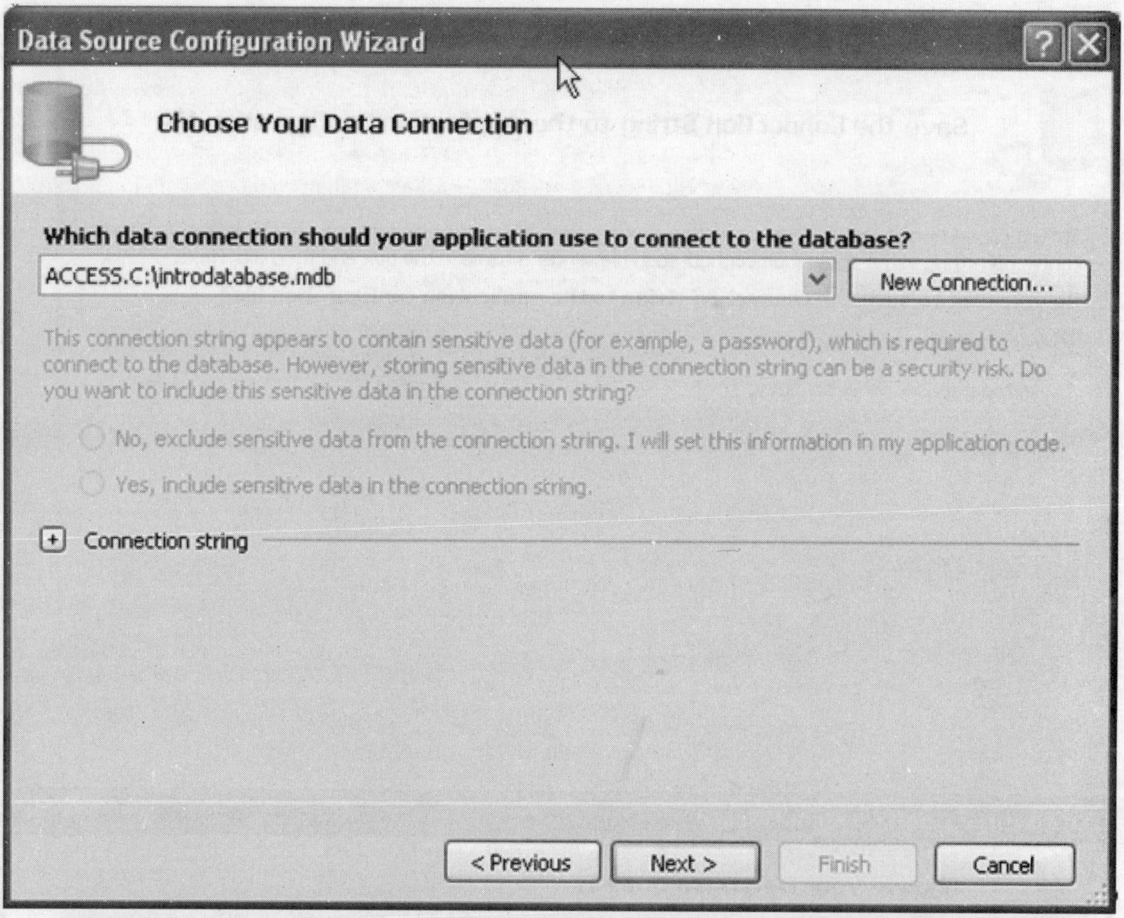

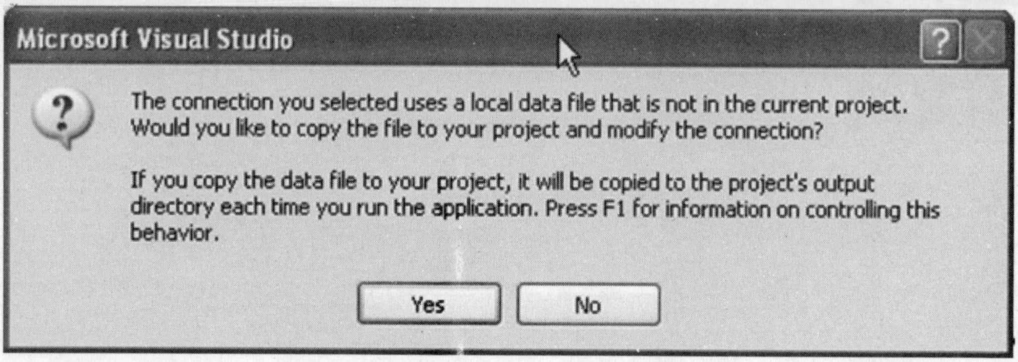

30. Keep default name as introdatabaseConnectionString
31. Click Next
32. Click + sign of Tables
33. At present you have one Table

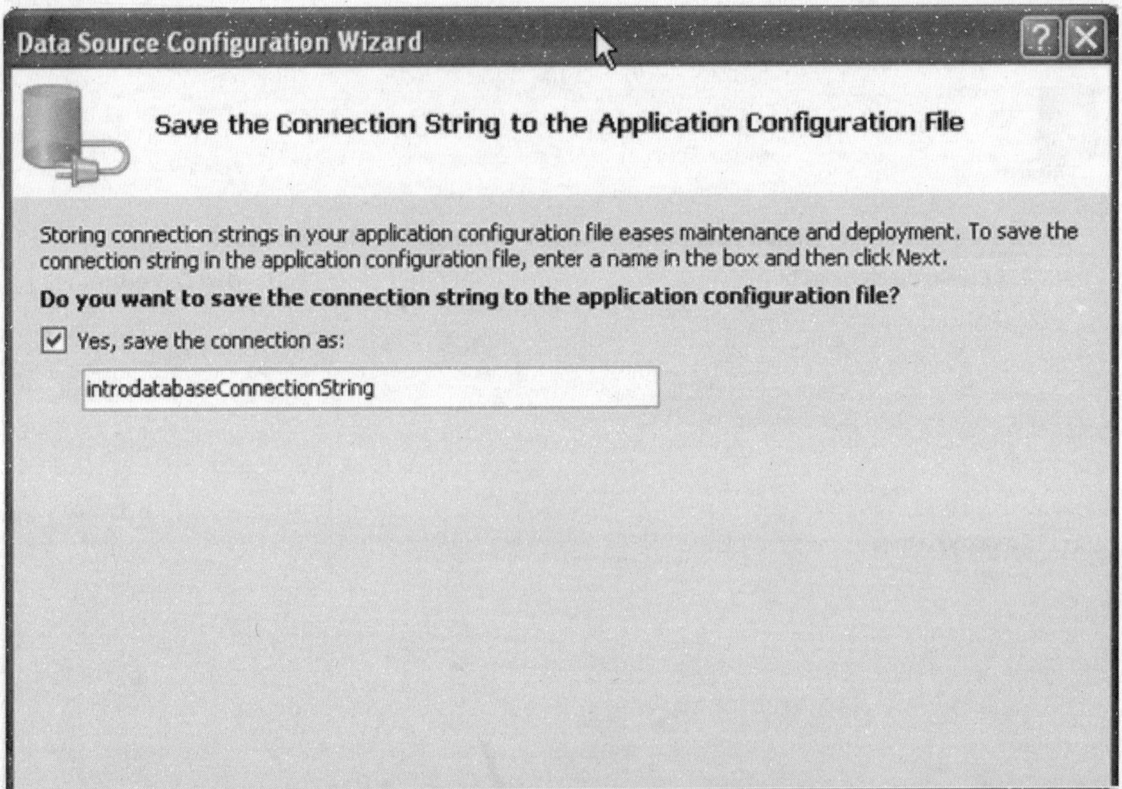
Data Source Configuration Wizard
Save the Connection String to the Application Configuration File
Storing connection strings in your application configuration file eases maintenance and deployment. To save the connection string in the application configuration file, enter a name in the box and then click Next.
Do you want to save the connection string to the application configuration file?
Yes, save the connection as:
introdatabaseConnectionString

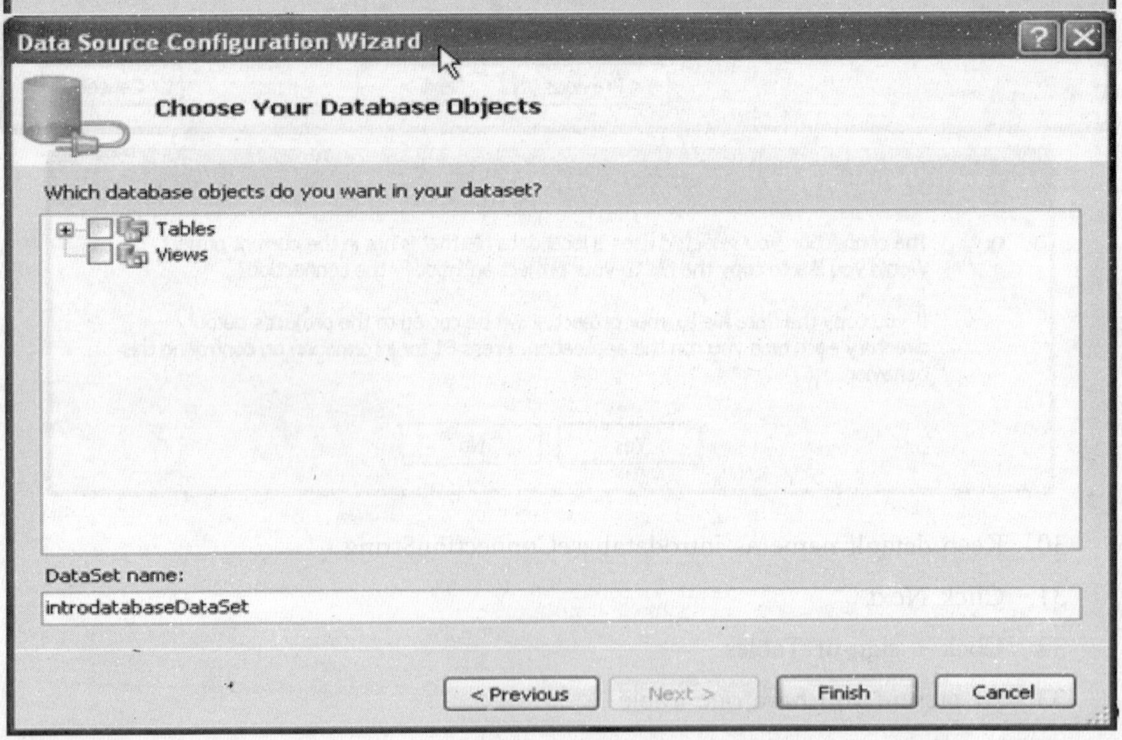
Data Source Configuration Wizard
Choose Your Database Objects
Which database objects do you want in your dataset?
Tables
Views
DataSet name:
introdatabaseDataSet
< Previous
Next >
Finish
Cancel

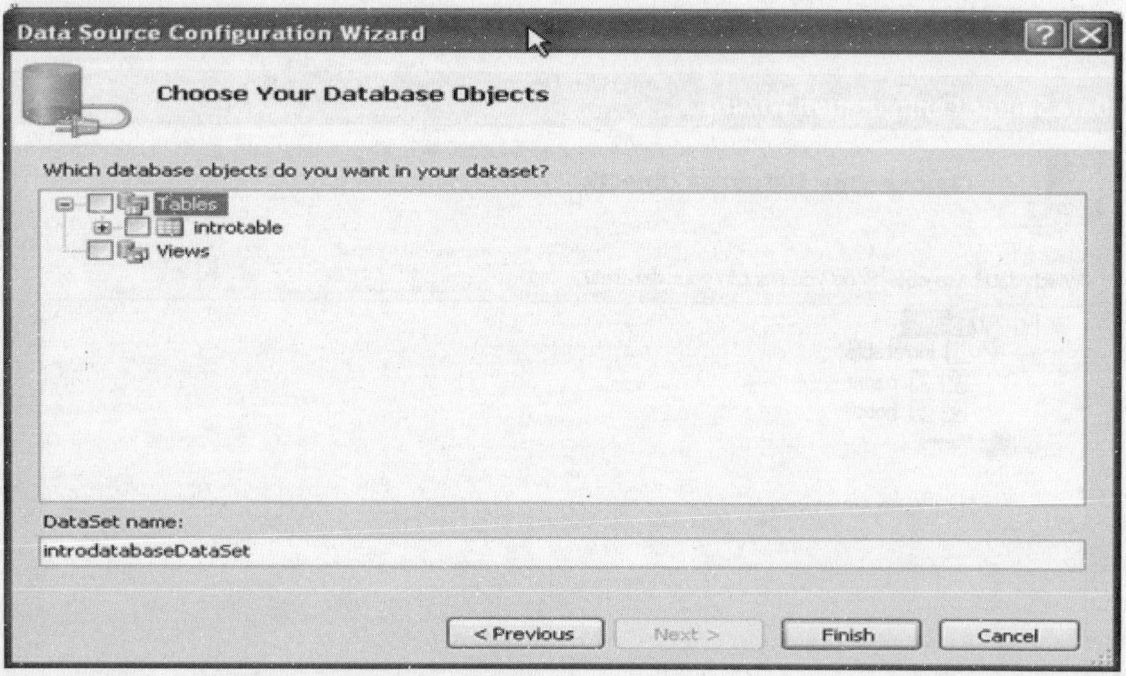

34. Now click on + sign of introtable

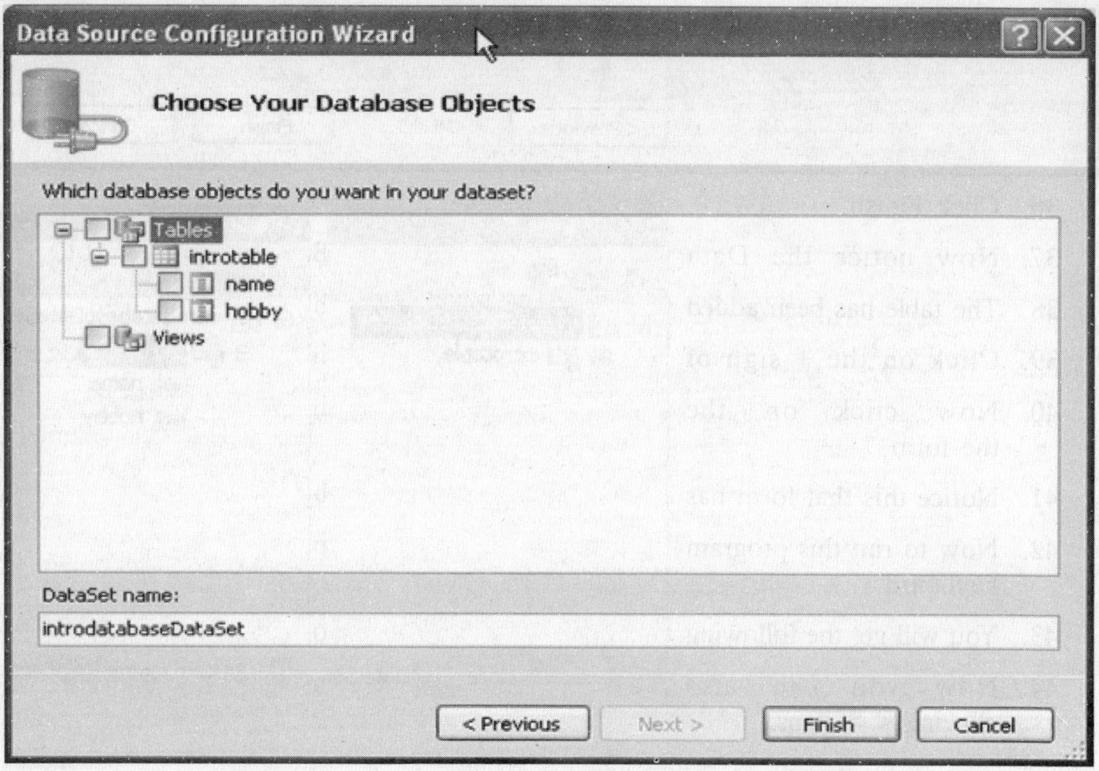

35. At present you have two fields, select both of them

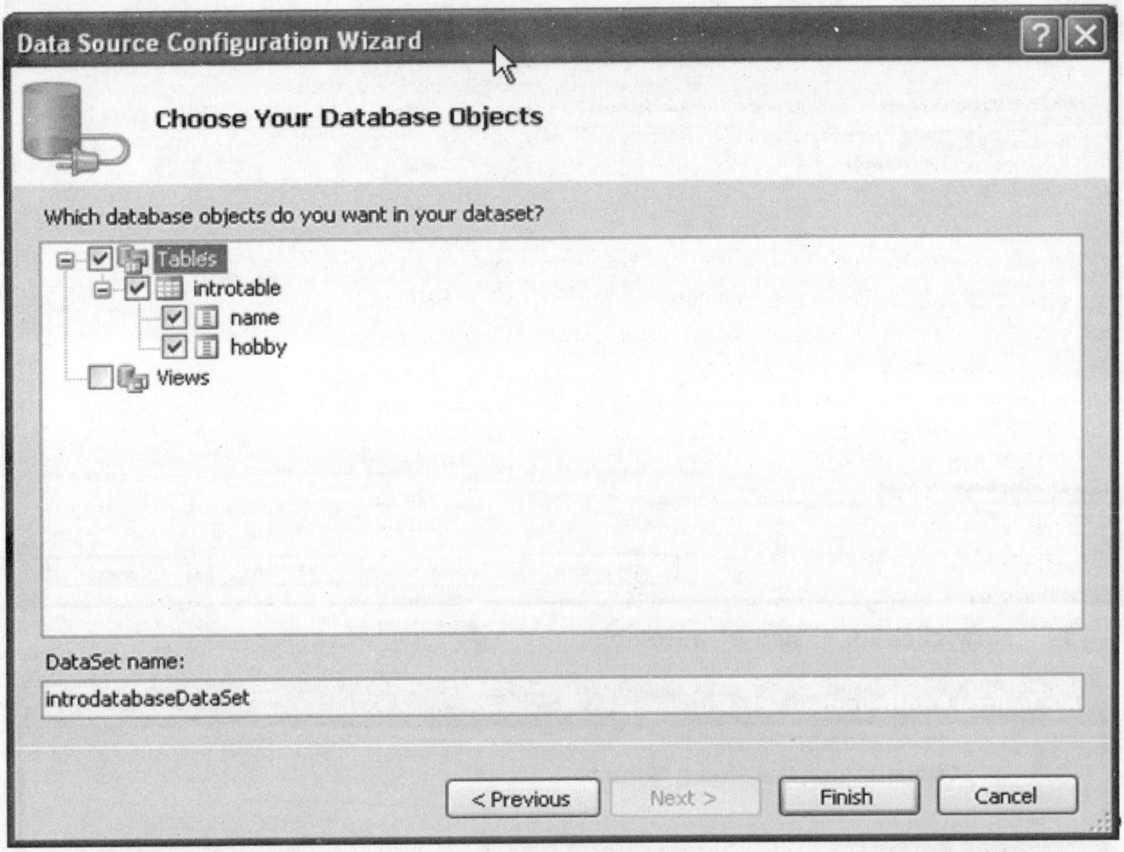

36. Click Finish
37. Now notice the Data S
38. The table has been added h
39. Click on the + sign of ir
40. Now click on the ir
the form
41. Notice this that form has b
42. Now to run this program p
keyboard
43. You will get the following o
44. Now you can also n
clicking < > signs.

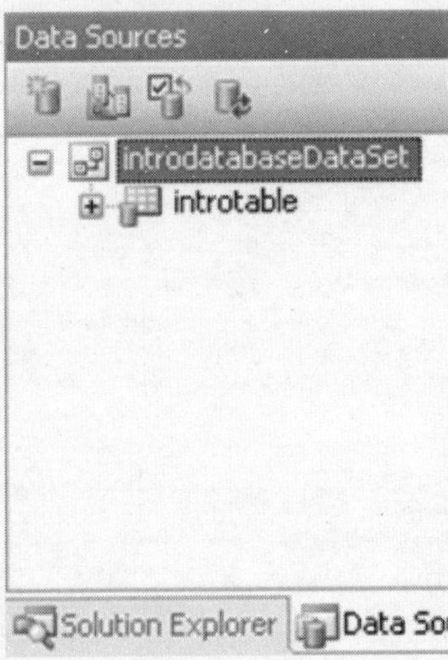

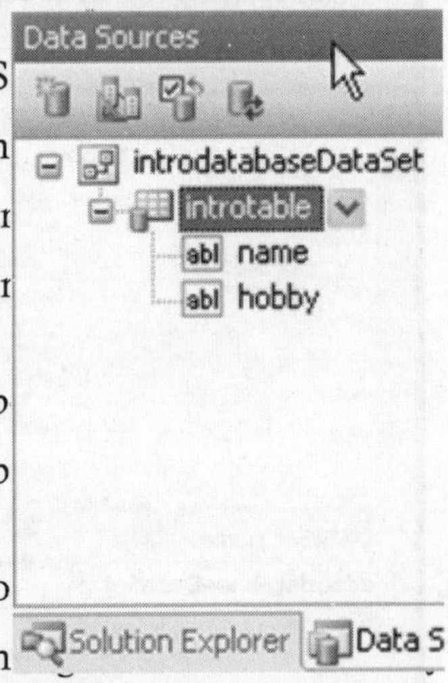

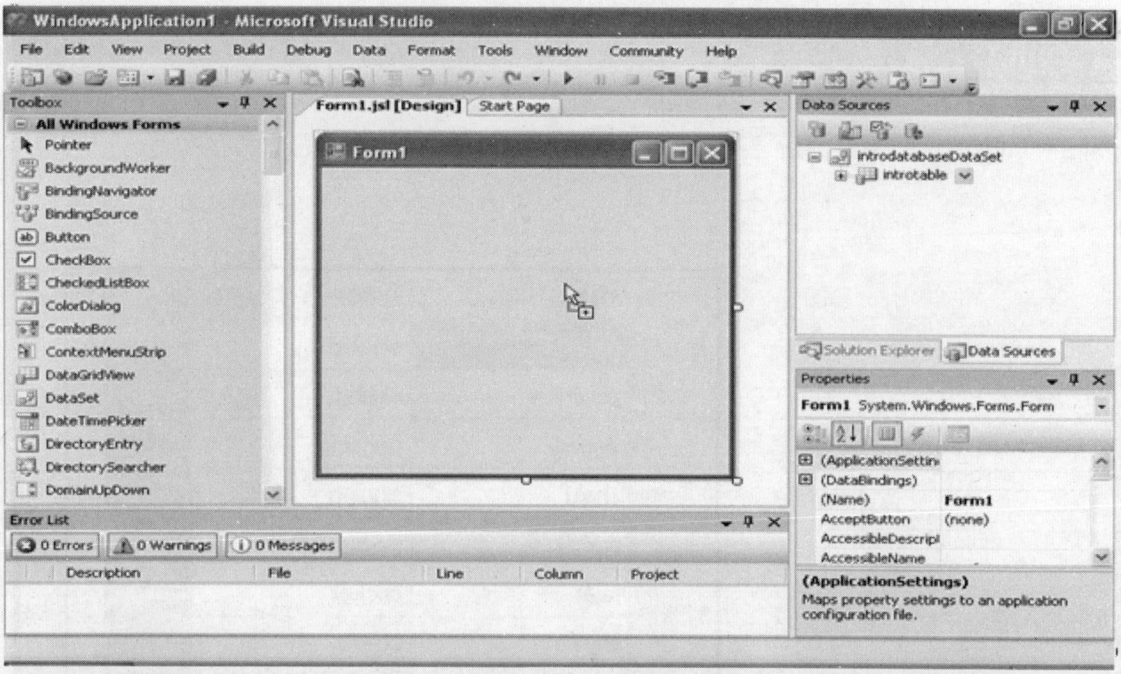

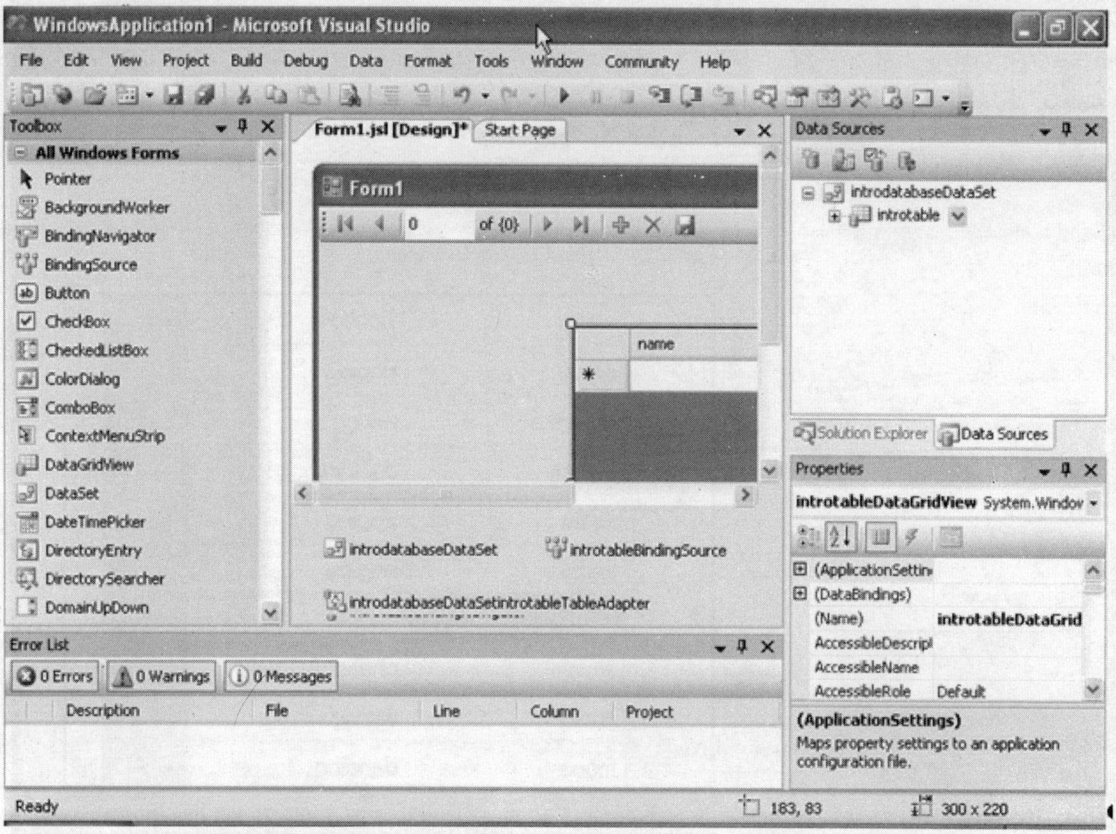

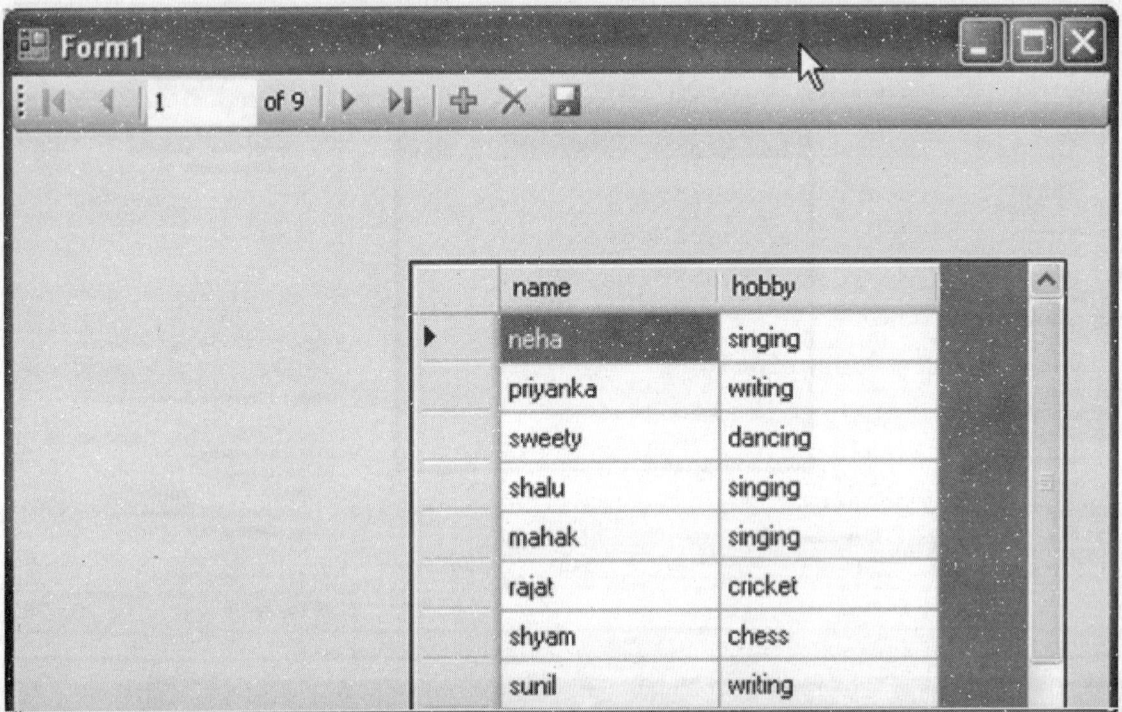
Form1
1
of 9
name
hobby
neha
singing
priyanka
writing
sweety
dancing
shalu
singing
mahak
singing
rajat
cricket
shyam
chess
sunil
writing

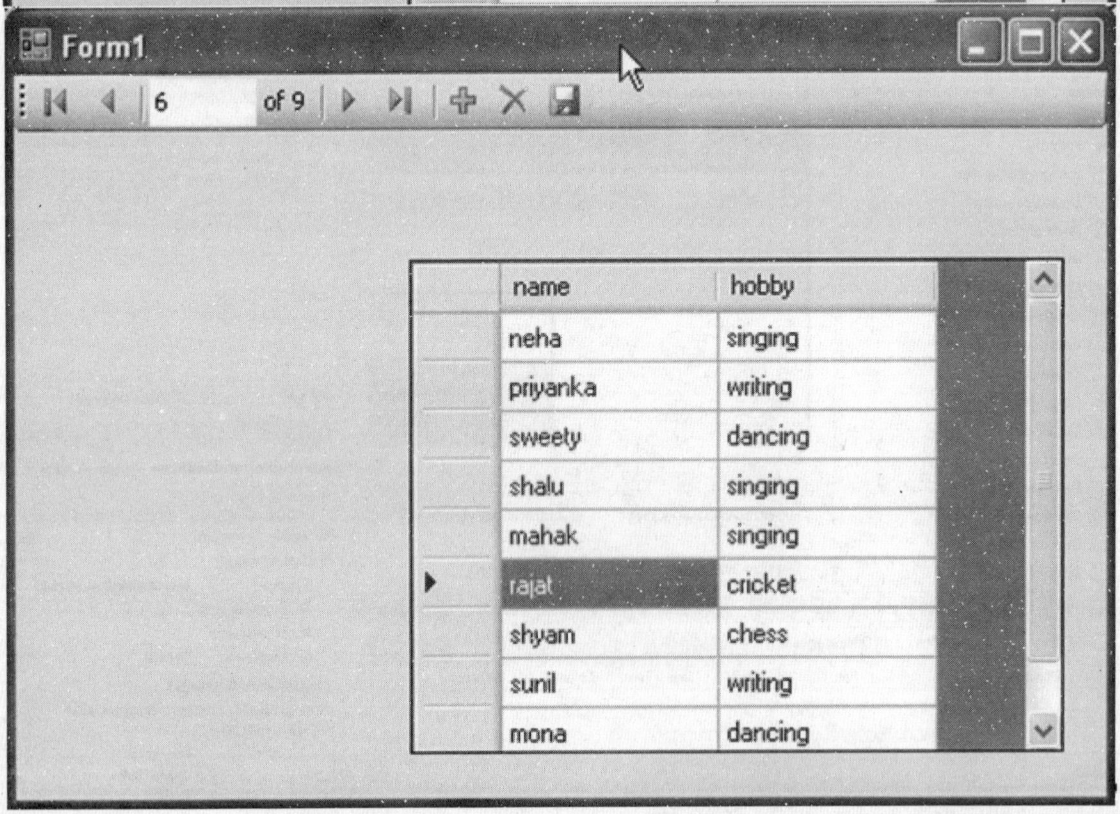
Form1
6
of 9
name
hobby
neha
singing
priyanka
writing
sweety
dancing
shalu
singing
mahak
singing
rajat
cricket
shyam
chess
sunil
writing
mona
dancing

— Code Form1.jsl —

```
package WindowsApplication1;
import System.Collections.Generic.*;
import System.Data.*;
import System.Drawing.*;
import System.ComponentModel.*;
import System.Windows.Forms.*;
/**
 * Summary description for Form1.
 */
public class Form1 extends System.Windows.Forms.Form
{
   private introdatabaseDataSet introdatabaseDataSet;
   private BindingSource introtableBindingSource;
   private introdatabaseDataSetintrotableTableAdapter
introdatabaseDataSetintrotableTableAdapter;
   private BindingNavigator introtableBindingNavigator;
   private ToolStripButton bindingNavigatorAddNewItem;
   private ToolStripLabel bindingNavigatorCountItem;
   private ToolStripButton bindingNavigatorDeleteItem;
   private ToolStripButton bindingNavigatorMoveFirstItem;
   private ToolStripButton bindingNavigatorMovePreviousItem;
   private ToolStripSeparator bindingNavigatorSeparator;
   private ToolStripTextBox bindingNavigatorPositionItem;
   private ToolStripSeparator bindingNavigatorSeparator1;
   private ToolStripButton bindingNavigatorMoveNextItem;
   private ToolStripButton bindingNavigatorMoveLastItem;
   private ToolStripSeparator bindingNavigatorSeparator2;
   private ToolStripButton introtableBindingNavigatorSaveItem;
   private DataGridView introtableDataGridView;
   private DataGridViewTextBoxColumn dataGridViewTextBoxColumn1;
   private DataGridViewTextBoxColumn dataGridViewTextBoxColumn2;
   /**
    * Required designer variable.
    */
```

```
private System.ComponentModel.IContainer components;
public Form1()
{
    //
    // Required for Windows Form Designer support
    //
    InitializeComponent();
    //
    // TODO: Add any constructor code after InitializeComponent
call
    //
}
#region Windows Form Designer generated code
/**
  * Clean up any resources being used.
  */
protected void Dispose(boolean disposing)
{
    if (disposing)
    {
    if (components != null)
    {
        components.Dispose();
    }
    }
    super.Dispose(disposing);
}
/**
 * Required method for Designer support - do not modify
  * the contents of this method with the code editor.
 */
private void InitializeComponent()
{
    this.components = new System.ComponentModel.Container();
    System.ComponentModel.ComponentResourceManager resources
```

```
= new System.ComponentModel.ComponentResourceManager
(Form1.class.ToType());
    this.introdatabaseDataSet = new WindowsApplication1.
introdatabaseDataSet();
    this.introtableBindingSource = new System.Windows.
Forms.BindingSource(this.components);
    this.introdatabaseDataSetintrotableTableAdapter = new
WindowsApplication1.introdatabaseDataSetintrotableTableAdapter();
    this.introtableBindingNavigator = new
System.Windows.Forms.BindingNavigator(this.components);
    this.bindingNavigatorMoveFirstItem = new
System.Windows.Forms.ToolStripButton();
    this.bindingNavigatorMovePreviousItem = new
System.Windows.Forms.ToolStripButton();
    this.bindingNavigatorSeparator = new
System.Windows.Forms.ToolStripSeparator();
    this.bindingNavigatorPositionItem = new
System.Windows.Forms.ToolStripTextBox();
    this.bindingNavigatorCountItem = new
System.Windows.Forms.ToolStripLabel();
    this.bindingNavigatorSeparator1 = new
System.Windows.Forms.ToolStripSeparator();
    this.bindingNavigatorMoveNextItem = new
System.Windows.Forms.ToolStripButton();
    this.bindingNavigatorMoveLastItem = new
System.Windows.Forms.ToolStripButton();
    this.bindingNavigatorSeparator2 = new
System.Windows.Forms.ToolStripSeparator();
    this.bindingNavigatorAddNewItem = new
System.Windows.Forms.ToolStripButton();
    this.bindingNavigatorDeleteItem = new
System.Windows.Forms.ToolStripButton();
    this.introtableBindingNavigatorSaveItem = new
System.Windows.Forms.ToolStripButton();
    this.introtableDataGridView = new
System.Windows.Forms.DataGridView();
    this.dataGridViewTextBoxColumn1 = new
System.Windows.Forms.DataGridViewTextBoxColumn();
```

```
    this.dataGridViewTextBoxColumn2 = new
System.Windows.Forms.DataGridViewTextBoxColumn();
    ((System.ComponentModel.ISupportInitialize)
(this.introdatabaseDataSet)).BeginInit();
    ((System.ComponentModel.ISupportInitialize)
(this.introtableBindingSource)).BeginInit();
    ((System.ComponentModel.ISupportInitialize)
(this.introtableBindingNavigator)).BeginInit();
    this.introtableBindingNavigator.SuspendLayout();
    ((System.ComponentModel.ISupportInitialize)
(this.introtableDataGridView)).BeginInit();
    this.SuspendLayout();
    //
    // introdatabaseDataSet
    //

this.introdatabaseDataSet.set_DataSetName("introdatabaseDataSet");
    this.introdatabaseDataSet.set_SchemaSerializationMode
(System.Data.SchemaSerializationMode.IncludeSchema);
    //
    // introtableBindingSource
    //

this.introtableBindingSource.set_DataMember("introtable");

this.introtableBindingSource.set_DataSource(this.introdatabaseDataSet);
    //
    // introdatabaseDataSetintrotableTableAdapter
    //
    this.introdatabaseDataSetintrotableTableAdapter.
set_ClearBeforeFill(true);
    //
    // introtableBindingNavigator
    //
    this.introtableBindingNavigator.set_AddNewItem
(this.bindingNavigatorAddNewItem);
    this.introtableBindingNavigator.set_BindingSource
```

```
(this.introtableBindingSource);
    this.introtableBindingNavigator.set_CountItem
(this.bindingNavigatorCountItem);
    this.introtableBindingNavigator.set_DeleteItem
(this.bindingNavigatorDeleteItem);
    this.introtableBindingNavigator.get_Items().AddRange(new
System.Windows.Forms.ToolStripItem[]  {
            this.bindingNavigatorMoveFirstItem,
            this.bindingNavigatorMovePreviousItem,
            this.bindingNavigatorSeparator,
            this.bindingNavigatorPositionItem,
            this.bindingNavigatorCountItem,
            this.bindingNavigatorSeparator1,
            this.bindingNavigatorMoveNextItem,
            this.bindingNavigatorMoveLastItem,
            this.bindingNavigatorSeparator2,
            this.bindingNavigatorAddNewItem,
            this.bindingNavigatorDeleteItem,
            this.introtableBindingNavigatorSaveItem}
    );
    this.introtableBindingNavigator.set_Location(new
System.Drawing.Point(0,  0));
    this.introtableBindingNavigator.set_MoveFirstItem
(this.bindingNavigatorMoveFirstItem);
    this.introtableBindingNavigator.set_MoveLastItem
(this.bindingNavigatorMoveLastItem);
    this.introtableBindingNavigator.set_MoveNextItem
(this.bindingNavigatorMoveNextItem);
    this.introtableBindingNavigator.set_MovePreviousItem
(this.bindingNavigatorMovePreviousItem);
    this.introtableBindingNavigator.set_Name
("introtableBindingNavigator");
    this.introtableBindingNavigator.set_PositionItem
(this.bindingNavigatorPositionItem);
    this.introtableBindingNavigator.set_Size(new
System.Drawing.Size(503,  25));
    this.introtableBindingNavigator.set_TabIndex(0);
```

```
this.introtableBindingNavigator.set_Text("bindingNavigator1");
    //
    // bindingNavigatorMoveFirstItem
    //

this.bindingNavigatorMoveFirstItem.set_DisplayStyle(System.
Windows.Forms.ToolStripItemDisplayStyle.Image);
    this.bindingNavigatorMoveFirstItem.set_Image(((System.
Drawing.Image) (resources.GetObject("bindingNavigator
MoveFirstItem.Image"))));
    this.bindingNavigatorMoveFirstItem.set_Name
("bindingNavigatorMoveFirstItem");
    this.bindingNavigatorMoveFirstItem.set_RightToLeft
AutoMirrorImage(true);
    this.bindingNavigatorMoveFirstItem.set_Size(new
System.Drawing.Size(23, 22));
    this.bindingNavigatorMoveFirstItem.set_Text("Move first");
    //
    // bindingNavigatorMovePreviousItem
    //
    this.bindingNavigatorMovePreviousItem.set_DisplayStyle
(System.Windows.Forms.ToolStripItemDisplayStyle.Image);

this.bindingNavigatorMovePreviousItem.set_Image(((System.Drawing.
Image) (resources.GetObject("bindingNavigatorMove
PreviousItem.Image"))));
    this.bindingNavigatorMovePreviousItem.set_Name
("bindingNavigatorMovePreviousItem");
    this.bindingNavigatorMovePreviousItem.
set_RightToLeftAutoMirrorImage(true);
    this.bindingNavigatorMovePreviousItem.set_Size(new
System.Drawing.Size(23, 22));
    this.bindingNavigatorMovePreviousItem.set_Text("Move
previous");
    //
    // bindingNavigatorSeparator
    //

this.bindingNavigatorSeparator.set_Name("bindingNavigatorSeparator");
```

```
    this.bindingNavigatorSeparator.set_Size(new
System.Drawing.Size(6, 25));
    //
    // bindingNavigatorPositionItem
    //

this.bindingNavigatorPositionItem.set_AccessibleName("Position");
    this.bindingNavigatorPositionItem.set_AutoSize(false);
    this.bindingNavigatorPositionItem.set_Name
("bindingNavigatorPositionItem");
    this.bindingNavigatorPositionItem.set_Size(new
System.Drawing.Size(50, 21));
    this.bindingNavigatorPositionItem.set_Text("0");

this.bindingNavigatorPositionItem.set_ToolTipText("Current
position");
    //
    // bindingNavigatorCountItem
    //

this.bindingNavigatorCountItem.set_Name("bindingNavigatorCountItem");
    this.bindingNavigatorCountItem.set_Size(new System.
Drawing.Size(36, 13));
    this.bindingNavigatorCountItem.set_Text("of {0}");
    this.bindingNavigatorCountItem.set_ToolTipText("Total
number of items");
    //
    // bindingNavigatorSeparator1
    //
    this.bindingNavigatorSeparator1.set_Name
("bindingNavigatorSeparator");
    this.bindingNavigatorSeparator1.set_Size(new
System.Drawing.Size(6, 6));
    //
    // bindingNavigatorMoveNextItem
    //
```

```
this.bindingNavigatorMoveNextItem.set_DisplayStyle(System.Windows.
Forms.ToolStripItemDisplayStyle.Image);

this.bindingNavigatorMoveNextItem.set_Image(((System.Drawing.Image)
(resources.GetObject("bindingNavigatorMoveNextItem.Image"))));
    this.bindingNavigatorMoveNextItem.set_Name
("bindingNavigatorMoveNextItem");
    this.bindingNavigatorMoveNextItem.set_RightToLeft
AutoMirrorImage(true);
    this.bindingNavigatorMoveNextItem.set_Size(new
System.Drawing.Size(23, 20));
    this.bindingNavigatorMoveNextItem.set_Text("Move next");
    //
    // bindingNavigatorMoveLastItem
    //
    this.bindingNavigatorMoveLastItem.set_DisplayStyle(
System.Windows.Forms.ToolStripItemDisplayStyle.Image);
    this.bindingNavigatorMoveLastItem.set_Image(((System.
Drawing.Image) (resources.GetObject("bindingNavigator
MoveLastItem.Image"))));
    this.bindingNavigatorMoveLastItem.set_Name
("bindingNavigatorMoveLastItem");
    this.bindingNavigatorMoveLastItem.set_Right
ToLeftAutoMirrorImage(true);
    this.bindingNavigatorMoveLastItem.set_Size(new
System.Drawing.Size(23, 20));
    this.bindingNavigatorMoveLastItem.set_Text("Move last");
    //
    // bindingNavigatorSeparator2
    //
    this.bindingNavigatorSeparator2.set_Name
("bindingNavigatorSeparator");
    this.bindingNavigatorSeparator2.set_Size(new
System.Drawing.Size(6, 6));
    //
    // bindingNavigatorAddNewItem
    //
```

```
this.bindingNavigatorAddNewItem.set_DisplayStyle
(System.Windows.Forms.ToolStripItemDisplayStyle.Image);
this.bindingNavigatorAddNewItem.set_Image(((System.Drawing.
Image)( resources.GetObject("bindingNavigatorAddNew
Item.Image"))));
this.bindingNavigatorAddNewItem.set_Name
("bindingNavigatorAddNewItem");
this.bindingNavigatorAddNewItem.set_RightToLeft
AutoMirrorImage(true);
this.bindingNavigatorAddNewItem.set_Size(new
System.Drawing.Size(23, 22));
this.bindingNavigatorAddNewItem.set_Text("Add new");
//
// bindingNavigatorDeleteItem
//
this.bindingNavigatorDeleteItem.set_DisplayStyle(System.
Windows.Forms.ToolStripItemDisplayStyle.Image);
this.bindingNavigatorDeleteItem.set_Image(((System.
Drawing.Image)( resources.GetObject("bindingNavigator
DeleteItem.Image"))));
this.bindingNavigatorDeleteItem.set_Name
("bindingNavigatorDeleteItem");
this.bindingNavigatorDeleteItem.set_RightToLeft
AutoMirrorImage(true);
this.bindingNavigatorDeleteItem.set_Size(new
System.Drawing.Size(23, 20));
this.bindingNavigatorDeleteItem.set_Text("Delete");
//
// introtableBindingNavigatorSaveItem
//
this.introtableBindingNavigatorSaveItem.set_DisplayStyle(
System.Windows.Forms.ToolStripItemDisplayStyle.Image);
this.introtableBindingNavigatorSaveItem.set_Image(((System.
Drawing.Image)( resources.GetObject("introtableBinding
NavigatorSaveItem.Image"))));
this.introtableBindingNavigatorSaveItem.set_Name
("introtableBindingNavigatorSaveItem");
```

```
     this.introtableBindingNavigatorSaveItem.set_Size(new
System.Drawing.Size(23, 23));
     this.introtableBindingNavigatorSaveItem.set_Text("Save
Data");
     this.introtableBindingNavigatorSaveItem.add_Click(new
System.EventHandler(this.introtableBinding
NavigatorSaveItem_Click_1));
     //
     // introtableDataGridView
     //

this.introtableDataGridView.set_AutoGenerateColumns(false);
     this.introtableDataGridView.get_Columns().AddRange(new
System.Windows.Forms.DataGridViewColumn[] {
               this.dataGridViewTextBoxColumn1,
               this.dataGridViewTextBoxColumn2}
     );
     this.introtableDataGridView.set_DataSource
(this.introtableBindingSource);
     this.introtableDataGridView.set_Location(new
System.Drawing.Point(183, 83));

this.introtableDataGridView.set_Name("introtableDataGridView");
     this.introtableDataGridView.set_Size(new
System.Drawing.Size(300, 220));
     this.introtableDataGridView.set_TabIndex(1);
     //
     // dataGridViewTextBoxColumn1
     //

this.dataGridViewTextBoxColumn1.set_DataPropertyName("name");
     this.dataGridViewTextBoxColumn1.set_HeaderText("name");
     this.dataGridViewTextBoxColumn1.set_Name
("dataGridViewTextBoxColumn1");
     //
     // dataGridViewTextBoxColumn2
     //
```

```
this.dataGridViewTextBoxColumn2.set_DataPropertyName("hobby");
    this.dataGridViewTextBoxColumn2.set_HeaderText("hobby");
    this.dataGridViewTextBoxColumn2.set_Name
("dataGridViewTextBoxColumn2");
    //
    // Form1
    //
    this.set_AutoScaleDimensions(new System.Drawing.SizeF(6F,
13F));
this.set_AutoScaleMode(System.Windows.Forms.AutoScaleMode.Font);
    this.set_ClientSize(new System.Drawing.Size(503, 323));
    this.get_Controls().Add(this.introtableDataGridView);
this.get_Controls().Add(this.introtableBindingNavigator);
    this.set_Name("Form1");
    this.set_Text("Form1");
    this.add_Load(new System.EventHandler(this.Form1_Load));
    ((System.ComponentModel.ISupportInitialize)
(this.introdatabaseDataSet)).EndInit();
    ((System.ComponentModel.ISupportInitialize)
(this.introtableBindingSource)).EndInit();
    ((System.ComponentModel.ISupportInitialize)
(this.introtableBindingNavigator)).EndInit();
    this.introtableBindingNavigator.ResumeLayout(false);
    this.introtableBindingNavigator.PerformLayout();
    ((System.ComponentModel.ISupportInitialize)
(this.introtableDataGridView)).EndInit();
    this.ResumeLayout(false);
    this.PerformLayout();
 }
 #endregion
 private void introtableBindingNavigatorSaveItem_Click(Object
sender, System.EventArgs e)
 {
    this.Validate();
    this.introtableBindingSource.EndEdit();
```

```
        this.introdatabaseDataSetintrotableTableAdapter.Update(
    this.introdatabaseDataSet.get_introtable());
      }
      private void introtableBindingNavigatorSaveItem_Click_1
    (Object sender, System.EventArgs e)
      {
        this.Validate();
        this.introtableBindingSource.EndEdit();
        this.introdatabaseDataSetintrotableTableAdapter.Update
    (this.introdatabaseDataSet.get_introtable());
      }
      private void Form1_Load(Object sender, System.EventArgs e)
      {
    // TODO: This line of code loads data into the
    'introdatabaseDataSet.introtable' table. You can move, or remove
    it, as needed.
    this.introdatabaseDataSetintrotableTableAdapter.Fill
    (this.introdatabaseDataSet.get_introtable());
      }
    }
```

— code Program.jsl —

```
    package WindowsApplication1;
    import System.Collections.Generic.*;
    import System.Windows.Forms.*;
    /**
      * Summary description for Program
      */
    public class Program
    {
      /**
        * The main entry point for the application.
        */
      /** @attribute System.STAThread() */
      public static void main(String[] args)
      {
        Application.EnableVisualStyles();
```

```
            Application.SetCompatibleTextRenderingDefault(false);
            Application.Run(new Form1());
        }
    }
```

If you wish you can also modify the above program. This way you can change the look and appearance. For this first take out everything from the form. Make it simple.

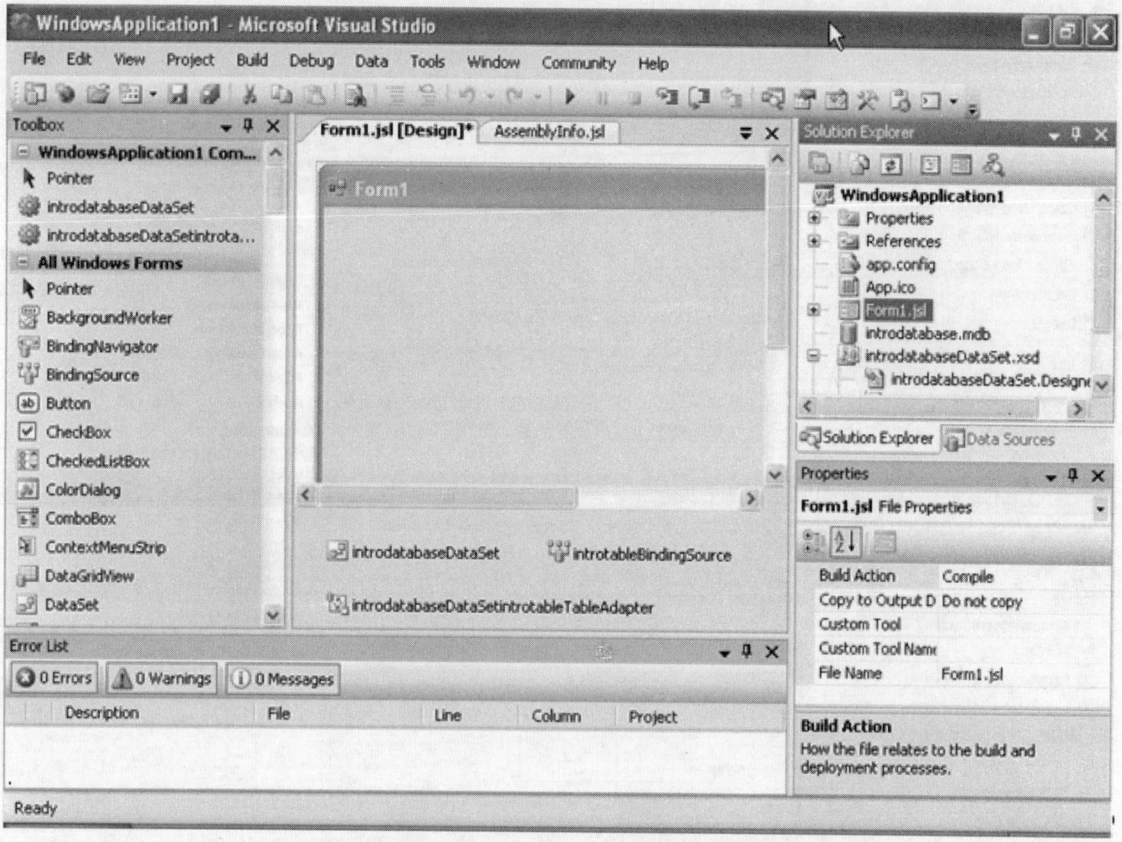

45. Now in Data Sources widow click the name field and drag it onto the form.
46. Now click the hobby field and drag it onto the form
47. Now in Toolbox click BindingNaviagtor control
48. Drag it onto the form
49. Now be sure that BindingNavigator control is selected and in Properties window select BindingSource property and choose IntrotableBindingSource
50. Now press F5 key on your keyboard
51. You will get following output in different layout:

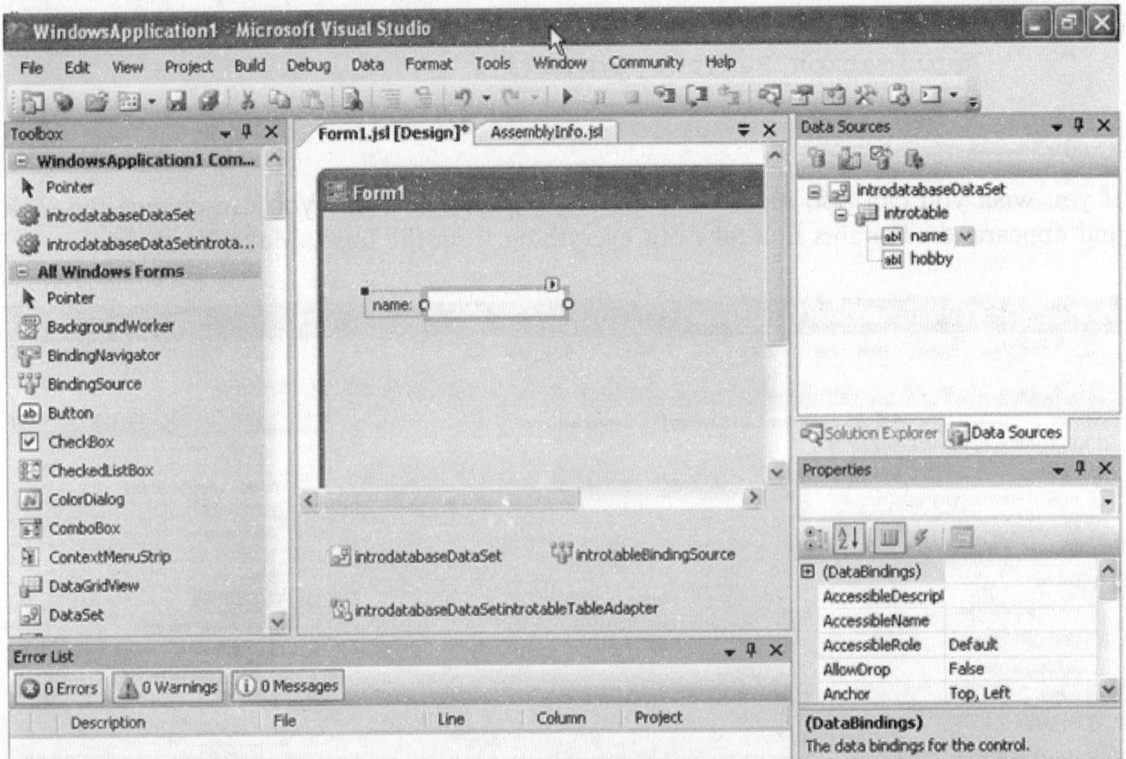
WindowsApplication1 - Microsoft Visual Studio
File Edit View Project Build Debug Data Format Tools Window Community Help
Toolbox
WindowsApplication1 Com...
Pointer
introdatabaseDataSet
introdatabaseDataSetintrota...
All Windows Forms
Pointer
BackgroundWorker
BindingNavigator
BindingSource
Button
CheckBox
CheckedListBox
ColorDialog
ComboBox
ContextMenuStrip
DataGridView
DataSet
Form1.jsl [Design]*
AssemblyInfo.jsl
Form1
name:
introdatabaseDataSet
introtableBindingSource
introdatabaseDataSetintrotableTableAdapter
Data Sources
introdatabaseDataSet
introtable
name
hobby
Solution Explorer
Data Sources
Properties
(DataBindings)
AccessibleDescripl
AccessibleName
AccessibleRole Default
AllowDrop False
Anchor Top, Left
(DataBindings)
The data bindings for the control.
Error List
0 Errors
0 Warnings
0 Messages
Description File Line Column Project

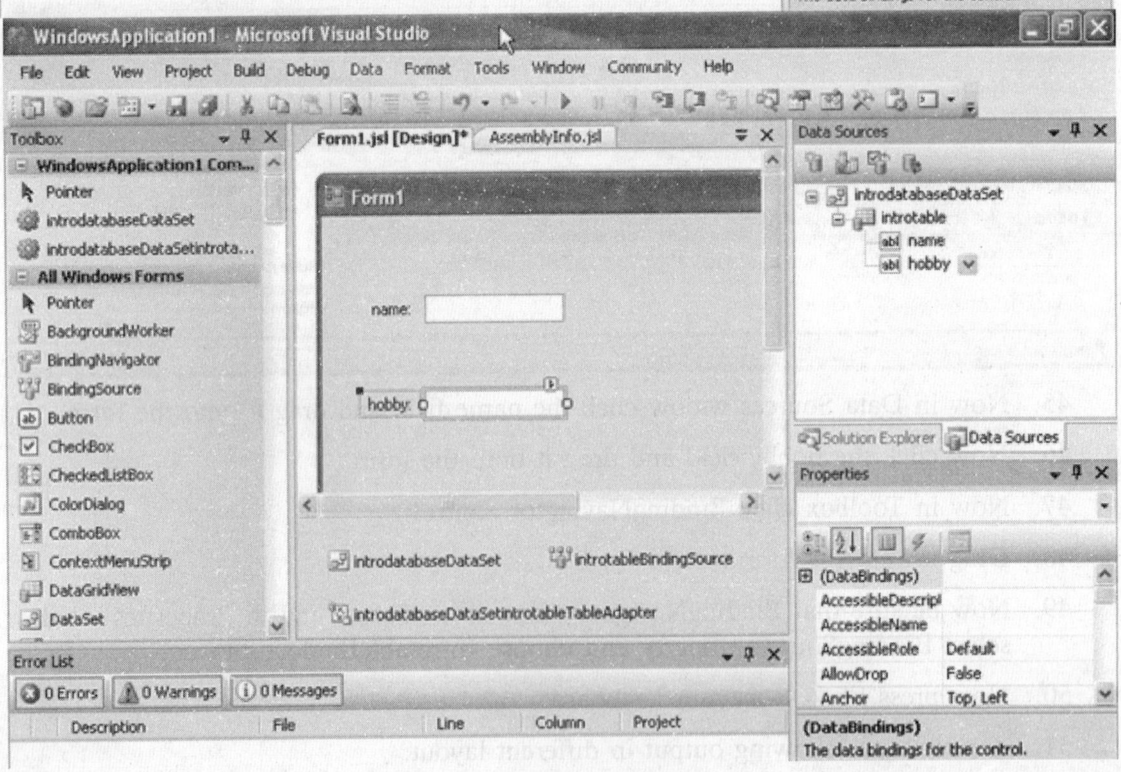
WindowsApplication1 - Microsoft Visual Studio
File Edit View Project Build Debug Data Format Tools Window Community Help
Toolbox
WindowsApplication1 Com...
Pointer
introdatabaseDataSet
introdatabaseDataSetintrota...
All Windows Forms
Pointer
BackgroundWorker
BindingNavigator
BindingSource
Button
CheckBox
CheckedListBox
ColorDialog
ComboBox
ContextMenuStrip
DataGridView
DataSet
Form1.jsl [Design]*
AssemblyInfo.jsl
Form1
name:
hobby:
introdatabaseDataSet
introtableBindingSource
introdatabaseDataSetintrotableTableAdapter
Data Sources
introdatabaseDataSet
introtable
name
hobby
Solution Explorer
Data Sources
Properties
(DataBindings)
AccessibleDescripl
AccessibleName
AccessibleRole Default
AllowDrop False
Anchor Top, Left
(DataBindings)
The data bindings for the control.
Error List
0 Errors
0 Warnings
0 Messages
Description File Line Column Project

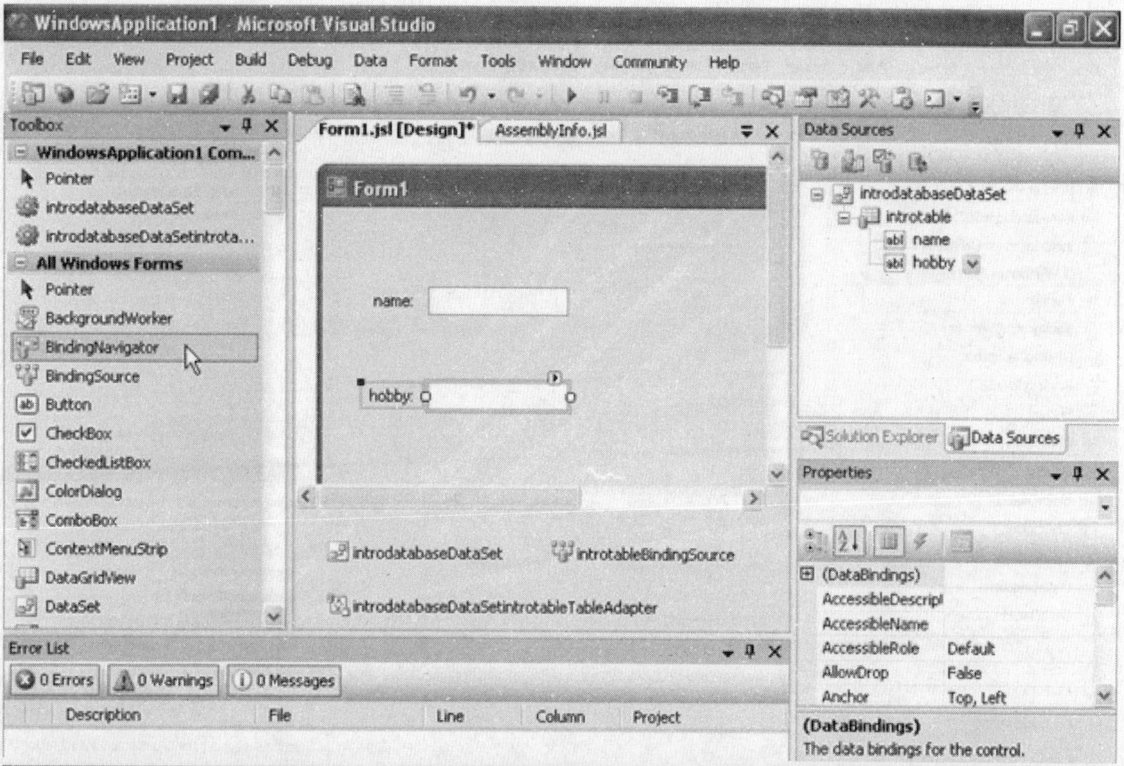
WindowsApplication1 - Microsoft Visual Studio
File Edit View Project Build Debug Data Format Tools Window Community Help
Toolbox
WindowsApplication1 Com...
Pointer
introdatabaseDataSet
introdatabaseDataSetintrota...
All Windows Forms
Pointer
BackgroundWorker
BindingNavigator
BindingSource
Button
CheckBox
CheckedListBox
ColorDialog
ComboBox
ContextMenuStrip
DataGridView
DataSet
Form1.jsl [Design]*
AssemblyInfo.jsl
Form1
name:
hobby:
introdatabaseDataSet
introtableBindingSource
introdatabaseDataSetintrotableTableAdapter
Data Sources
introdatabaseDataSet
introtable
name
hobby
Solution Explorer
Data Sources
Properties
(DataBindings)
AccessibleDescripl
AccessibleName
AccessibleRole Default
AllowDrop False
Anchor Top, Left
(DataBindings)
The data bindings for the control.
Error List
0 Errors
0 Warnings
0 Messages
Description
File
Line
Column
Project

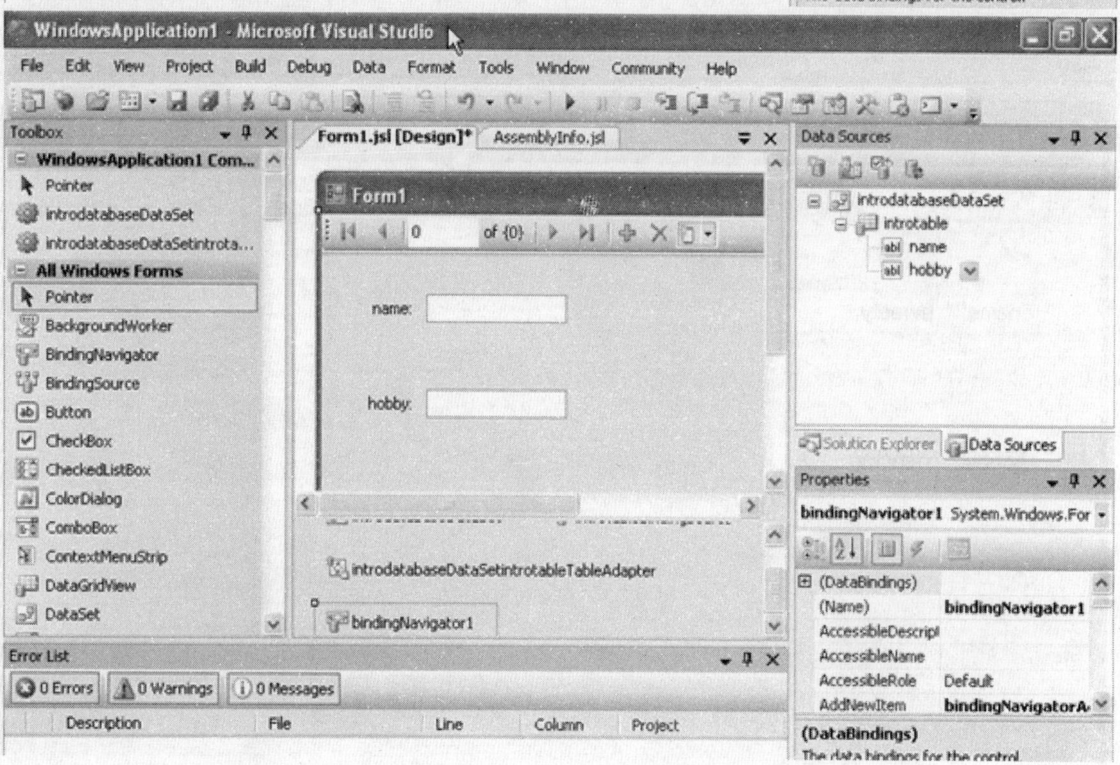
WindowsApplication1 - Microsoft Visual Studio
File Edit View Project Build Debug Data Format Tools Window Community Help
Toolbox
WindowsApplication1 Com...
Pointer
introdatabaseDataSet
introdatabaseDataSetintrota...
All Windows Forms
Pointer
BackgroundWorker
BindingNavigator
BindingSource
Button
CheckBox
CheckedListBox
ColorDialog
ComboBox
ContextMenuStrip
DataGridView
DataSet
Form1.jsl [Design]*
AssemblyInfo.jsl
Form1
0
of {0}
name:
hobby:
introdatabaseDataSetintrotableTableAdapter
bindingNavigator1
Data Sources
introdatabaseDataSet
introtable
name
hobby
Solution Explorer
Data Sources
Properties
bindingNavigator1 System.Windows.For
(DataBindings)
(Name) bindingNavigator1
AccessibleDescripl
AccessibleName
AccessibleRole Default
AddNewItem bindingNavigatorA
(DataBindings)
Error List
0 Errors
0 Warnings
0 Messages
Description
File
Line
Column
Project

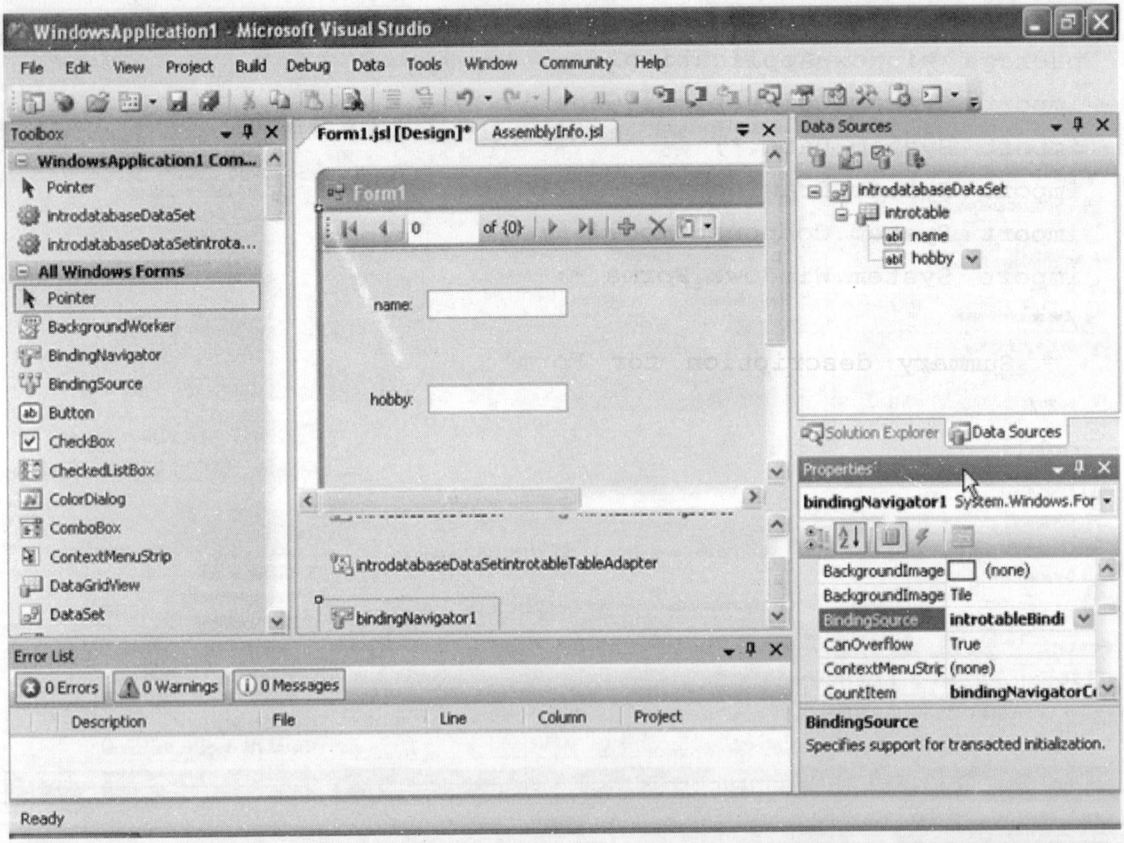
WindowsApplication1 - Microsoft Visual Studio
File Edit View Project Build Debug Data Tools Window Community Help
Toolbox
WindowsApplication1 Com...
Pointer
introdatabaseDataSet
introdatabaseDataSetintrota...
All Windows Forms
Pointer
BackgroundWorker
BindingNavigator
BindingSource
Button
CheckBox
CheckedListBox
ColorDialog
ComboBox
ContextMenuStrip
DataGridView
DataSet
Form1.jsl [Design]*
AssemblyInfo.jsl
Form1
of {0}
name:
hobby:
introdatabaseDataSetintrotableTableAdapter
bindingNavigator1
Data Sources
introdatabaseDataSet
introtable
name
hobby
Solution Explorer
Data Sources
Properties
bindingNavigator1 System.Windows.For
BackgroundImage (none)
BackgroundImage Tile
BindingSource introtableBindi
CanOverflow True
ContextMenuStrip (none)
CountItem bindingNavigatorC
BindingSource
Specifies support for transacted initialization.
Error List
0 Errors
0 Warnings
0 Messages
Description
File
Line
Column
Project
Ready

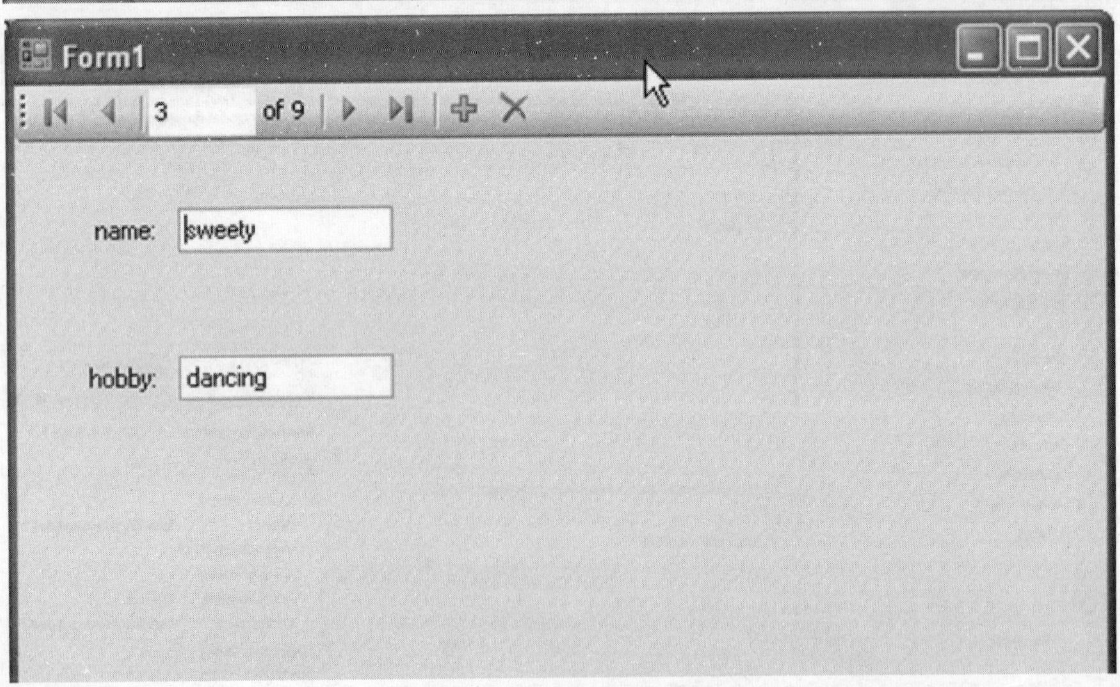
Form1
3
of 9
name:
sweety
hobby:
dancing

— Form1.jsl —

```
package WindowsApplication1;
import System.Collections.Generic.*;
import System.Data.*;
import System.Drawing.*;
import System.ComponentModel.*;
import System.Windows.Forms.*;
/**
  * Summary description for Form1.
  */
public class Form1 extends System.Windows.Forms.Form
{
   private introdatabaseDataSet introdatabaseDataSet;
   private BindingSource introtableBindingSource;
   private introdatabaseDataSetintrotableTableAdapter
introdatabaseDataSetintrotableTableAdapter;
   private TextBox nameTextBox;
   private TextBox hobbyTextBox;
   private BindingNavigator bindingNavigator1;
   private ToolStripButton bindingNavigatorAddNewItem;
   private ToolStripLabel bindingNavigatorCountItem;
   private ToolStripButton bindingNavigatorDeleteItem;
   private ToolStripButton bindingNavigatorMoveFirstItem;
   private ToolStripButton bindingNavigatorMovePreviousItem;
   private ToolStripSeparator bindingNavigatorSeparator;
   private ToolStripTextBox bindingNavigatorPositionItem;
   private ToolStripSeparator bindingNavigatorSeparator1;
   private ToolStripButton bindingNavigatorMoveNextItem;
   private ToolStripButton bindingNavigatorMoveLastItem;
   private ToolStripSeparator bindingNavigatorSeparator2;
   /**
   * Required designer variable.
     */
   private System.ComponentModel.IContainer components;
   public Form1()
```

```
    {
        //
        // Required for Windows Form Designer support
        //
        InitializeComponent();
        //
        // TODO: Add any constructor code after InitializeComponent
call
        //
    }
    #region Windows Form Designer generated code
    /**
      * Clean up any resources being used.
      */
   protected void Dispose(boolean disposing)
    {
        if (disposing)
        {
            if (components != null)
            {
                components.Dispose();
            }
        }
        super.Dispose(disposing);
    }
    /**
     * Required method for Designer support - do not modify
     * the contents of this method with the code editor.
     */
    private void InitializeComponent()
    {
        this.components = new System.ComponentModel.Container();
        System.Windows.Forms.Label nameLabel;
        System.Windows.Forms.Label hobbyLabel;
        System.ComponentModel.ComponentResourceManager resources
```

```
= new System.ComponentModel.ComponentResourceManager
(Form1.class.ToType());
    this.introdatabaseDataSet = new
WindowsApplication1.introdatabaseDataSet();
    this.introtableBindingSource = new
System.Windows.Forms.BindingSource(this.components);
    this.introdatabaseDataSetintrotableTableAdapter = new
WindowsApplication1.introdatabaseDataSetintrotableTableAdapter();
    this.nameTextBox = new System.Windows.Forms.TextBox();
    this.hobbyTextBox = new System.Windows.Forms.TextBox();
    this.bindingNavigator1 = new
System.Windows.Forms.BindingNavigator(this.components);
    this.bindingNavigatorMoveFirstItem = new
System.Windows.Forms.ToolStripButton();
    this.bindingNavigatorMovePreviousItem = new
System.Windows.Forms.ToolStripButton();
    this.bindingNavigatorSeparator = new
System.Windows.Forms.ToolStripSeparator();
    this.bindingNavigatorPositionItem = new
System.Windows.Forms.ToolStripTextBox();
    this.bindingNavigatorCountItem = new
System.Windows.Forms.ToolStripLabel();
    this.bindingNavigatorSeparator1 = new
System.Windows.Forms.ToolStripSeparator();
    this.bindingNavigatorMoveNextItem = new
System.Windows.Forms.ToolStripButton();
    this.bindingNavigatorMoveLastItem = new
System.Windows.Forms.ToolStripButton();
    this.bindingNavigatorSeparator2 = new
System.Windows.Forms.ToolStripSeparator();
    this.bindingNavigatorAddNewItem = new
System.Windows.Forms.ToolStripButton();
    this.bindingNavigatorDeleteItem = new
System.Windows.Forms.ToolStripButton();
    nameLabel = new System.Windows.Forms.Label();
    hobbyLabel = new System.Windows.Forms.Label();
    ((System.ComponentModel.ISupportInitialize)
(this.introdatabaseDataSet)).BeginInit();
```

```
    ((System.ComponentModel.ISupportInitialize)
 (this.introtableBindingSource)).BeginInit();
    ((System.ComponentModel.ISupportInitialize)
 (this.bindingNavigator1)).BeginInit();
    this.bindingNavigator1.SuspendLayout();
    this.SuspendLayout();
    //
    // introdatabaseDataSet
    //
    this.introdatabaseDataSet.set_DataSetName
 ("introdatabaseDataSet");
   this.introdatabaseDataSet.set_SchemaSerializationMode
 (System.Data.SchemaSerializationMode.IncludeSchema);
    //
    // introtableBindingSource
    //

this.introtableBindingSource.set_DataMember("introtable");
    this.introtableBindingSource.set_DataSource
 (this.introdatabaseDataSet);
    //
    // introdatabaseDataSetintrotableTableAdapter
    //
    this.introdatabaseDataSetintrotableTableAdapter.
 set_ClearBeforeFill(true);
    //
    // nameLabel
    //
    nameLabel.set_AutoSize(true);
    nameLabel.set_Location(new System.Drawing.Point(33, 58));
    nameLabel.set_Name("nameLabel");
    nameLabel.set_Size(new System.Drawing.Size(36, 13));
    nameLabel.set_TabIndex(0);
    nameLabel.set_Text("name:");
    //
    // nameTextBox
```

```
    //
    this.nameTextBox.get_DataBindings().Add(new
System.Windows.Forms.Binding("Text",
this.introtableBindingSource, "name", true));
    this.nameTextBox.set_Location(new System.Drawing.Point(75,
55));
    this.nameTextBox.set_Name("nameTextBox");
    this.nameTextBox.set_Size(new System.Drawing.Size(100,
20));
    this.nameTextBox.set_TabIndex(1);
    //
    // hobbyLabel
    //
    hobbyLabel.set_AutoSize(true);
    hobbyLabel.set_Location(new System.Drawing.Point(30,
124));
    hobbyLabel.set_Name("hobbyLabel");
    hobbyLabel.set_Size(new System.Drawing.Size(39, 13));
    hobbyLabel.set_TabIndex(2);
    hobbyLabel.set_Text("hobby:");
    //
    // hobbyTextBox
    //
    this.hobbyTextBox.get_DataBindings().Add(new
System.Windows.Forms.Binding("Text",
this.introtableBindingSource, "hobby", true));
    this.hobbyTextBox.set_Location(new
System.Drawing.Point(75, 121));
    this.hobbyTextBox.set_Name("hobbyTextBox");
    this.hobbyTextBox.set_Size(new System.Drawing.Size(100,
20));
    this.hobbyTextBox.set_TabIndex(3);
    //
    // bindingNavigator1
    //
    this.bindingNavigator1.set_AddNewItem
(this.bindingNavigatorAddNewItem);
```

```
this.bindingNavigator1.set_BindingSource
(this.introtableBindingSource);
this.bindingNavigator1.set_CountItem
(this.bindingNavigatorCountItem);
this.bindingNavigator1.set_DeleteItem
(this.bindingNavigatorDeleteItem);
this.bindingNavigator1.get_Items().AddRange(new
System.Windows.Forms.ToolStripItem[] {
            this.bindingNavigatorMoveFirstItem,
            this.bindingNavigatorMovePreviousItem,
            this.bindingNavigatorSeparator,
            this.bindingNavigatorPositionItem,
            this.bindingNavigatorCountItem,
            this.bindingNavigatorSeparator1,
            this.bindingNavigatorMoveNextItem,
            this.bindingNavigatorMoveLastItem,
            this.bindingNavigatorSeparator2,
            this.bindingNavigatorAddNewItem,
            this.bindingNavigatorDeleteItem}
);
this.bindingNavigator1.set_Location(new
System.Drawing.Point(0, 0));
this.bindingNavigator1.set_MoveFirstItem
(this.bindingNavigatorMoveFirstItem);
this.bindingNavigator1.set_MoveLastItem
(this.bindingNavigatorMoveLastItem);
this.bindingNavigator1.set_MoveNextItem
(this.bindingNavigatorMoveNextItem);
this.bindingNavigator1.set_MovePreviousItem
(this.bindingNavigatorMovePreviousItem);
this.bindingNavigator1.set_Name("bindingNavigator1");
this.bindingNavigator1.set_PositionItem
(this.bindingNavigatorPositionItem);
this.bindingNavigator1.set_Size(new
System.Drawing.Size(503, 25));
this.bindingNavigator1.set_TabIndex(4);
this.bindingNavigator1.set_Text("bindingNavigator1");
```

```
      //
      // bindingNavigatorMoveFirstItem
      //

this.bindingNavigatorMoveFirstItem.set_DisplayStyle(System.
Windows.Forms.ToolStripItemDisplayStyle.Image);

this.bindingNavigatorMoveFirstItem.set_Image(((System.Drawing.Image)(
resources.GetObject("bindingNavigatorMoveFirstItem.Image"))));
      this.bindingNavigatorMoveFirstItem.set_Name
("bindingNavigatorMoveFirstItem");
      this.bindingNavigatorMoveFirstItem.set_RightToLeft
AutoMirrorImage(true);
      this.bindingNavigatorMoveFirstItem.set_Size(new
System.Drawing.Size(23, 22));
      this.bindingNavigatorMoveFirstItem.set_Text("Move first");
      //
      // bindingNavigatorMovePreviousItem
      //
      this.bindingNavigatorMovePreviousItem.set_DisplayStyle
(System.Windows.Forms.ToolStripItemDisplayStyle.Image);

this.bindingNavigatorMovePreviousItem.set_Image(((System.Drawing.Image)
(resources.GetObject("bindingNavigatorMovePrevious
Item.Image"))));
      this.bindingNavigatorMovePreviousItem.set_Name("binding
NavigatorMovePreviousItem");
      this.bindingNavigatorMovePreviousItem.set_RightToLeft
AutoMirrorImage(true);
      this.bindingNavigatorMovePreviousItem.set_Size(new
System.Drawing.Size(23, 22));
      this.bindingNavigatorMovePreviousItem.set_Text("Move
previous");
      //
      // bindingNavigatorSeparator
      //
      this.bindingNavigatorSeparator.set_Name
("bindingNavigatorSeparator");
```

```
    this.bindingNavigatorSeparator.set_Size(new
System.Drawing.Size(6, 25));
    //
    // bindingNavigatorPositionItem
    //
this.bindingNavigatorPositionItem.set_AccessibleName("Position");
    this.bindingNavigatorPositionItem.set_AutoSize(false);
    this.bindingNavigatorPositionItem.set_Name
("bindingNavigatorPositionItem");
    this.bindingNavigatorPositionItem.set_Size(new
System.Drawing.Size(50, 21));
    this.bindingNavigatorPositionItem.set_Text("0");

this.bindingNavigatorPositionItem.set_ToolTipText("Current
position");
    //
    // bindingNavigatorCountItem
    //
    this.bindingNavigatorCountItem.set_Name
("bindingNavigatorCountItem");
    this.bindingNavigatorCountItem.set_Size(new
System.Drawing.Size(36, 22));
    this.bindingNavigatorCountItem.set_Text("of {0}");
    this.bindingNavigatorCountItem.set_ToolTipText("Total
number of items");
    //
    // bindingNavigatorSeparator1
    //
    this.bindingNavigatorSeparator1.set_Name
("bindingNavigatorSeparator");
    this.bindingNavigatorSeparator1.set_Size(new
System.Drawing.Size(6, 25));
    //
    // bindingNavigatorMoveNextItem
    //
this.bindingNavigatorMoveNextItem.set_DisplayStyle(System.
Windows.Forms.ToolStripItemDisplayStyle.Image);
```

```
this.bindingNavigatorMoveNextItem.set_Image(((System.Drawing.Image)
(resources.GetObject("bindingNavigatorMoveNextItem.Image"))));
      this.bindingNavigatorMoveNextItem.set_Name
("bindingNavigatorMoveNextItem");
      this.bindingNavigatorMoveNextItem.set_RightToLeft
AutoMirrorImage(true);
      this.bindingNavigatorMoveNextItem.set_Size(new
System.Drawing.Size(23, 22));
      this.bindingNavigatorMoveNextItem.set_Text("Move next");
      //
      // bindingNavigatorMoveLastItem
      //
this.bindingNavigatorMoveLastItem.set_DisplayStyle(System.
Windows. Forms.ToolStripItemDisplayStyle.Image);

this.bindingNavigatorMoveLastItem.set_Image(((System.Drawing.
Image)(resources.GetObject("bindingNavigatorMoveLastItem.
Image"))));

this.bindingNavigatorMoveLastItem.set_Name("bindingNavigator
MoveLastItem");
      this.bindingNavigatorMoveLastItem.set_RightToLeftAuto
MirrorImage(true);
      this.bindingNavigatorMoveLastItem.set_Size(new
System.Drawing.Size(23, 22));
      this.bindingNavigatorMoveLastItem.set_Text("Move last");
      //
      // bindingNavigatorSeparator2
      //
      this.bindingNavigatorSeparator2.set_Name("binding
NavigatorSeparator");
      this.bindingNavigatorSeparator2.set_Size(new
System.Drawing.Size(6, 25));
      //
      // bindingNavigatorAddNewItem
      //
      this.bindingNavigatorAddNewItem.set_DisplayStyle
(System.Windows.Forms.ToolStripItemDisplayStyle.Image);
```

```
this.bindingNavigatorAddNewItem.set_Image(((System.Drawing.
Image) (resources.GetObject("bindingNavigatorAddNew
Item.Image"))));
    this.bindingNavigatorAddNewItem.set_Name
("bindingNavigatorAddNewItem");
    this.bindingNavigatorAddNewItem.set_RightToLeft
AutoMirrorImage(true);
    this.bindingNavigatorAddNewItem.set_Size(new System.
Drawing.Size(23, 22));
    this.bindingNavigatorAddNewItem.set_Text("Add new");
    //
    // bindingNavigatorDeleteItem
    //
    this.bindingNavigatorDeleteItem.set_DisplayStyle
(System.Windows.Forms.ToolStripItemDisplayStyle.Image);
    this.bindingNavigatorDeleteItem.set_Image
(((System.Drawing.Image)(resources.GetObject ("bindingNavigator
DeleteItem.Image"))));
    this.bindingNavigatorDeleteItem.set_Name
("bindingNavigatorDeleteItem");
    this.bindingNavigatorDeleteItem.set_Right
ToLeftAutoMirrorImage(true);
    this.bindingNavigatorDeleteItem.set_Size(new
System.Drawing.Size(23, 22));
    this.bindingNavigatorDeleteItem.set_Text("Delete");
    //
    // Form1
    //
    this.set_AutoScaleDimensions(new System.Drawing.SizeF(6F,
13F));
this.set_AutoScaleMode(System.Windows.Forms.AutoScaleMode.Font);
    this.set_ClientSize(new System.Drawing.Size(503, 323));
    this.get_Controls().Add(this.bindingNavigator1);
    this.get_Controls().Add(hobbyLabel);
    this.get_Controls().Add(this.hobbyTextBox);
    this.get_Controls().Add(nameLabel);
```

```
        this.get_Controls().Add(this.nameTextBox);
        this.set_Name("Form1");
        this.set_Text("Form1");
        this.add_Load(new System.EventHandler(this.Form1_Load));
        ((System.ComponentModel.ISupportInitialize)
(this.introdatabaseDataSet)).EndInit();
        ((System.ComponentModel.ISupportInitialize)
(this.introtableBindingSource)).EndInit();
        ((System.ComponentModel.ISupportInitialize)
(this.bindingNavigator1)).EndInit();
        this.bindingNavigator1.ResumeLayout(false);
        this.bindingNavigator1.PerformLayout();
        this.ResumeLayout(false);
        this.PerformLayout();
    }
    #endregion
    private void introtableBindingNavigatorSaveItem_Click(Object
sender, System.EventArgs e)
    {
        this.Validate();
        this.introtableBindingSource.EndEdit();
        this.introdatabaseDataSetintrotableTableAdapter.Update
(this.introdatabaseDataSet.get_introtable());
    }
    private void introtableBindingNavigatorSaveItem_Click_1
(Object sender, System.EventArgs e)
    {
        this.Validate();
        this.introtableBindingSource.EndEdit();
        this.introdatabaseDataSetintrotableTableAdapter.Update
(this.introdatabaseDataSet.get_introtable());
    }
    private void Form1_Load(Object sender, System.EventArgs e)
    {
        // TODO: This line of code loads data into the
'introdatabaseDataSet.introtable' table. You can move, or remove
it, as needed.
```

```
this.introdatabaseDataSetintrotableTableAdapter.Fill(
this.introdatabaseDataSet.get_introtable());
    }
}
```

— app.config —

```
<?xml version="1.0" encoding="utf-8" ?>
<configuration>
     <configSections>
     </configSections>
     <connectionStrings>
          <add name="WindowsApplication1.Properties.Settings.
introdatabaseConnectionString"
          connectionString="Provider=Microsoft.Jet.OLEDB.4.0;Data
Source=|DataDirectory|\introdatabase.mdb"
               providerName="System.Data.OleDb" />
     </connectionStrings>
</configuration>
```

— Program.jsl —

```
package WindowsApplication1;
import System.Collections.Generic.*;
import System.Windows.Forms.*;
/**
  * Summary description for Program
  */
public class Program
{
     * The main entry point for the application.
   /** @attribute System.STAThread() */
   public static void main(String[] args)
   {
      Application.EnableVisualStyles();
      Application.SetCompatibleTextRenderingDefault(false);
      Application.Run(new Form1());
   }
}
```

6 Visual C++ and ADO.Net

INTRODUCTION

Similar to what we had done earlier, we will this time use Visual C++ 2005 with ADO.Net.

Let us perform the following steps:

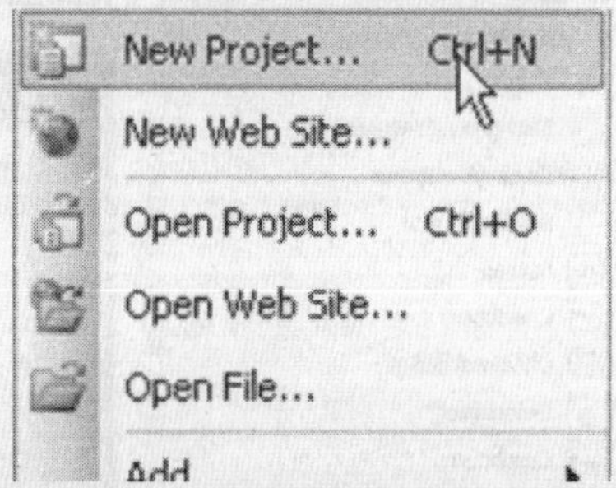

1. Start Visual Studio 2005
2. On menu bar click File
3. Click New Project
4. You will get New Project dialog box
5. Under Project types select Visual C++

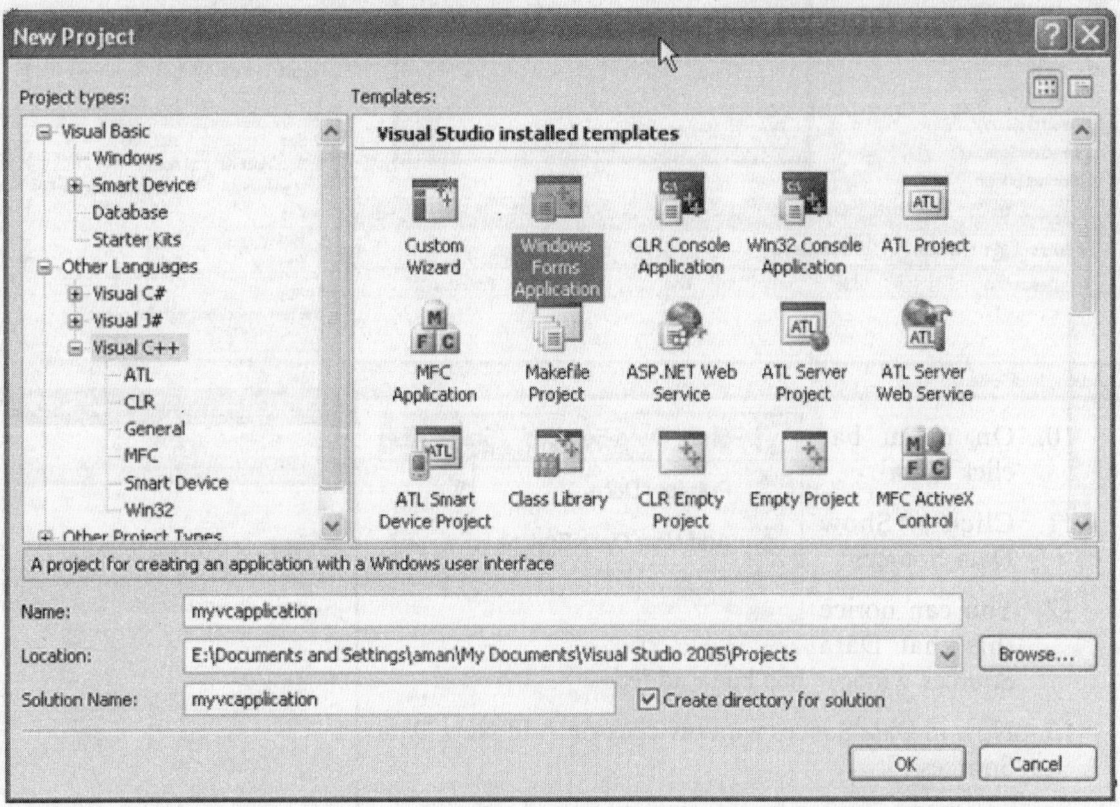

6. Under Templates select Windows Forms Applications
7. In Name field type, myvcapplication
8. Click OK
9. At present you have following scenario

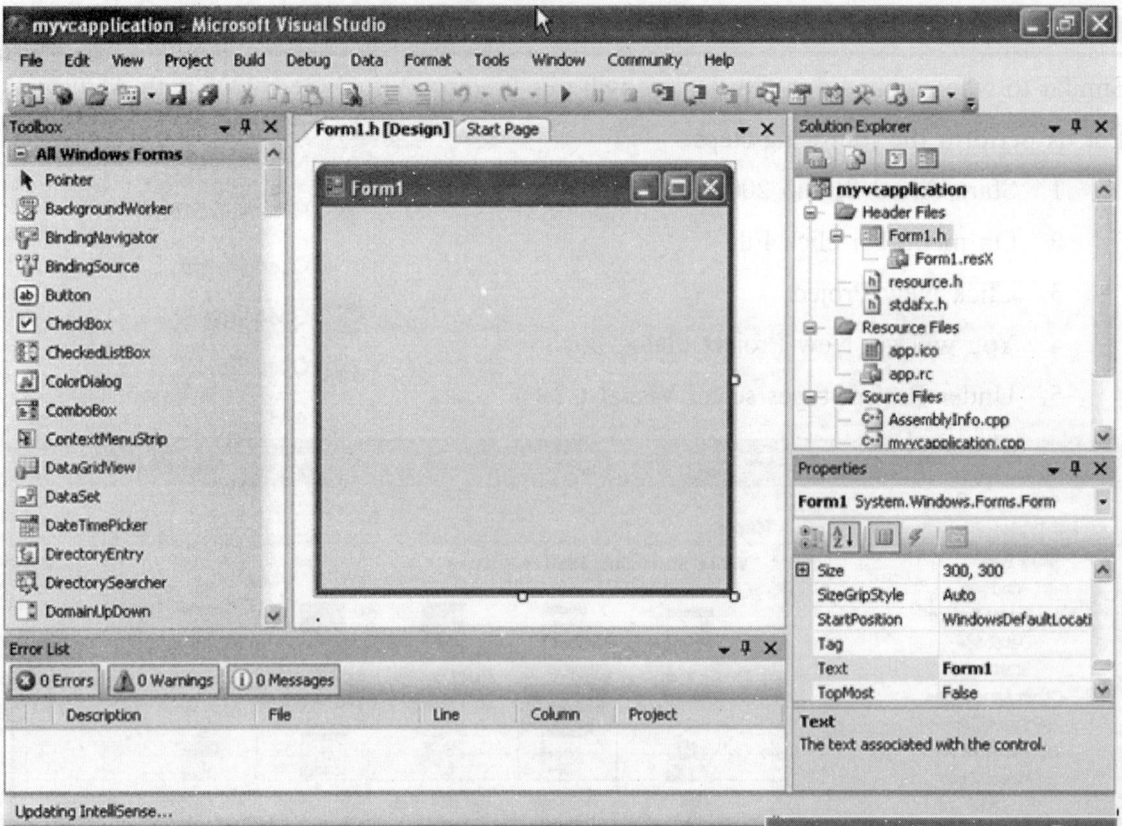

10. On menu bar click Data
11. Click Show Data Sources
12. You can notice this that Data Sources window has been added

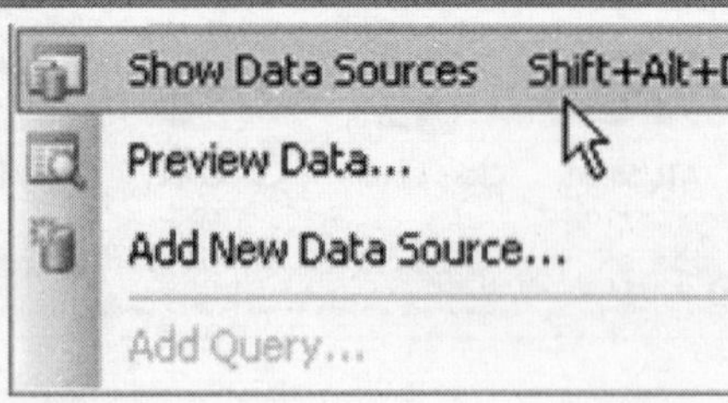

13. Now in Data Souces window click on Add New Data Sources
14. You will get Data Source Configuration Wizard
15. Select Database

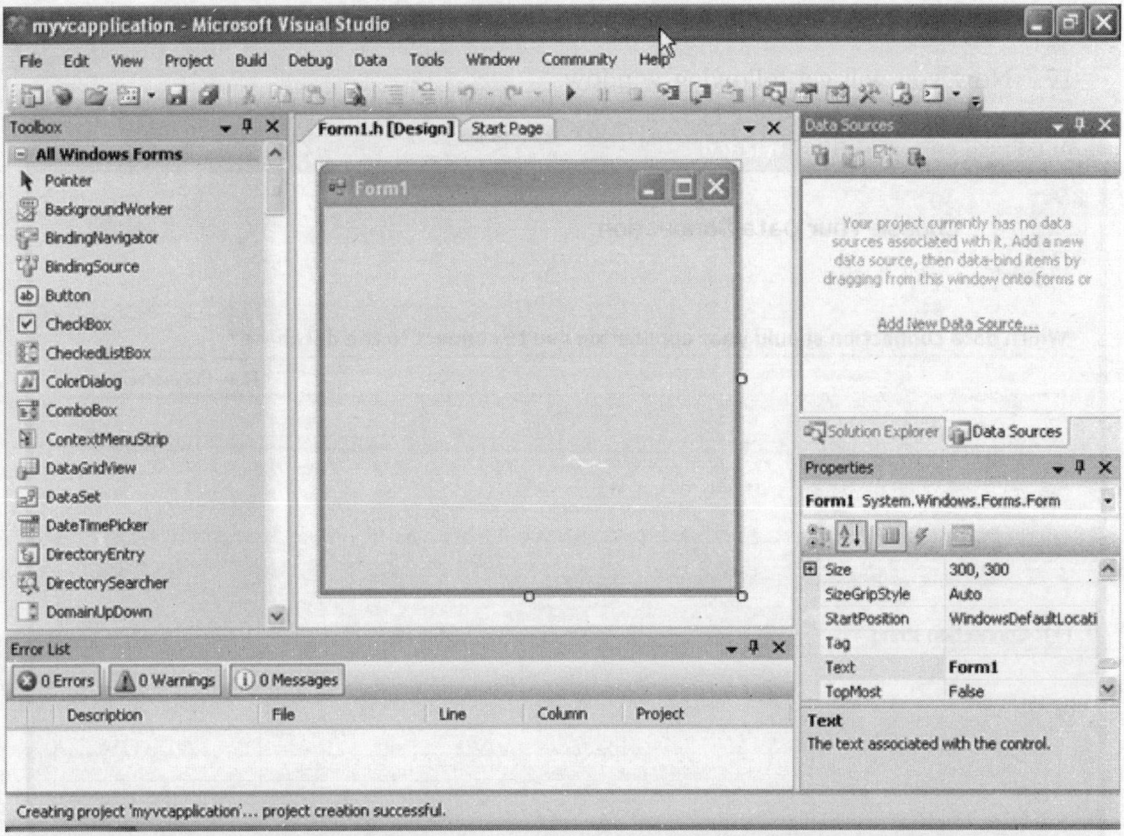
myvcapplication - Microsoft Visual Studio
File Edit View Project Build Debug Data Tools Window Community Help
Toolbox
All Windows Forms
Pointer
BackgroundWorker
BindingNavigator
BindingSource
Button
CheckBox
CheckedListBox
ColorDialog
ComboBox
ContextMenuStrip
DataGridView
DataSet
DateTimePicker
DirectoryEntry
DirectorySearcher
DomainUpDown
Form1.h [Design]
Start Page
Form1
Data Sources
Your project currently has no data sources associated with it. Add a new data source, then data-bind items by dragging from this window onto forms or
Add New Data Source...
Solution Explorer
Data Sources
Properties
Form1 System.Windows.Forms.Form
Size 300, 300
SizeGripStyle Auto
StartPosition WindowsDefaultLocati
Tag
Text Form1
TopMost False
Text
The text associated with the control.
Error List
0 Errors
0 Warnings
0 Messages
Description File Line Column Project
Creating project 'myvcapplication'... project creation successful.

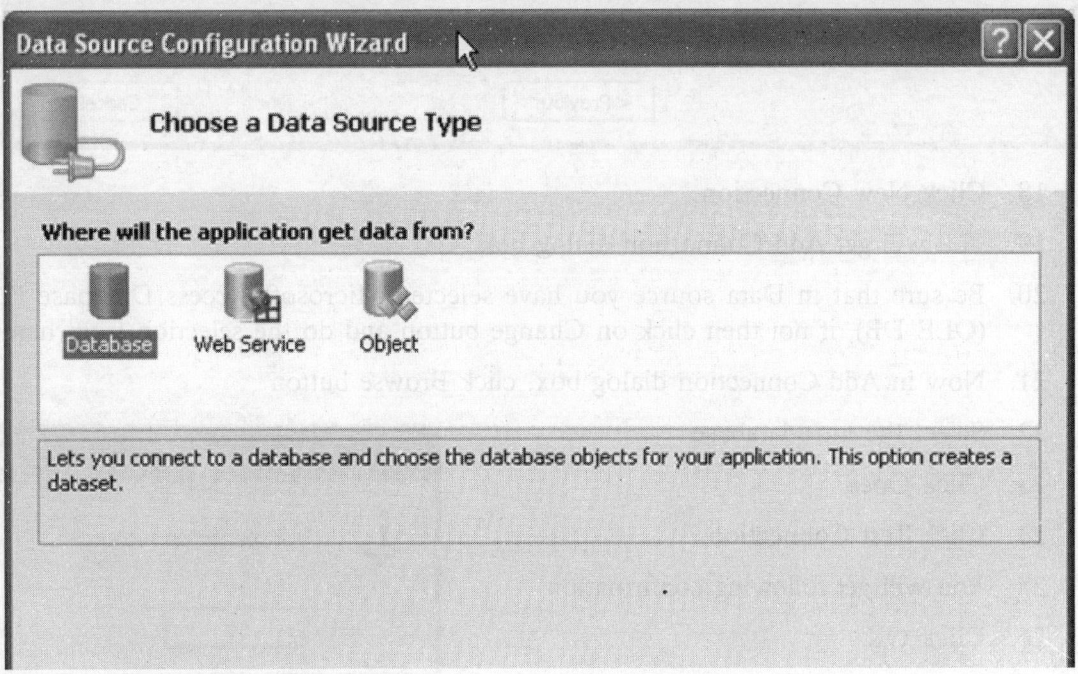
Data Source Configuration Wizard
Choose a Data Source Type
Where will the application get data from?
Database
Web Service
Object
Lets you connect to a database and choose the database objects for your application. This option creates a dataset.

16. Click Next
17. Now you will get following window

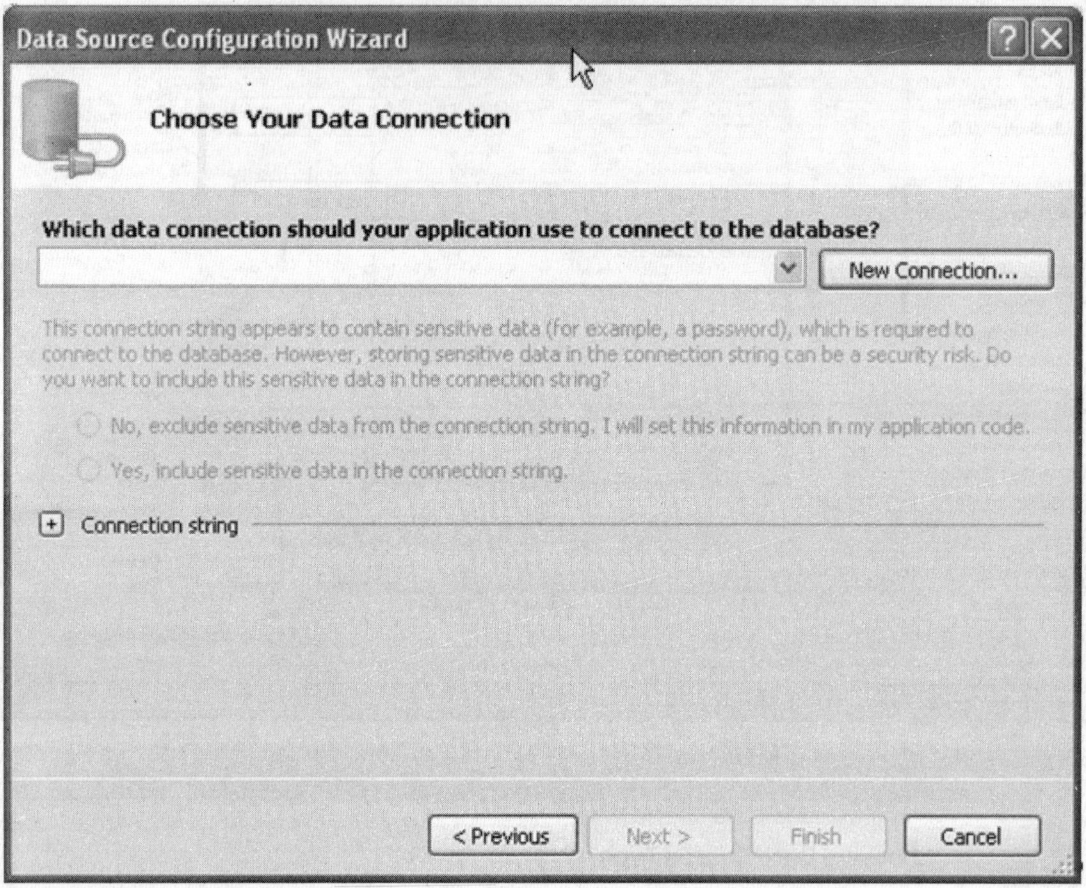

18. Click New Connection...
19. You will get Add Connection dialog box
20. Be sure that in Data source you have selected Microsoft Access Database File (OLE DB), if not then click on Change button and do the selection from here
21. Now in Add Connection dialog box, click Browse button
22. Select the introdatabase
23. Click Open
24. Click Test Connection
25. You will get following confirmation
26. Click OK

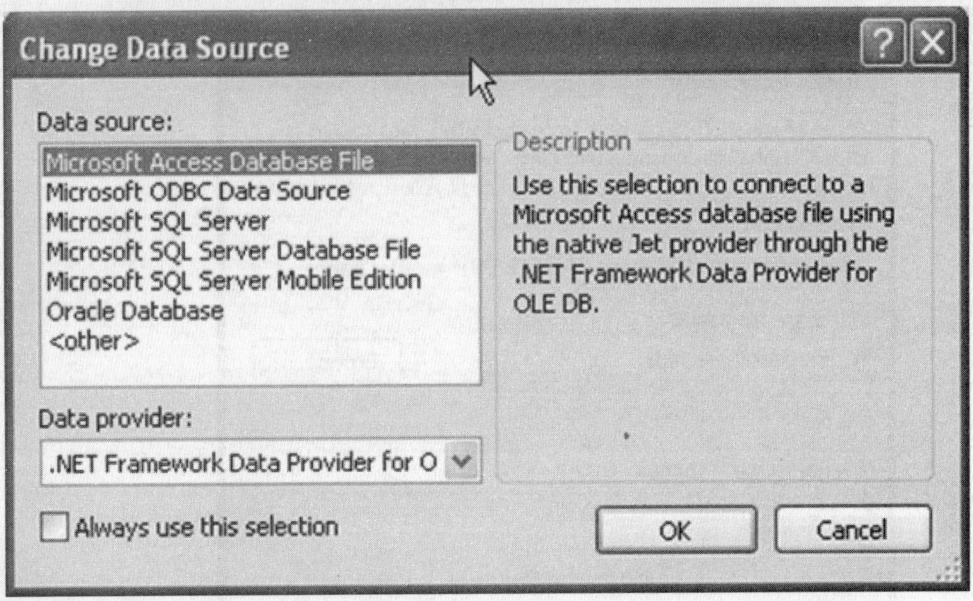

27. Now click Next
28. You will get following message
29. Click Yes

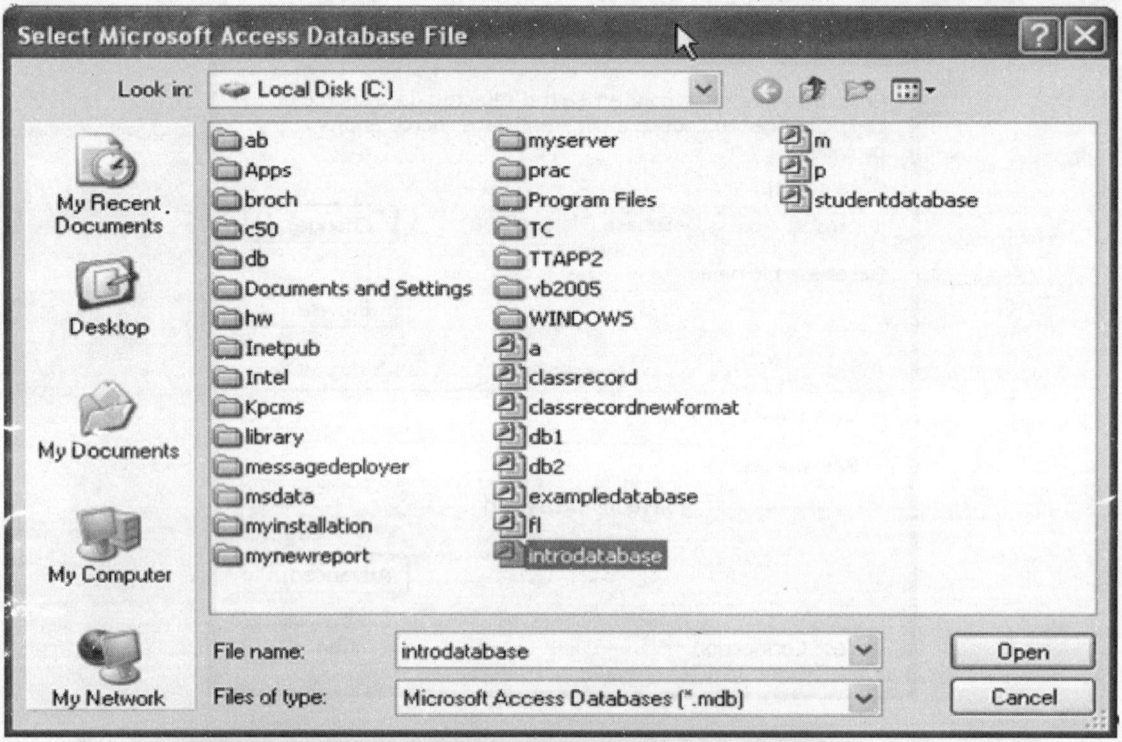
Select Microsoft Access Database File
Look in:
Local Disk (C:)
My Recent Documents
Desktop
My Documents
My Computer
My Network
ab
Apps
broch
c50
db
Documents and Settings
hw
Inetpub
Intel
Kpcms
library
messagedeployer
msdata
myinstallation
mynewreport
myserver
prac
Program Files
TC
TTAPP2
vb2005
WINDOWS
a
classrecord
classrecordnewformat
db1
db2
exampledatabase
fl
introdatabase
m
p
studentdatabase
File name:
introdatabase
Files of type:
Microsoft Access Databases (*.mdb)
Open
Cancel

Add Connection
Enter information to connect to the selected data source or click "Change" to choose a different data source and/or provider.
Data source:
Microsoft Access Database File (OLE DB)
Change...
Database file name:
C:\introdatabase.mdb
Browse...
Log on to the database
User name:
Admin
Password:
Save my password
Advanced...
Test Connection
OK
Cancel

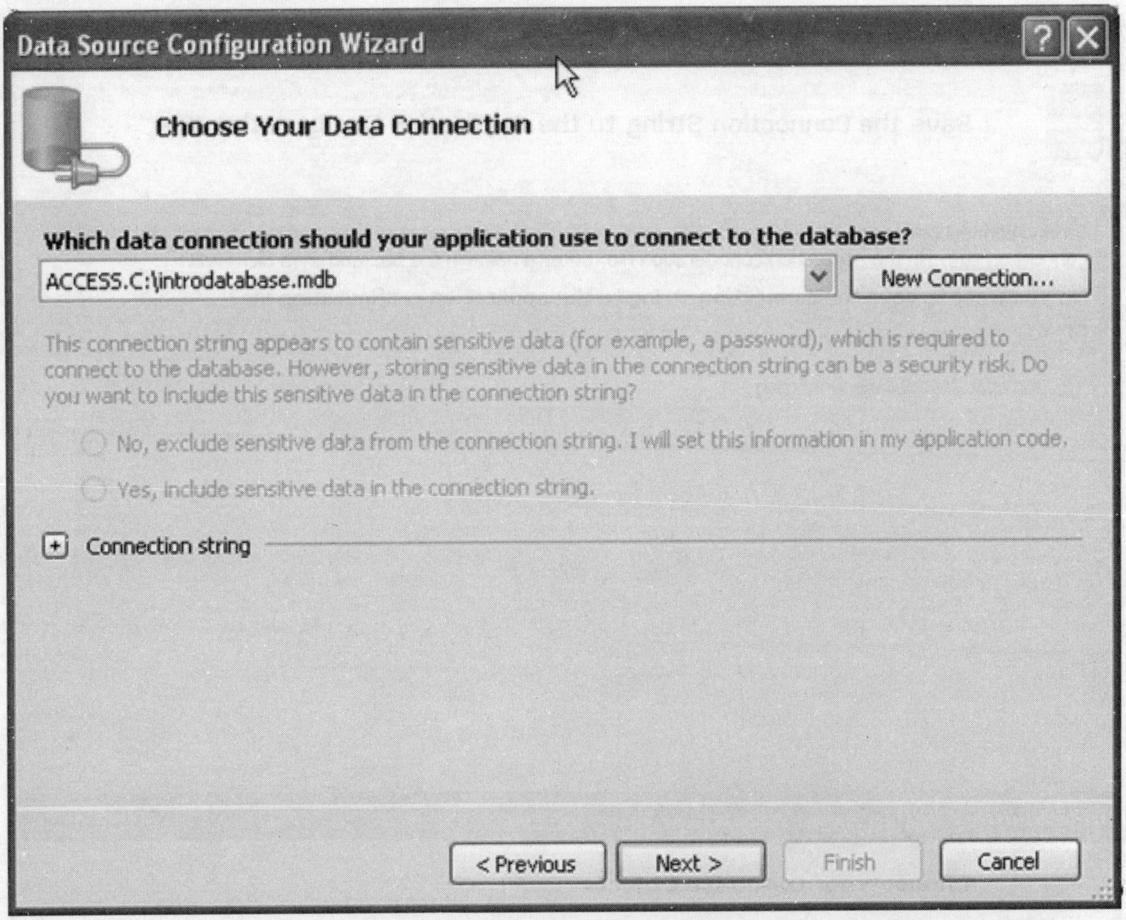

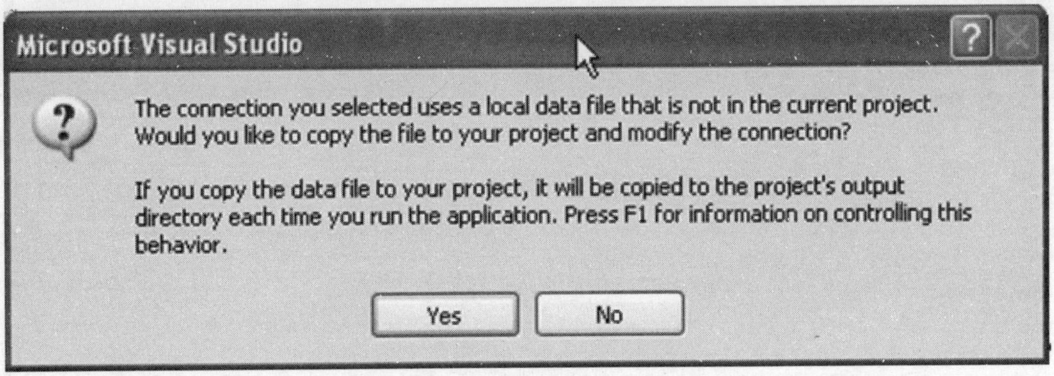

30. Keep default name as introdatabaseConnectionString
31. Click Next
32. Click + sign of Tables
33. At present you have one Table

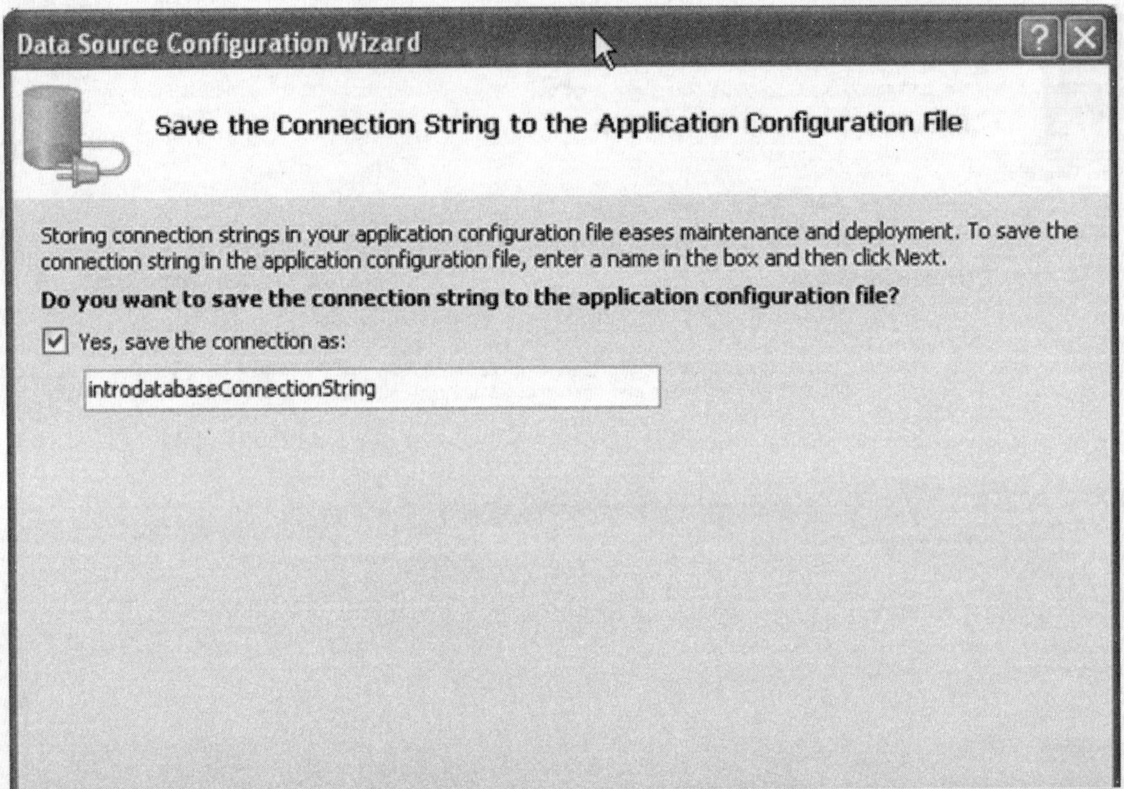
Data Source Configuration Wizard
Save the Connection String to the Application Configuration File
Storing connection strings in your application configuration file eases maintenance and deployment. To save the connection string in the application configuration file, enter a name in the box and then click Next.
Do you want to save the connection string to the application configuration file?
Yes, save the connection as:
introdatabaseConnectionString

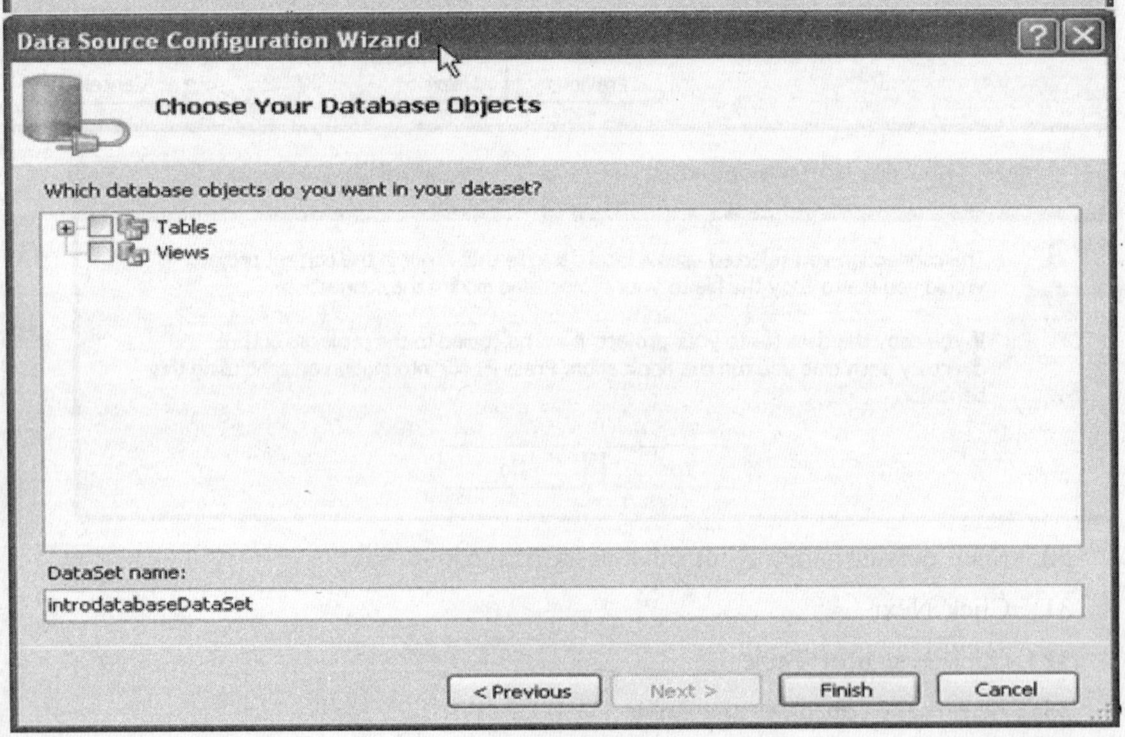
Data Source Configuration Wizard
Choose Your Database Objects
Which database objects do you want in your dataset?
Tables
Views
DataSet name:
introdatabaseDataSet
< Previous
Next >
Finish
Cancel

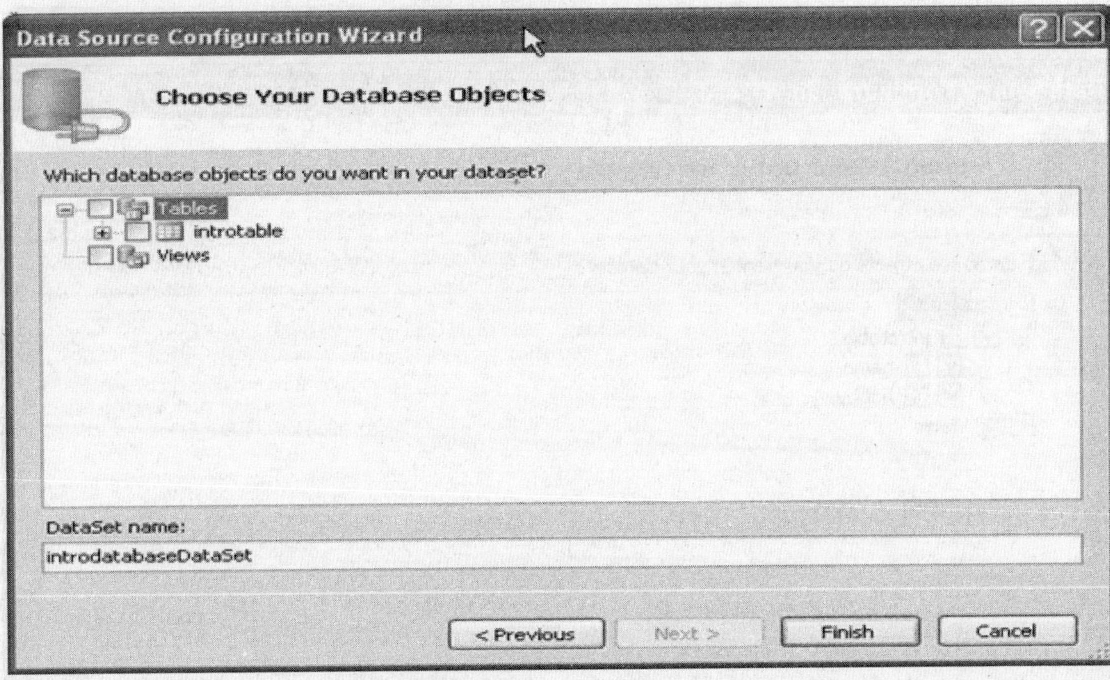

34. Now click on + sign of introtable

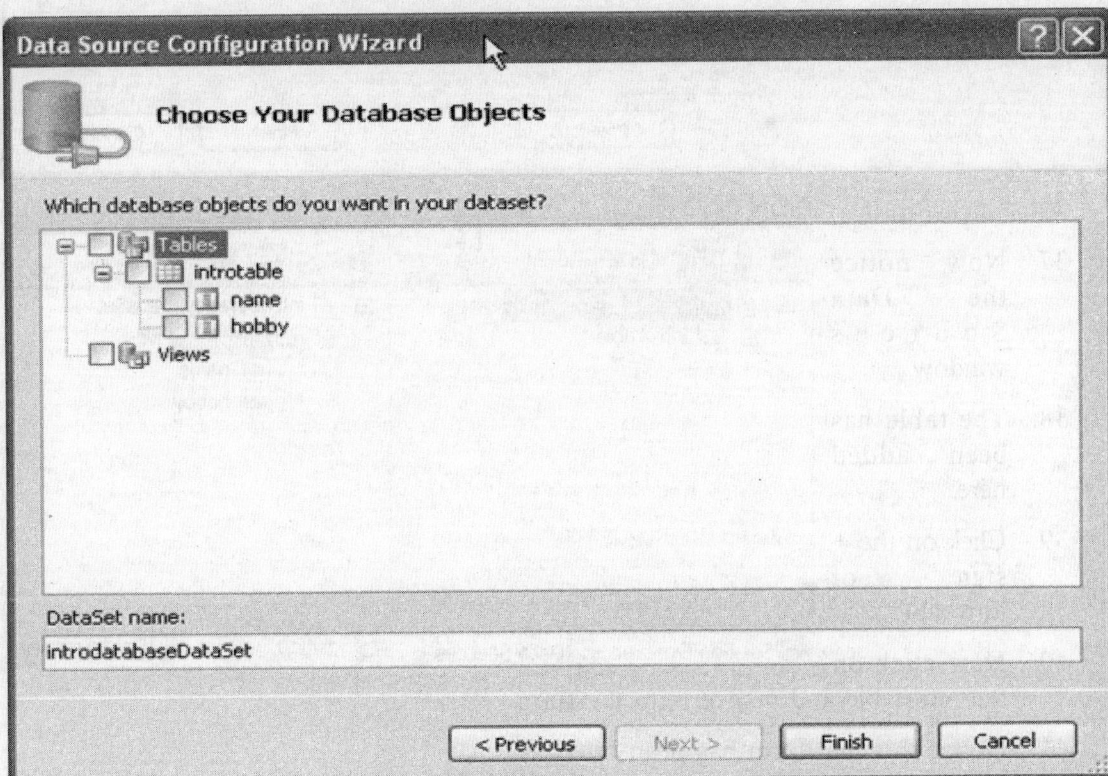

35. At present you have two fields, select both of them

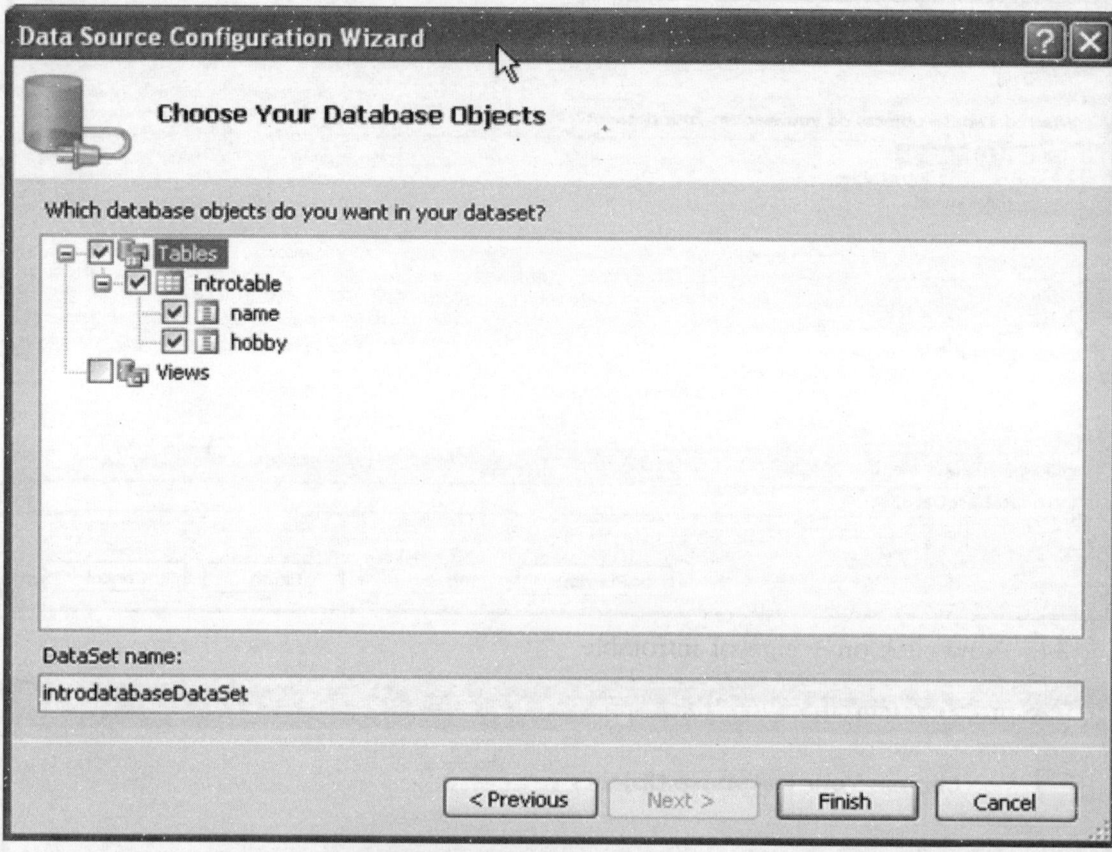

36. Click Finish
37. Now notice the Data Sources window
38. The table has been added here.
39. Click on the + sign of introtable
40. Now click on the introtable and drag it onto the form
41. Notice this that form has been filled up

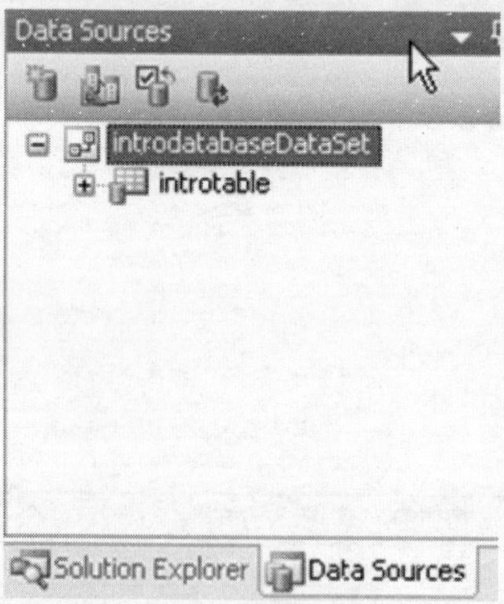

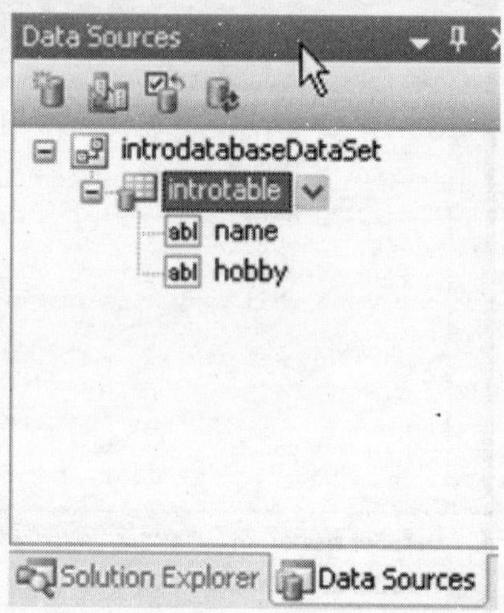

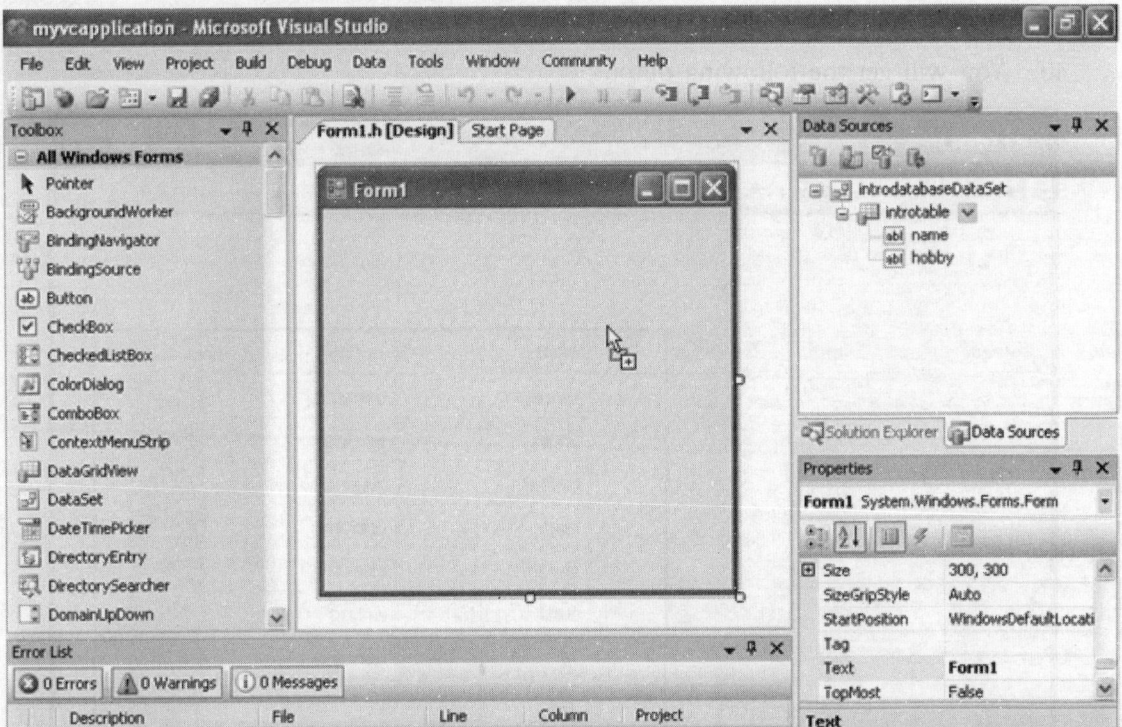
myvcapplication - Microsoft Visual Studio
File Edit View Project Build Debug Data Tools Window Community Help
Toolbox
All Windows Forms
Pointer
BackgroundWorker
BindingNavigator
BindingSource
Button
CheckBox
CheckedListBox
ColorDialog
ComboBox
ContextMenuStrip
DataGridView
DataSet
DateTimePicker
DirectoryEntry
DirectorySearcher
DomainUpDown
Form1.h [Design]
Start Page
Form1
Data Sources
introdatabaseDataSet
introtable
name
hobby
Solution Explorer
Data Sources
Properties
Form1 System.Windows.Forms.Form
Size 300, 300
SizeGripStyle Auto
StartPosition WindowsDefaultLocati
Tag
Text Form1
TopMost False
Text
Error List
0 Errors
0 Warnings
0 Messages
Description File Line Column Project

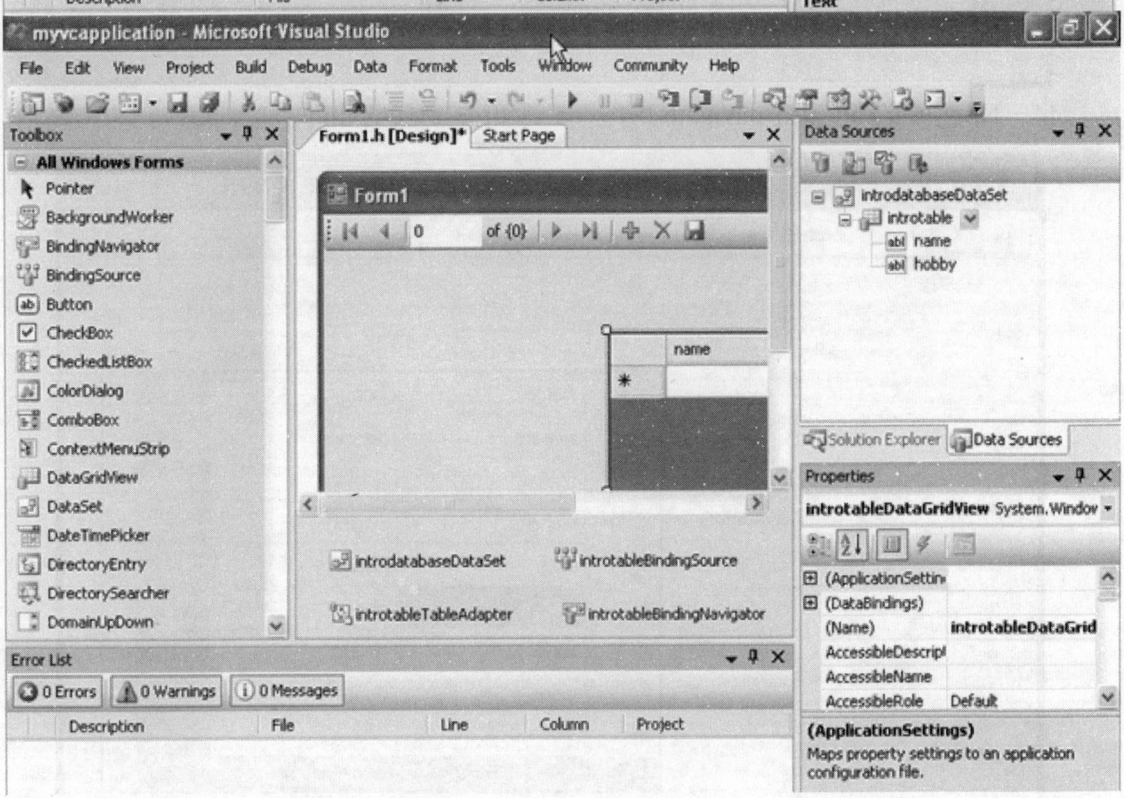
myvcapplication - Microsoft Visual Studio
File Edit View Project Build Debug Data Format Tools Window Community Help
Toolbox
All Windows Forms
Pointer
BackgroundWorker
BindingNavigator
BindingSource
Button
CheckBox
CheckedListBox
ColorDialog
ComboBox
ContextMenuStrip
DataGridView
DataSet
DateTimePicker
DirectoryEntry
DirectorySearcher
DomainUpDown
Form1.h [Design]*
Start Page
Form1
0
of {0}
name
introdatabaseDataSet
introtableBindingSource
introtableTableAdapter
introtableBindingNavigator
Data Sources
introdatabaseDataSet
introtable
name
hobby
Solution Explorer
Data Sources
Properties
introtableDataGridView System.Windov
(ApplicationSettin
(DataBindings)
(Name) introtableDataGrid
AccessibleDescript
AccessibleName
AccessibleRole Default
(ApplicationSettings)
Maps property settings to an application configuration file.
Error List
0 Errors
0 Warnings
0 Messages
Description File Line Column Project

42. Now to run this program press F5 key on your keyboard
43. You will get the following output:

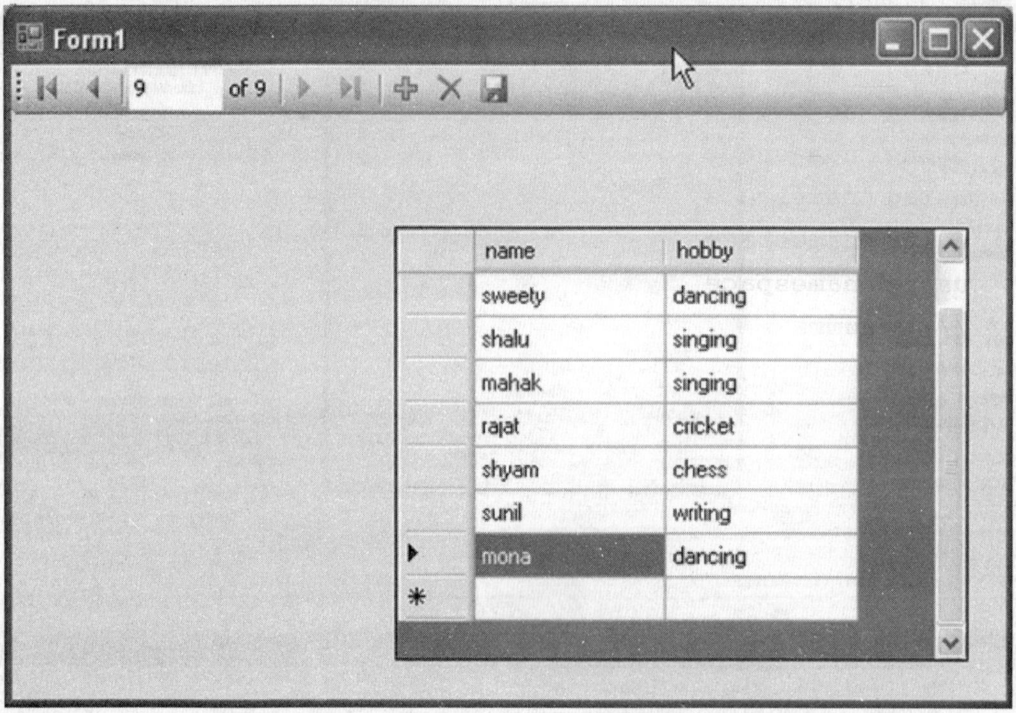

44. Now you can also navigate between records by clicking < > signs.

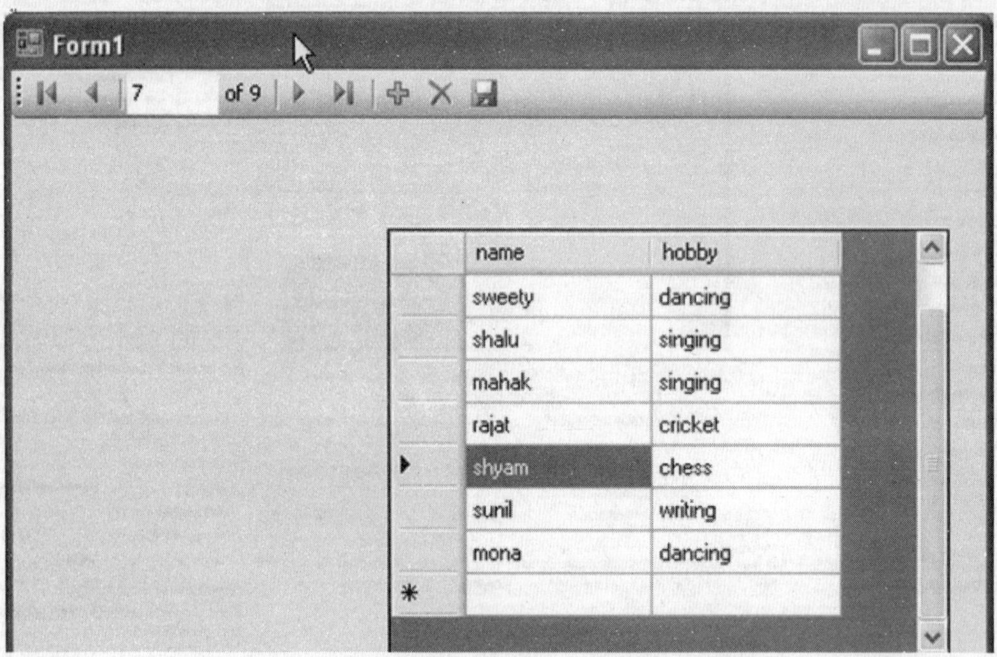

— Form1.h —

```
#pragma once
namespace myvcapplication {
  using namespace System;
  using namespace System::ComponentModel;
  using namespace System::Collections;
  using namespace System::Windows::Forms;
  using namespace System::Data;
  using namespace System::Drawing;
  /// <summary>
  /// Summary for Form1
  ///
  /// WARNING: If you change the name of this class, you will
need to change the 'Resource File Name' property for the managed
resource compiler tool associated with all .resx files this
class depends on.  Otherwise, the designers will not be able
to interact properly with localized resources associated with
this form.
  /// </summary>
  public ref class Form1 : public System::Windows::Forms::Form
  {
  public:
     Form1(void)
     {
        InitializeComponent();
        //
        //TODO: Add the constructor code here
        //
     }
  protected:
     /// <summary>
     /// Clean up any resources being used.
     /// </summary>
     ~Form1()
     {
        if (components)
```

```
        {
            delete components;
        }
    }
    private:  myvcapplication::introdatabaseDataSet^
  introdatabaseDataSet;
    protected:
    private:  System::Windows::Forms::BindingSource^
  introtableBindingSource;
    private: myvcapplication::introdatabaseDataSetTableAdapters::
  introtableTableAdapter^  introtableTableAdapter;
    private: System::Windows::Forms::BindingNavigator^
  introtableBindingNavigator;
    private: System::Windows::Forms::ToolStripButton^
  bindingNavigatorAddNewItem;
    private: System::Windows::Forms::ToolStripLabel^
  bindingNavigatorCountItem;
    private: System::Windows::Forms::ToolStripButton^
  bindingNavigatorDeleteItem;
    private: System::Windows::Forms::ToolStripButton^
  bindingNavigatorMoveFirstItem;
    private: System::Windows::Forms::ToolStripButton^
  bindingNavigatorMovePreviousItem;
    private: System::Windows::Forms::ToolStripSeparator^
  bindingNavigatorSeparator;
    private: System::Windows::Forms::ToolStripTextBox^
  bindingNavigatorPositionItem;
    private: System::Windows::Forms::ToolStripSeparator^
  bindingNavigatorSeparator1;
    private: System::Windows::Forms::ToolStripButton^
  bindingNavigatorMoveNextItem;
    private: System::Windows::Forms::ToolStripButton^
  bindingNavigatorMoveLastItem;
    private: System::Windows::Forms::ToolStripSeparator^
  bindingNavigatorSeparator2;
    private: System::Windows::Forms::ToolStripButton^
  introtableBindingNavigatorSaveItem;
    private:    System::Windows::Forms::DataGridView^
```

```
introtableDataGridView;
   private: System::Windows::Forms::DataGridViewTextBoxColumn^
dataGridViewTextBoxColumn1;
   private: System::Windows::Forms::DataGridViewTextBoxColumn^
dataGridViewTextBoxColumn2;
   private: System::ComponentModel::IContainer^ components;
   private:
      /// <summary>
      /// Required designer variable.
      /// </summary>
#pragma region Windows Form Designer generated code
      /// <summary>
      /// Required method for Designer support - do not modify
      /// the contents of this method with the code editor.
      /// </summary>
      void InitializeComponent(void)
      {
         this->components = (gcnew
   System::ComponentModel::Container());
         System::ComponentModel::ComponentResourceManager^
   resources = (gcnew System::ComponentModel::
   ComponentResourceManager(Form1::typeid));
         this->introdatabaseDataSet = (gcnew myvcapplication::
   introdatabaseDataSet());
         this->introtableBindingSource = (gcnew System::
   Windows::Forms::BindingSource(this->components));
         this->introtableTableAdapter = (gcnew myvcapplication::
   introdatabaseDataSetTableAdapters::introtableTableAdapter());
         this->introtableBindingNavigator = (gcnew System::
   Windows::Forms::BindingNavigator(this->components));
         this->bindingNavigatorMoveFirstItem = (gcnew System::
   Windows::Forms::ToolStripButton());
         this->bindingNavigatorMovePreviousItem = (gcnew
   System:: Windows::Forms::ToolStripButton());
         this->bindingNavigatorSeparator = (gcnew System::
   Windows::Forms::ToolStripSeparator());
```

```
        this->bindingNavigatorPositionItem = (gcnew System::
    Windows::Forms::ToolStripTextBox());
        this->bindingNavigatorCountItem = (gcnew System::
    Windows::Forms::ToolStripLabel());
        this->bindingNavigatorSeparator1 = (gcnew System::
    Windows::Forms::ToolStripSeparator());
        this->bindingNavigatorMoveNextItem = (gcnew System::
    Windows::Forms::ToolStripButton());
        this->bindingNavigatorMoveLastItem = (gcnew System::
    Windows::Forms::ToolStripButton());
        this->bindingNavigatorSeparator2 = (gcnew System::
    Windows::Forms::ToolStripSeparator());
        this->bindingNavigatorAddNewItem = (gcnew System::
    Windows::Forms::ToolStripButton());
        this->bindingNavigatorDeleteItem = (gcnew System::
    Windows::Forms::ToolStripButton());
        this->introtableBindingNavigatorSaveItem = (gcnew
    System:: Windows::Forms::ToolStripButton());
        this->introtableDataGridView = (gcnew System::
    Windows::Forms::DataGridView());
        this->dataGridViewTextBoxColumn1 = (gcnew System::
    Windows::Forms::DataGridViewTextBoxColumn());
        this->dataGridViewTextBoxColumn2 = (gcnew System::
    Windows::Forms::DataGridViewTextBoxColumn());

    (cli::safe_cast<System::ComponentModel::ISupportInitialize^
    >(this->introdatabaseDataSet))->BeginInit();

    (cli::safe_cast<System::ComponentModel::ISupportInitialize^
    >(this->introtableBindingSource))->BeginInit();

    (cli::safe_cast<System::ComponentModel::ISupportInitialize^
    >(this->introtableBindingNavigator))->BeginInit();
        this->introtableBindingNavigator->SuspendLayout();

    (cli::safe_cast<System::ComponentModel::ISupportInitialize^
    >(this->introtableDataGridView))->BeginInit();
        this->SuspendLayout();
```

```
//
// introdatabaseDataSet
//
this->introdatabaseDataSet->DataSetName = L"introdatabaseDataSet";
this->introdatabaseDataSet->SchemaSerializationMode = System::Data::SchemaSerializationMode::IncludeSchema;
//
// introtableBindingSource
//
this->introtableBindingSource->DataMember = L"introtable";
this->introtableBindingSource->DataSource = this->introdatabaseDataSet;
//
// introtableTableAdapter
//
this->introtableTableAdapter->ClearBeforeFill = true;
//
// introtableBindingNavigator
//
this->introtableBindingNavigator->AddNewItem = this->bindingNavigatorAddNewItem;
this->introtableBindingNavigator->BindingSource = this->introtableBindingSource;
this->introtableBindingNavigator->CountItem = this->bindingNavigatorCountItem;
this->introtableBindingNavigator->DeleteItem = this->bindingNavigatorDeleteItem;
this->introtableBindingNavigator->Items->AddRange(gcnew cli::array< System::Windows::Forms::ToolStripItem^ >(12) {this->bindingNavigatorMoveFirstItem,
    this->bindingNavigatorMovePreviousItem, this->bindingNavigatorSeparator, this->bindingNavigatorPositionItem, this->bindingNavigatorCountItem,
    this->bindingNavigatorSeparator1, this->bindingNavigatorMoveNextItem, this->bindingNavigatorMoveLastItem, this->bindingNavigatorSeparator2,
```

```
this->bindingNavigatorAddNewItem, this->bindingNavigatorDeleteItem, this->introtableBindingNavigatorSaveItem});
this->introtableBindingNavigator->Location = System::Drawing::Point(0, 0);
this->introtableBindingNavigator->MoveFirstItem = this->bindingNavigatorMoveFirstItem;
this->introtableBindingNavigator->MoveLastItem = this->bindingNavigatorMoveLastItem;
this->introtableBindingNavigator->MoveNextItem = this->bindingNavigatorMoveNextItem;
this->introtableBindingNavigator->MovePreviousItem = this->bindingNavigatorMovePreviousItem;
this->introtableBindingNavigator->Name = L"introtableBindingNavigator";
this->introtableBindingNavigator->PositionItem = this->bindingNavigatorPositionItem;
this->introtableBindingNavigator->Size = System::Drawing::Size(522, 25);
this->introtableBindingNavigator->TabIndex = 0;
this->introtableBindingNavigator->Text = L"bindingNavigator1";
//
// bindingNavigatorMoveFirstItem
//
this->bindingNavigatorMoveFirstItem->DisplayStyle = System::Windows::Forms::ToolStripItemDisplayStyle::Image;
this->bindingNavigatorMoveFirstItem->Image = (cli::safe_cast<System::Drawing::Image^ >(resources->GetObject(L"bindingNavigatorMoveFirstItem.Image")));
this->bindingNavigatorMoveFirstItem->Name = L"bindingNavigatorMoveFirstItem";
this->bindingNavigatorMoveFirstItem->RightToLeftAutoMirrorImage = true;
this->bindingNavigatorMoveFirstItem->Size = System::Drawing::Size(23, 22);
this->bindingNavigatorMoveFirstItem->Text = L"Move first";
```

```
        //
        // bindingNavigatorMovePreviousItem
        //
        this->bindingNavigatorMovePreviousItem->DisplayStyle =
System::Windows::Forms::ToolStripItemDisplayStyle::Image;
        this->bindingNavigatorMovePreviousItem->Image =
(cli::safe_cast<System::Drawing::Image^ >(resources-
>GetObject(L"bindingNavigatorMovePreviousItem.Image")));
        this->bindingNavigatorMovePreviousItem->Name =
L"bindingNavigatorMovePreviousItem";
        this->bindingNavigatorMovePreviousItem-
>RightToLeftAutoMirrorImage = true;
        this->bindingNavigatorMovePreviousItem->Size =
System::Drawing::Size(23, 22);
        this->bindingNavigatorMovePreviousItem->Text = L"Move
previous";
        //
        // bindingNavigatorSeparator
        //
        this->bindingNavigatorSeparator->Name =
L"bindingNavigatorSeparator";
        this->bindingNavigatorSeparator->Size =
System::Drawing::Size(6, 25);
        //
        // bindingNavigatorPositionItem
        //
        this->bindingNavigatorPositionItem->AccessibleName =
L"Position";
        this->bindingNavigatorPositionItem->AutoSize = false;
        this->bindingNavigatorPositionItem->Name =
L"bindingNavigatorPositionItem";
        this->bindingNavigatorPositionItem->Size =
System::Drawing::Size(50, 21);
        this->bindingNavigatorPositionItem->Text = L"0";
        this->bindingNavigatorPositionItem->ToolTipText =
L"Current position";
        //
```

```
        // bindingNavigatorCountItem
        //
        this->bindingNavigatorCountItem->Name =
L"bindingNavigatorCountItem";
        this->bindingNavigatorCountItem->Size =
System::Drawing::Size(36, 13);
        this->bindingNavigatorCountItem->Text = L"of {0}";
        this->bindingNavigatorCountItem->ToolTipText = L"Total
number of items";
        //
        // bindingNavigatorSeparator1
        //
        this->bindingNavigatorSeparator1->Name =
L"bindingNavigatorSeparator";
        this->bindingNavigatorSeparator1->Size =
System::Drawing::Size(6, 6);
        //
        // bindingNavigatorMoveNextItem
        //
        this->bindingNavigatorMoveNextItem->DisplayStyle =
System::Windows::Forms::ToolStripItemDisplayStyle::Image;
        this->bindingNavigatorMoveNextItem->Image =
(cli::safe_cast<System::Drawing::Image^  >(resources-
>GetObject(L"bindingNavigatorMoveNextItem.Image")));
        this->bindingNavigatorMoveNextItem->Name =
L"bindingNavigatorMoveNextItem";
        this->bindingNavigatorMoveNextItem-
>RightToLeftAutoMirrorImage = true;
        this->bindingNavigatorMoveNextItem->Size =
System::Drawing::Size(23, 20);
        this->bindingNavigatorMoveNextItem->Text = L"Move next";
        //
        // bindingNavigatorMoveLastItem
        //
        this->bindingNavigatorMoveLastItem->DisplayStyle =
System::Windows::Forms::ToolStripItemDisplayStyle::Image;
        this->bindingNavigatorMoveLastItem->Image =
```

```
(cli::safe_cast<System::Drawing::Image^ >(resources->GetObject(L"bindingNavigatorMoveLastItem.Image")));
        this->bindingNavigatorMoveLastItem->Name = L"bindingNavigatorMoveLastItem";
        this->bindingNavigatorMoveLastItem->RightToLeftAutoMirrorImage = true;
        this->bindingNavigatorMoveLastItem->Size = System::Drawing::Size(23, 20);
        this->bindingNavigatorMoveLastItem->Text = L"Move last";
        //
        // bindingNavigatorSeparator2
        //
        this->bindingNavigatorSeparator2->Name = L"bindingNavigatorSeparator";
        this->bindingNavigatorSeparator2->Size = System::Drawing::Size(6, 6);
        //
        // bindingNavigatorAddNewItem
        //
        this->bindingNavigatorAddNewItem->DisplayStyle = System::Windows::Forms::ToolStripItemDisplayStyle::Image;
        this->bindingNavigatorAddNewItem->Image = (cli::safe_cast<System::Drawing::Image^ >(resources->GetObject(L"bindingNavigatorAddNewItem.Image")));
        this->bindingNavigatorAddNewItem->Name = L"bindingNavigatorAddNewItem";
        this->bindingNavigatorAddNewItem->RightToLeftAutoMirrorImage = true;
        this->bindingNavigatorAddNewItem->Size = System::Drawing::Size(23, 22);
        this->bindingNavigatorAddNewItem->Text = L"Add new";
        //
        // bindingNavigatorDeleteItem
        //
        this->bindingNavigatorDeleteItem->DisplayStyle = System::Windows::Forms::ToolStripItemDisplayStyle::Image;
        this->bindingNavigatorDeleteItem->Image =
```

```
(cli::safe_cast<System::Drawing::Image^ >(resources->GetObject(L"bindingNavigatorDeleteItem.Image")));
        this->bindingNavigatorDeleteItem->Name = L"bindingNavigatorDeleteItem";
        this->bindingNavigatorDeleteItem->RightToLeftAutoMirrorImage = true;
        this->bindingNavigatorDeleteItem->Size = System::Drawing::Size(23, 20);
        this->bindingNavigatorDeleteItem->Text = L"Delete";
        //
        // introtableBindingNavigatorSaveItem
        //
        this->introtableBindingNavigatorSaveItem->DisplayStyle = System::Windows::Forms::ToolStripItemDisplayStyle::Image;
        this->introtableBindingNavigatorSaveItem->Image = (cli::safe_cast<System::Drawing::Image^ >(resources->GetObject(L"introtableBindingNavigatorSaveItem.Image")));
        this->introtableBindingNavigatorSaveItem->Name = L"introtableBindingNavigatorSaveItem";
        this->introtableBindingNavigatorSaveItem->Size = System::Drawing::Size(23, 23);
        this->introtableBindingNavigatorSaveItem->Text = L"Save Data";
        this->introtableBindingNavigatorSaveItem->Click += gcnew System::EventHandler(this, &Form1::introtableBindingNavigatorSaveItem_Click);
        //
        // introtableDataGridView
        //
        this->introtableDataGridView->AutoGenerateColumns = false;
        this->introtableDataGridView->Columns->AddRange(gcnew cli::array< System::Windows::Forms::DataGridViewColumn^ >(2) {this->dataGridViewTextBoxColumn1,
            this->dataGridViewTextBoxColumn2});
        this->introtableDataGridView->DataSource = this->introtableBindingSource;
```

```
        this->introtableDataGridView->Location =
  System::Drawing::Point(202, 82);
        this->introtableDataGridView->Name =
  L"introtableDataGridView";
        this->introtableDataGridView->Size =
  System::Drawing::Size(300, 220);
        this->introtableDataGridView->TabIndex = 1;
        //
        // dataGridViewTextBoxColumn1
        //
        this->dataGridViewTextBoxColumn1->DataPropertyName =
  L"name";
        this->dataGridViewTextBoxColumn1->HeaderText = L"name";
        this->dataGridViewTextBoxColumn1->Name =
  L"dataGridViewTextBoxColumn1";
        //
        // dataGridViewTextBoxColumn2
        //
        this->dataGridViewTextBoxColumn2->DataPropertyName =
  L"hobby";
        this->dataGridViewTextBoxColumn2->HeaderText = L"hobby";
        this->dataGridViewTextBoxColumn2->Name =
  L"dataGridViewTextBoxColumn2";
        //
        // Form1
        //
        this->AutoScaleDimensions = System::Drawing::SizeF(6,
  13);
        this->AutoScaleMode =
  System::Windows::Forms::AutoScaleMode::Font;
        this->ClientSize = System::Drawing::Size(522, 322);
        this->Controls->Add(this->introtableDataGridView);
        this->Controls->Add(this->introtableBindingNavigator);
        this->Name = L"Form1";
        this->Text = L"Form1";
        this->Load += gcnew System::EventHandler(this,
  &Form1::Form1_Load);
```

```
(cli::safe_cast<System::ComponentModel::ISupportInitialize^
>(this->introdatabaseDataSet))->EndInit();

(cli::safe_cast<System::ComponentModel::ISupportInitialize^
>(this->introtableBindingSource))->EndInit();

(cli::safe_cast<System::ComponentModel::ISupportInitialize^
>(this->introtableBindingNavigator))->EndInit();
        this->introtableBindingNavigator->ResumeLayout(false);
        this->introtableBindingNavigator->PerformLayout();

(cli::safe_cast<System::ComponentModel::ISupportInitialize^
>(this->introtableDataGridView))->EndInit();
        this->ResumeLayout(false);
        this->PerformLayout();
    }
#pragma endregion
  private:                                        System::Void
introtableBindingNavigatorSaveItem_Click(System::Object^
sender, System::EventArgs^  e) {
            this->Validate();
            this->introtableBindingSource->EndEdit();
            this->introtableTableAdapter->Update(this-
>introdatabaseDataSet->introtable);
        }
private: System::Void Form1_Load(System::Object^  sender,
System::EventArgs^  e) {
        // TODO: This line of code loads data into the
'introdatabaseDataSet.introtable' table. You can move, or remove
it, as needed.
            this->introtableTableAdapter->Fill(this-
>introdatabaseDataSet->introtable);
      }
};
}
```

If you wish you can also modify the above program. This way you can change the look and appearance. For this first take out everything from the form. Make it simple.

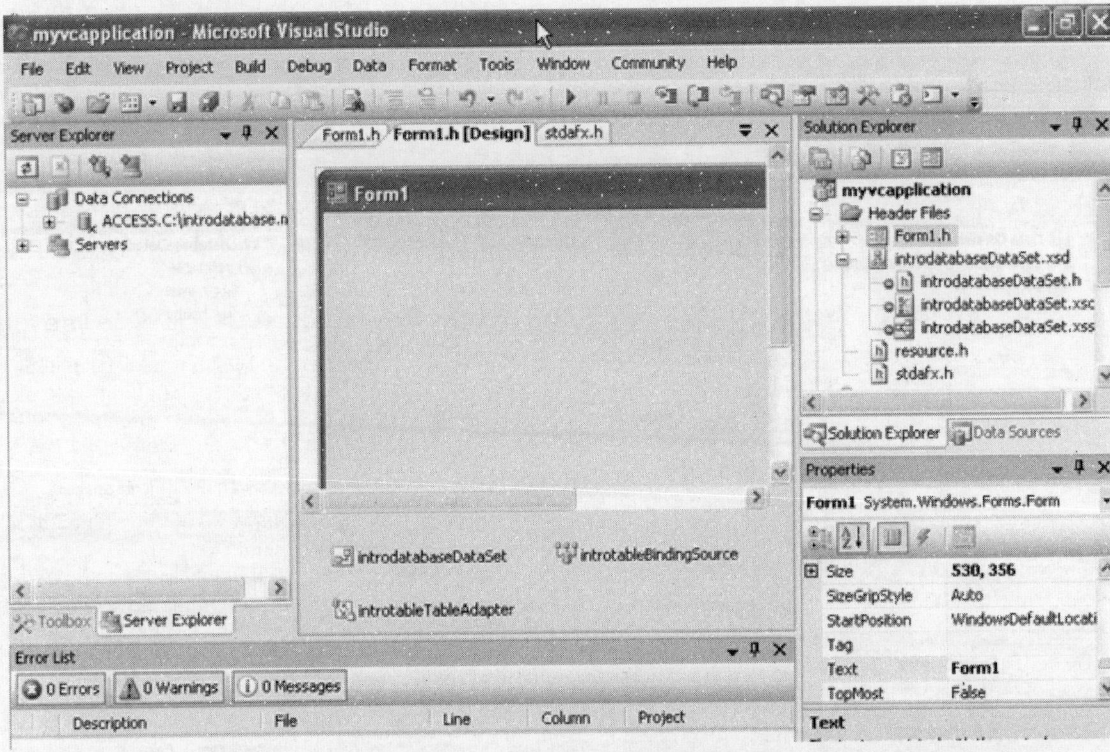

45. Now in Data Sources widow click the name field and drag it onto the form.

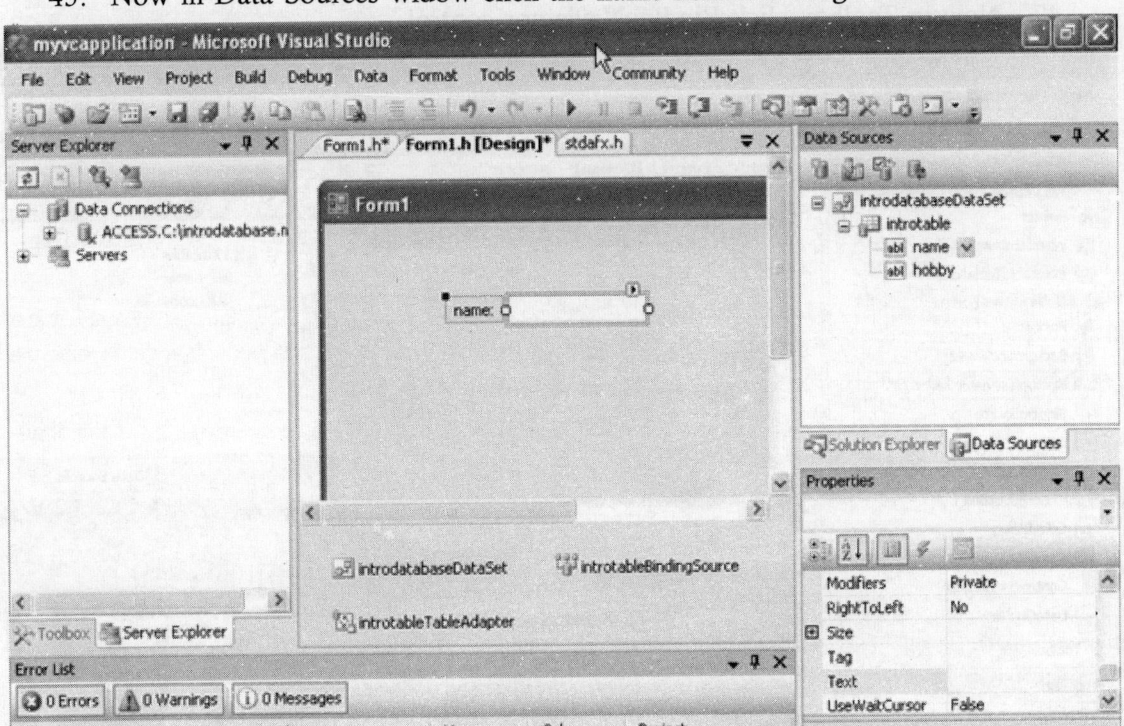

46. Now click the hobby field and drag it onto the form

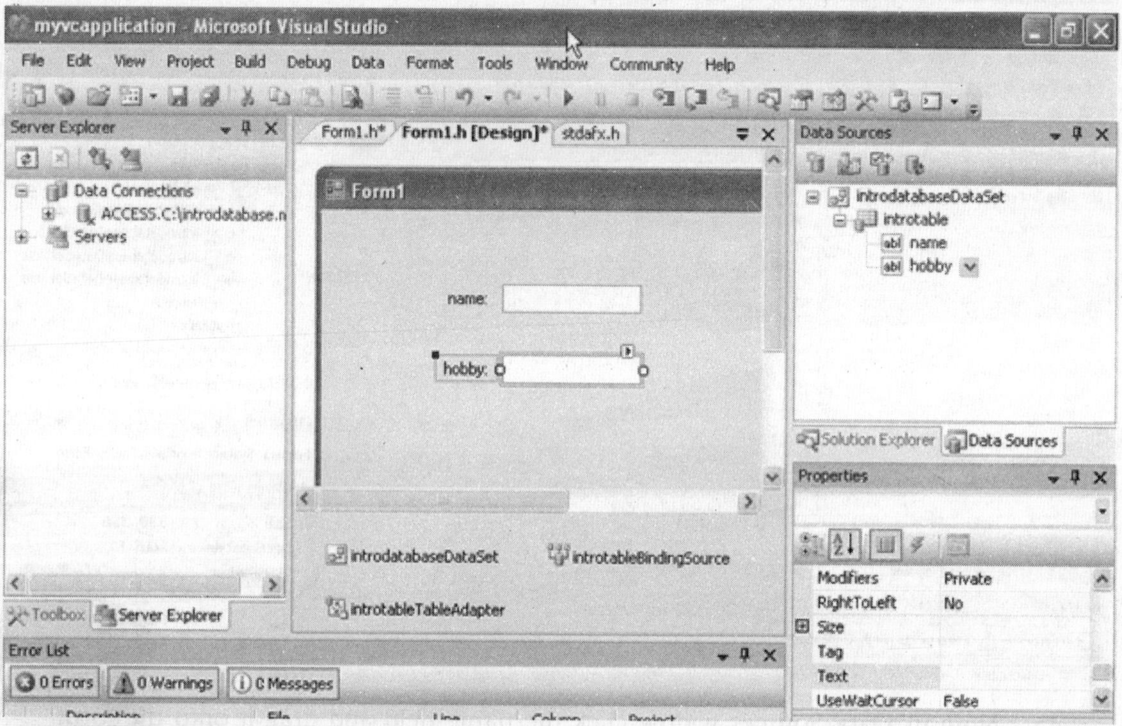

47. Now in Toolbox click BindingNaviagtor control

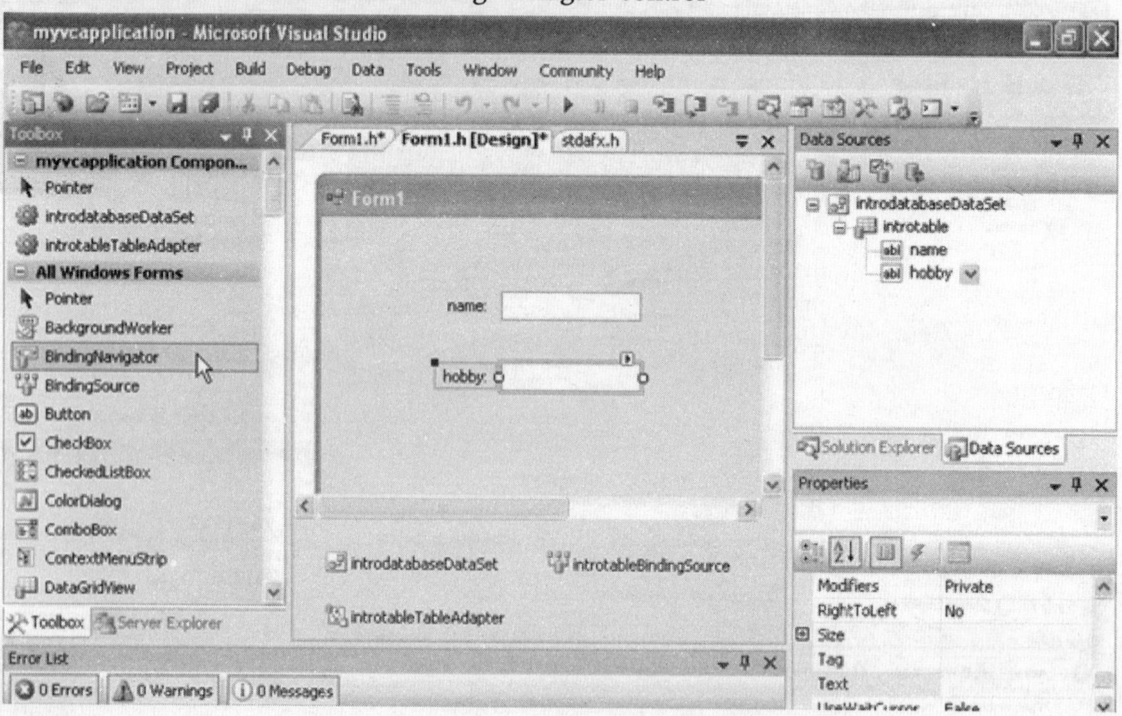

48. Drag it onto the form

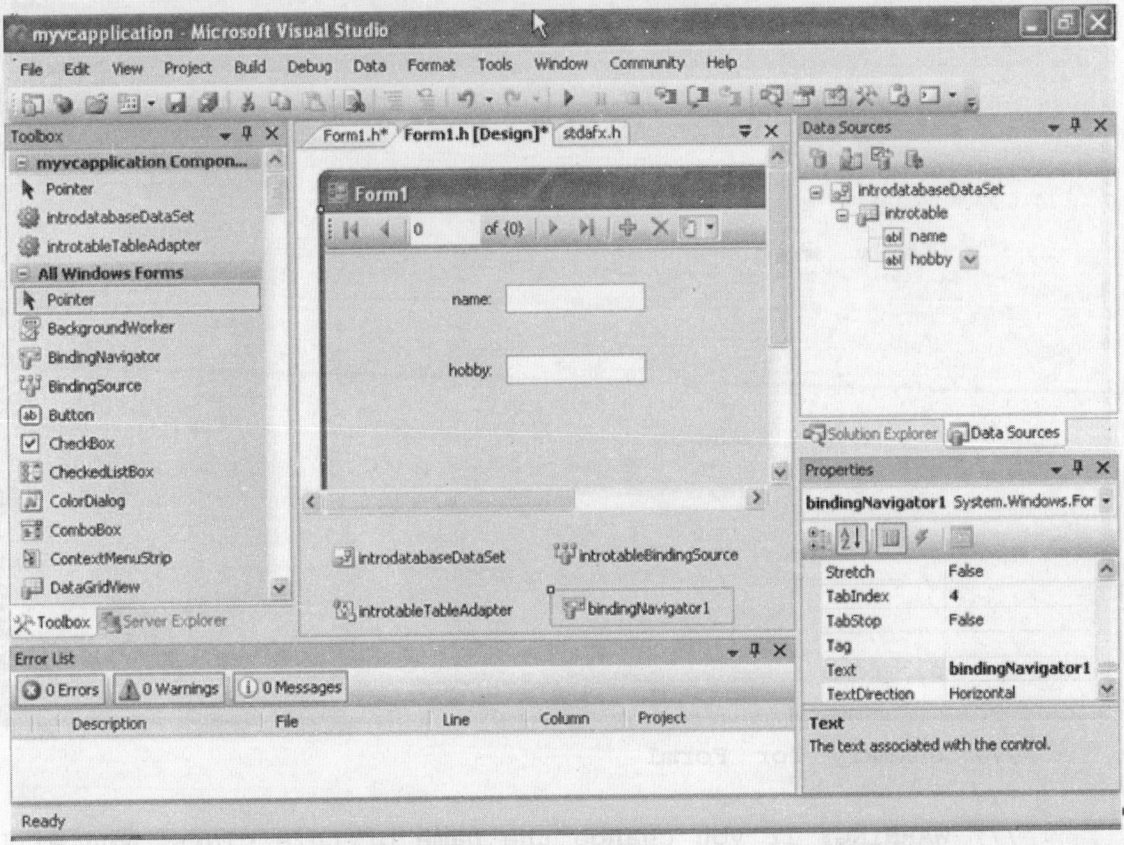

49. Now be sure that BindingNavigator control is selected and in Properties window select BindingSource property and choose IntrotableBindingSource

50. Now press F5 key on your keyboard

51. You will get following output in different layout:

— Form1.h —

```
#pragma once
namespace myvcapplication {
  using namespace System;
  using namespace System::ComponentModel;
  using namespace System::Collections;
  using namespace System::Windows::Forms;
  using namespace System::Data;
  using namespace System::Drawing;
  /// <summary>
```

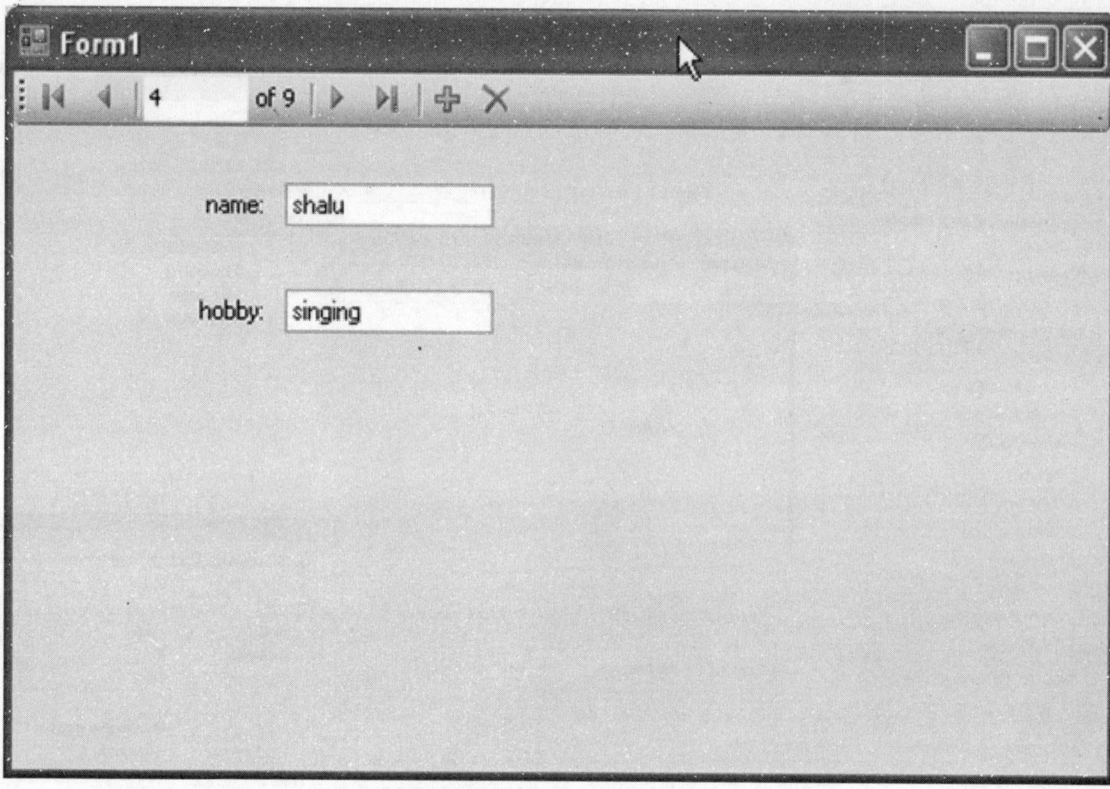


```
/// Summary for Form1
///
/// WARNING: If you change the name of this class, you will need to change the
///          'Resource File Name' property for the managed resource compiler tool
///          associated with all .resx files this class depends on.  Otherwise,
///          the designers will not be able to interact properly with localized
///          resources associated with this form.
/// </summary>
public ref class Form1 : public System::Windows::Forms::Form
{
public:
   Form1(void)
   {
      InitializeComponent();
```

```
        //
        //TODO: Add the constructor code here
        //
    }
  protected:
    /// <summary>
    /// Clean up any resources being used.
    /// </summary>
    ~Form1()
    {
      if (components)
      {
        delete components;
      }
    }
  private: myvcapplication::introdatabaseDataSet^
introdatabaseDataSet;
  protected:
  private: System::Windows::Forms::BindingSource^
introtableBindingSource;
  private: myvcapplication::introdatabaseDataSetTableAdapters::
introtableTableAdapter^ introtableTableAdapter;
  private: System::Windows::Forms::TextBox^ nameTextBox;
  private: System::Windows::Forms::TextBox^ hobbyTextBox;
  private: System::Windows::Forms::BindingNavigator^
bindingNavigator1;
  private: System::Windows::Forms::ToolStripButton^
bindingNavigatorAddNewItem;
  private: System::Windows::Forms::ToolStripLabel^
bindingNavigatorCountItem;
  private: System::Windows::Forms::ToolStripButton^
bindingNavigatorDeleteItem;
  private: System::Windows::Forms::ToolStripButton^
bindingNavigatorMoveFirstItem;
  private: System::Windows::Forms::ToolStripButton^
bindingNavigatorMovePreviousItem;
  private: System::Windows::Forms::ToolStripSeparator^
bindingNavigatorSeparator;
```

```
   private:  System::Windows::Forms::ToolStripTextBox^
bindingNavigatorPositionItem;
   private:  System::Windows::Forms::ToolStripSeparator^
bindingNavigatorSeparator1;
   private:  System::Windows::Forms::ToolStripButton^
bindingNavigatorMoveNextItem;
   private:  System::Windows::Forms::ToolStripButton^
bindingNavigatorMoveLastItem;
   private:  System::Windows::Forms::ToolStripSeparator^
bindingNavigatorSeparator2;
private:  System::ComponentModel::IContainer^   components;
   private:
      /// <summary>
      /// Required designer variable.
      /// </summary>
#pragma region Windows Form Designer generated code
      /// <summary>
      /// Required method for Designer support - do not modify
      /// the contents of this method with the code editor.
      /// </summary>
      void InitializeComponent(void)
      {
         this->components = (gcnew
System::ComponentModel::Container());
         System::Windows::Forms::Label^  nameLabel;
         System::Windows::Forms::Label^  hobbyLabel;
         System::ComponentModel::ComponentResourceManager^
resources = (gcnew System::ComponentModel::
ComponentResourceManager(Form1::typeid));
         this->introdatabaseDataSet = (gcnew myvcapplication::
introdatabaseDataSet());
         this->introtableBindingSource = (gcnew
System::Windows::Forms::BindingSource(this->components));
         this->introtableTableAdapter = (gcnew
myvcapplication::introdatabaseDataSetTableAdapters::
introtableTableAdapter());
         this->nameTextBox = (gcnew System::Windows::Forms::
TextBox());
```

```
        this->hobbyTextBox = (gcnew System::Windows::Forms::
  TextBox());
        this->bindingNavigator1 = (gcnew System::Windows::
  Forms::BindingNavigator(this->components));
        this->bindingNavigatorMoveFirstItem = (gcnew System::
  Windows::Forms::ToolStripButton());
        this->bindingNavigatorMovePreviousItem = (gcnew
  System::Windows::Forms::ToolStripButton());
        this->bindingNavigatorSeparator = (gcnew System::
  Windows::Forms::ToolStripSeparator());
        this->bindingNavigatorPositionItem = (gcnew System::
  Windows::Forms::ToolStripTextBox());
        this->bindingNavigatorCountItem = (gcnew System::
  Windows::Forms::ToolStripLabel());
        this->bindingNavigatorSeparator1 = (gcnew System::
  Windows::Forms::ToolStripSeparator());
        this->bindingNavigatorMoveNextItem = (gcnew System::
  Windows::Forms::ToolStripButton());
        this->bindingNavigatorMoveLastItem = (gcnew System::
  Windows::Forms::ToolStripButton());
        this->bindingNavigatorSeparator2 = (gcnew System::
  Windows::Forms::ToolStripSeparator());
        this->bindingNavigatorAddNewItem = (gcnew System::
  Windows::Forms::ToolStripButton());
        this->bindingNavigatorDeleteItem = (gcnew System::
  Windows::Forms::ToolStripButton());
        nameLabel = (gcnew System::Windows::Forms::Label());
        hobbyLabel = (gcnew System::Windows::Forms::Label());

  (cli::safe_cast<System::ComponentModel::ISupportInitialize^
  >(this->introdatabaseDataSet))->BeginInit();

  (cli::safe_cast<System::ComponentModel::ISupportInitialize^
  >(this->introtableBindingSource))->BeginInit();

  (cli::safe_cast<System::ComponentModel::ISupportInitialize^
  >(this->bindingNavigator1))->BeginInit();
        this->bindingNavigator1->SuspendLayout();
        this->SuspendLayout();
        //
        // introdatabaseDataSet
```

```
        //
        this->introdatabaseDataSet->DataSetName =
L"introdatabaseDataSet";
        this->introdatabaseDataSet->SchemaSerializationMode =
System::Data::SchemaSerializationMode::IncludeSchema;
        //
        // introtableBindingSource
        //
        this->introtableBindingSource->DataMember =
L"introtable";
        this->introtableBindingSource->DataSource = this-
>introdatabaseDataSet;
        //
        // introtableTableAdapter
        //
        this->introtableTableAdapter->ClearBeforeFill = true;
        //
        // nameLabel
        //
        nameLabel->AutoSize = true;
        nameLabel->Location = System::Drawing::Point(88, 54);
        nameLabel->Name = L"nameLabel";
        nameLabel->Size = System::Drawing::Size(36, 13);
        nameLabel->TabIndex = 0;
        nameLabel->Text = L"name:";
        //
        // nameTextBox
        //
        this->nameTextBox->DataBindings->Add((gcnew
System::Windows::Forms::Binding(L"Text", this-
>introtableBindingSource, L"name",true)));
        this->nameTextBox->Location = System::Drawing::
Point(130, 51);
      this->nameTextBox->Name = L"nameTextBox";
      this->nameTextBox->Size = System::Drawing::Size(100, 20);
      this->nameTextBox->TabIndex = 1;
      //
      // hobbyLabel
```

```
        //
        hobbyLabel->AutoSize = true;
        hobbyLabel->Location = System::Drawing::Point(85, 103);
        hobbyLabel->Name = L"hobbyLabel";
        hobbyLabel->Size = System::Drawing::Size(39, 13);
        hobbyLabel->TabIndex = 2;
        hobbyLabel->Text = L"hobby:";
        //
        // hobbyTextBox
        //
        this->hobbyTextBox->DataBindings->Add((gcnew
System::Windows::Forms::Binding(L"Text", this-
>introtableBindingSource, L"hobby", true)));
        this->hobbyTextBox->Location = System::Drawing::
Point(130, 100);
        this->hobbyTextBox->Name = L"hobbyTextBox";
        this->hobbyTextBox->Size = System::Drawing::Size(100, 20);
        this->hobbyTextBox->TabIndex = 3;
        //
        // bindingNavigator1
        //
        this->bindingNavigator1->AddNewItem = this-
>bindingNavigatorAddNewItem;
        this->bindingNavigator1->BindingSource = this-
>introtableBindingSource;
        this->bindingNavigator1->CountItem = this-
>bindingNavigatorCountItem;
        this->bindingNavigator1->DeleteItem = this-
>bindingNavigatorDeleteItem;
        this->bindingNavigator1->Items->AddRange(gcnew cli::array<
System::Windows::Forms::ToolStripItem^ >(11) {this-
>bindingNavigatorMoveFirstItem,
        this->bindingNavigatorMovePreviousItem, this-
>bindingNavigatorSeparator, this->bindingNavigatorPositionItem,
this->bindingNavigatorCountItem,
        this->bindingNavigatorSeparator1, this-
>bindingNavigatorMoveNextItem, this->bindingNavigatorMove
LastItem, this->bindingNavigatorSeparator2,
      this->bindingNavigatorAddNewItem, this-
>bindingNavigatorDeleteItem});
```

```
        this->bindingNavigator1->Location =
System::Drawing::Point(0, 0);
        this->bindingNavigator1->MoveFirstItem = this-
>bindingNavigatorMoveFirstItem;
        this->bindingNavigator1->MoveLastItem = this-
>bindingNavigatorMoveLastItem;
        this->bindingNavigator1->MoveNextItem = this-
>bindingNavigatorMoveNextItem;
        this->bindingNavigator1->MovePreviousItem = this-
>bindingNavigatorMovePreviousItem;
        this->bindingNavigator1->Name = L"bindingNavigator1";
        this->bindingNavigator1->PositionItem = this-
>bindingNavigatorPositionItem;
        this->bindingNavigator1->Size =
System::Drawing::Size(522, 25);
        this->bindingNavigator1->TabIndex = 4;
        this->bindingNavigator1->Text = L"bindingNavigator1";
        //
        // bindingNavigatorMoveFirstItem
        //
        this->bindingNavigatorMoveFirstItem->DisplayStyle =
System::Windows::Forms::ToolStripItemDisplayStyle::Image;
        this->bindingNavigatorMoveFirstItem->Image =
(cli::safe_cast<System::Drawing::Image^ >(resources-
>GetObject(L"bindingNavigatorMoveFirstItem.Image")));
        this->bindingNavigatorMoveFirstItem->Name =
L"bindingNavigatorMoveFirstItem";
        this->bindingNavigatorMoveFirstItem-
>RightToLeftAutoMirrorImage = true;
        this->bindingNavigatorMoveFirstItem->Size =
System::Drawing::Size(23, 22);
    this->bindingNavigatorMoveFirstItem->Text = L"Move first";
        //
        // bindingNavigatorMovePreviousItem
        //
        this->bindingNavigatorMovePreviousItem->DisplayStyle =
System::Windows::Forms::ToolStripItemDisplayStyle::Image;
        this->bindingNavigatorMovePreviousItem->Image =
(cli::safe_cast<System::Drawing::Image^ >(resources-
>GetObject(L"bindingNavigatorMovePreviousItem.Image")));
```

```
        this->bindingNavigatorMovePreviousItem->Name =
L"bindingNavigatorMovePreviousItem";
        this->bindingNavigatorMovePreviousItem-
>RightToLeftAutoMirrorImage = true;
        this->bindingNavigatorMovePreviousItem->Size =
System::Drawing::Size(23, 22);
        this->bindingNavigatorMovePreviousItem->Text = L"Move
previous";
        //
        // bindingNavigatorSeparator
        //
        this->bindingNavigatorSeparator->Name =
L"bindingNavigatorSeparator";
        this->bindingNavigatorSeparator->Size = System::
Drawing::Size(6, 25);
        //
        // bindingNavigatorPositionItem
        //
        this->bindingNavigatorPositionItem->AccessibleName =
L"Position";
        this->bindingNavigatorPositionItem->AutoSize = false;
        this->bindingNavigatorPositionItem->Name =
L"bindingNavigatorPositionItem";
        this->bindingNavigatorPositionItem->Size =
System::Drawing::Size(50, 21);
        this->bindingNavigatorPositionItem->Text = L"0";
        this->bindingNavigatorPositionItem->ToolTipText =
L"Current position";
        //
        // bindingNavigatorCountItem
        //
        this->bindingNavigatorCountItem->Name =
L"bindingNavigatorCountItem";
        this->bindingNavigatorCountItem->Size =
System::Drawing::Size(36, 22);
        this->bindingNavigatorCountItem->Text = L"of {0}";
        this->bindingNavigatorCountItem->ToolTipText = L"Total
number of items";
        //
```

```
        // bindingNavigatorSeparator1
        //
        this->bindingNavigatorSeparator1->Name =
L"bindingNavigatorSeparator";
        this->bindingNavigatorSeparator1->Size =
System::Drawing::Size(6, 25);
        //
        // bindingNavigatorMoveNextItem
        //
        this->bindingNavigatorMoveNextItem->DisplayStyle =
System::Windows::Forms::ToolStripItemDisplayStyle::Image;
        this->bindingNavigatorMoveNextItem->Image =
(cli::safe_cast<System::Drawing::Image^ >(resources-
>GetObject(L"bindingNavigatorMoveNextItem.Image")));
        this->bindingNavigatorMoveNextItem->Name =
L"bindingNavigatorMoveNextItem";
        this->bindingNavigatorMoveNextItem-
>RightToLeftAutoMirrorImage = true;
        this->bindingNavigatorMoveNextItem->Size =
System::Drawing::Size(23, 22);
        this->bindingNavigatorMoveNextItem->Text = L"Move next";
        //
        // bindingNavigatorMoveLastItem
        //
        this->bindingNavigatorMoveLastItem->DisplayStyle =
System::Windows::Forms::ToolStripItemDisplayStyle::Image;
        this->bindingNavigatorMoveLastItem->Image =
(cli::safe_cast<System::Drawing::Image^ >(resources-
>GetObject(L"bindingNavigatorMoveLastItem.Image")));
        this->bindingNavigatorMoveLastItem->Name =
L"bindingNavigatorMoveLastItem";
        this->bindingNavigatorMoveLastItem-
>RightToLeftAutoMirrorImage = true;
        this->bindingNavigatorMoveLastItem->Size =
System::Drawing::Size(23, 22);
        this->bindingNavigatorMoveLastItem->Text = L"Move last";
        //
        // bindingNavigatorSeparator2
        //
```

```
        this->bindingNavigatorSeparator2->Name =
L"bindingNavigatorSeparator";
        this->bindingNavigatorSeparator2->Size = System::
Drawing::Size(6, 25);
        //
        // bindingNavigatorAddNewItem
        //
        this->bindingNavigatorAddNewItem->DisplayStyle =
System::Windows::Forms::ToolStripItemDisplayStyle::Image;
        this->bindingNavigatorAddNewItem->Image =
(cli::safe_cast<System::Drawing::Image^ >(resources-
>GetObject(L"bindingNavigatorAddNewItem.Image")));
        this->bindingNavigatorAddNewItem->Name =
L"bindingNavigatorAddNewItem";
        this->bindingNavigatorAddNewItem-
>RightToLeftAutoMirrorImage = true;
        this->bindingNavigatorAddNewItem->Size =
System::Drawing::Size(23, 22);
        this->bindingNavigatorAddNewItem->Text = L"Add new";
        //
        // bindingNavigatorDeleteItem
        //
        this->bindingNavigatorDeleteItem->DisplayStyle =
System::Windows::Forms::ToolStripItemDisplayStyle::Image;
        this->bindingNavigatorDeleteItem->Image =
(cli::safe_cast<System::Drawing::Image^ >(resources-
>GetObject(L"bindingNavigatorDeleteItem.Image")));
        this->bindingNavigatorDeleteItem->Name =
L"bindingNavigatorDeleteItem";
        this->bindingNavigatorDeleteItem-
>RightToLeftAutoMirrorImage = true;
        this->bindingNavigatorDeleteItem->Size =
System::Drawing::Size(23, 22);
        this->bindingNavigatorDeleteItem->Text = L"Delete";
        // Form1
    this->AutoScaleDimensions = System::Drawing::SizeF(6, 13);
        this->AutoScaleMode =
System::Windows::Forms::AutoScaleMode::Font;
    this->ClientSize = System::Drawing::Size(522, 322);
```

```
      this->Controls->Add(this->bindingNavigator1);
      this->Controls->Add(hobbyLabel);
      this->Controls->Add(this->hobbyTextBox);
      this->Controls->Add(nameLabel);
      this->Controls->Add(this->nameTextBox);
      this->Name = L"Form1";
      this->Text = L"Form1";
      this->Load += gcnew System::EventHandler(this,
&Form1::Form1_Load);
(cli::safe_cast<System::ComponentModel::ISupportInitialize^
>(this->introdatabaseDataSet))->EndInit();
(cli::safe_cast<System::ComponentModel::ISupportInitialize^
>(this->introtableBindingSource))->EndInit();
(cli::safe_cast<System::ComponentModel::ISupportInitialize^
>(this->bindingNavigator1))->EndInit();
        this->bindingNavigator1->ResumeLayout(false);
        this->bindingNavigator1->PerformLayout();
        this->ResumeLayout(false);
        this->PerformLayout();
      }
#pragma endregion
  private: System::Void introtableBindingNavigator
SaveItem_Click(System::Object^ sender, System::EventArgs^ e)
{
      this->Validate();
      this->introtableBindingSource->EndEdit();
      this->introtableTableAdapter->Update(this-
>introdatabaseDataSet->introtable);
         }
private: System::Void Form1_Load(System::Object^ sender,
System::EventArgs^ e) {
// TODO: This line of code loads data into the
'introdatabaseDataSet.introtable' table. You can move, or remove
it, as needed.
      this->introtableTableAdapter->Fill(this-
>introdatabaseDataSet->introtable);
      }
};
}
```

7 Questions

Descriptive Type Questions

ANSWER THE FOLLOWING QUESTIONS

Chapter 1 — Introduction to ADO.Net

1. How would you create a database using MS Access?
2. Describe the process of linking this database with ADO.Net.

Chapter 2 — ADO.Net and ASP.Net

1. Describe the process of linking ASP.Net with ADO.Net.

Chapter 3 — Database Connectivity with Visual Basic 2005

1. Describe the process of connecting Visual Basic 2005 with ADO.Net.

Chapter 4 — Visual C# and ADO.Net

1. Describe the process of connecting Visual C# with ADO.Net.

Chapter 5 — Visual J# and ADO.Net

1. Describe the process of connecting Visual J# with ADO.Net.

Chapter 6 — Visual C++ and ADO.Net

1. Describe the process of connecting Visual C++ with ADO.Net.

FIREWALL MEDIA

(An imprint of Laxmi Publications Pvt. Ltd.)

Computer Books *for School, BCA, MCA, IGNOU, DOEACC and Engineering Students and Professionals*

ISBN	TITLE	AUTHOR	PRICE	PAGES
	.NET			
8170087155	**Building Business Intelligence Applications with .Net**	Robert Ericsson	Rs. 295.00	404
8170083567	**Learning VB.Net Through Applications**	Clayton Crooks	Rs. 295.00	450
8131800865	**Magic of C# with .Net Frame Work**	Shibi Panikkar, Kumar Sanjeev	Rs. 495.00	950
8170082471	**Magic of ASP.Net with C#**	Shibi Panikkar, Kumar Sanjeev	Rs. 395.00	828
8170089662	**ASP.Net Interview Questions and Answers**	J. Rajaram	Rs. 95.00	175
	A TO Z SERIES			
8170083214	**Access 2002 from A to Z**	Julia Kelly, Stephen L. Nelson	Rs. 75.00	185
8170083222	**Excel 2002 from A to Z**	Stephen L. Nelson	Rs. 75.00	193
8170083230	**Front Page 2002 from A to Z**	Heather Williamson	Rs. 85.00	219
8170083249	**Outlook 2002 from A to Z**	Stephen L. Nelson	Rs. 75.00	202
8170083257	**Page Maker 7 from A to Z**	Marc Campbell	Rs. 75.00	202
8170083265	**PowerPoint 2002 from A to Z**	Stephen L. Nelson	Rs. 75.00	202
8170083273	**Windows XP from A to Z**	Pat Coleman	Rs. 95.00	249
8170083281	**Word 2002 from A to Z**	Stephen L. Nelson	Rs. 75.00	199
817008329X	**XML from A to Z**	Heather Williamson	Rs. 75.00	200
8170083303	**Dreamweaver 4 from A to Z**	Heather Williamson	Rs. 85.00	215
	BEGINNERS & GENERAL INTEREST			
817008248X	**Shortcuts to Success in Computing**	Dheeraj Mehrotra	Rs. 55.00	110
8170083311	**Pictorial Computer Dictionary**	Dheeraj Mehrotra	Rs. 45.00	156
8170083486	**Pocket Net Browser**	Dheeraj Mehrotra	Rs. 95.00	302
8170084261	**1000 IT Quizzes**	Dheeraj Mehrotra	Rs. 75.00	120
8131800679	**Information Technology Bible**	Remesh Bangia	Rs. 295.00	567
8131800377	**Fundamentals of Information Technology Including MS Office**	Dinesh Maidasani, Jai Narayan Yadav	Rs. 175.00	356
813180089X	**Fundamentals of Information Technology Including MS Office (Hindi Medium)**	Dinesh Maidasani, Jai Narayan Yadav	Rs. 175.00	425
8170089719	**Foundations of Computer Science**	Ashok Arora	Rs. 250.00	386

Please write for a free color Firewall Media Catalog for details on the above books.

ISBN	TITLE	AUTHOR	PRICE	PAGES
	CALL CENTERS			
8170082196	**Call Centers Made Easy**	Stephen Medcroft	Rs. 195.00	310
	CISCO			
8170087481	**Enabling IP Routing with Cisco Routers**	R. Das, K. Chakrabarty	Rs. 295.00	486
817008749X	**Designing Networks with Cisco**	H. Pasricha, D. Jagu	Rs. 195.00	316
8170087503	**Cisco IP Routing Protocols: Troubleshooting Techniques**	V. Anand, K. Chakrabarty	Rs. 295.00	409
	DATABASES			
8170089530	**DBMS—Complete Practical Approach**	Sharad Maheshwari, Ruchin Jain	Rs. 350.00	656
8170082404	**Learn to Program Visual Basic-Examples**	John Smiley	Rs. 295.00	482
8170082412	**Learn to Program Visual Basic-Databases**	John Smiley	Rs. 325.00	653
8170082420	**Learn to Program Visual Basic-Objects**	John Smiley	Rs. 325.00	670
817008475X	**IT Resources-Access 2002 VBA Programming Access**	Michele Amelot	Rs. 195.00	424
8170084512	**The Power of Oracle 9i**	Rajiv Parida, Vinod Sharma	Rs. 475.00	1035
8170088518	**Principles and Implementation of Data Warehousing**	Rajiv A. Parida	Rs. 295.00	487
817008864X	**DBA Study Guide OCP Prep Guide**	Nazar Abdul	Rs. 295.00	474
8170088658	**Oracle 11i—The Complete Reference**	Rashmi Anandi	Rs. 495.00	975
8131800067	**Toxonomy of Database Management System**	Aditya Kumar Gupta	Rs. 75.00	146
8131800385	**Introduction to SQL and PL/SQL**	Sharad Maheshwari, Ruchin Jain	Rs. 200.00	389
	DOEACC 'O' LEVEL			
8170088089	**DOEACC 'O' Level Model Test Papers**	Ramesh Bangia	Rs. 175.00	296
8170089115	**DOEACC 'O' & 'A' Level Programming & Problem Solving Through 'C' Language (Model Test Paper with Solutions)**	Mukesh Sharma	Rs. 95.00	213
8170089069	**DOEACC 'O' & 'A' Level Business Systems (Model Test Paper with Solutions)**	Mukesh Sharma	Rs. 100.00	252
8170085640	**Programming and Problem Solving Through "C" Language**	Harsha Priya, R. Ranjeet	Rs. 95.00	306

ISBN	TITLE	AUTHOR	PRICE	PAGES
8170084474	**IT Tools and Applications**	Ramesh Bangia	Rs. 145.00	370
8170085594	**Business Systems**	Ramesh Bangia	Rs. 175.00	452
8170089514	**Internet & Web Design**	Ramesh Bangia	Rs. 150.00	300

ELECTRONIC COMMERCE

ISBN	TITLE	AUTHOR	PRICE	PAGES
8170085497	**Electronic Commerce**	Pete Loshin, John Vacca	Rs. 295.00	472
817008119X	**E-Commerce**	Mamta Bhusry	Rs. 95.00	215
8170083524	**Marketing in the Cyber Age**	Kurt Rohner	Rs. 295.00	223

HARDWARE/EMBEDDED SYSTEMS

ISBN	TITLE	AUTHOR	PRICE	PAGES
8170087473	**Essential Electronics for PC Technicians**	John W. Farber	Rs. 295.00	546
8170086264	**Grid Computing: A Practical Guide to Technology and Applications**	Ahmar Abbas	Rs. 295.00	408
8170088186	**CD Cracking Uncovered Protection Against Unsanctioned CD Copy**	Kris Kaspersky	Rs. 295.00	422
8170083435	**Practical Linux Programming: Device Drivers, Embedded Systems and the Internet**	Ashfaq A. Khan	Rs. 295.00	420
8170083575	**TCP/IP Application Layer Protocols for Embedded Systems**	M. Tim Jones	Rs. 295.00	460
8131800520	**PC Repair and Maintenance : A Practical Guide**	Joel Rosenthal, Kevin Irwin	Rs. 195.00	362
8131800768	**The A+ Certification and PC Repair Handbook**	Christopher A Crayton, Joel Z. Rosenthal	Rs. 495.00	888

INTERNET & WEB TECHNOLOGY

ISBN	TITLE	AUTHOR	PRICE	PAGES
8170083206	**The Internet Handbook for Writers, Students and Teachers**	Mary McGuire, Linda Stilborne	Rs. 195.00	276
8170084776	**Way in-Internet Getting Started**	Elizabeth Bramire	Rs. 95.00	165
8170088976	**Web Technology**	Ramesh Bangia	Rs. 250.00	560
8170087163	**Web Design with Macromedia Studio MX 2004**	Eric Hunley	Rs. 295.00	558
8170083400	**Professional Web Design (Techniques and Templates)**	Clint Eccher	Rs. 295.00	425
8170088046	**HTML, XHTML, CSS and XML**	Teodoru Gugoiu	Rs. 195.00	355
8170083583	**FrontPage 2000 for Visual Learners**	Chris Charuhas	Rs. 95.00	200
8170083591	**HTML & Java Script for Visual Learners**	Chris Charuhas	Rs. 95.00	200

Please write for a free color Firewall Media Catalog for details on the above books.

ISBN	TITLE	AUTHOR	PRICE	PAGES
8170083605	**The Visual Learners Guide to Managing Web Projects**	Chris Charuhas	Rs. 95.00	130
8170083613	**Dreamweaver 4 for Visual Learners**	Chris Charuhas	Rs. 95.00	200
8170084768	**IT Resource-Implementing XML: Managing and Formatting Data**	Johhny Brochard	Rs. 125.00	279
8170089476	**Design Your Web World**	Sunil Jalota	Rs. 75.00	146

KEEPING AHEAD SERIES

ISBN	TITLE	AUTHOR	PRICE	PAGES
8170084652	**Keeping Ahead-Exchange 2000 Server**	Philippe Levesque	Rs. 145.00	285
8170084660	**Keeping Ahead-Windows 2000 Professional**	Jose Dardoigne	Rs. 175.00	388
8170084679	**Keeping Ahead-Windows 2000 Server**	Philippe Mathon	Rs. 175.00	360
8170084687	**Keeping Ahead-Linux Administration Kernel Version 2.0 to 2.2**	Bruno Guèrin	Rs. 125.00	240
8170084695	**Keeping Ahead-Using Linux Kernel Version 2.0 to 2.2**	Bruno Guèrin	Rs. 125.00	258
8170084709	**Keeping Ahead-Java 2**	Benjamin Aumaille	Rs. 145.00	284
8170084717	**Keeping Ahead-SQL Server 7**	Joelle Mosset	Rs. 145.00	329
8170084725	**Keeping Ahead-JavaScript and VBScript**	Benjamin Aumaille	Rs. 145.00	313
8170084733	**Keeping Ahead-C++ Programming Language**	Bruno Dubois	Rs. 125.00	234
8170084741	**Keeping Ahead-TCP/IP in the NT Environment**	Bruno Ferec	Rs. 125.00	230

MCSE

ISBN	TITLE	AUTHOR	PRICE	PAGES
817008489X	**MCSE-Administering SQL Server 7.0**	Jerome Gabillaud	Rs. 295.00	580
8170084903	**MCSE-Networking Essentials**	Jose Dordoigne	Rs. 245.00	453
8170084911	**MCSE-Windows 2000 Professional**	Jose Dordoigne	Rs. 325.00	665
817008492X	**MCSE-Windows 2000 Server**	Phillippe Mathon	Rs. 345.00	712

MULTIMEDIA AND ANIMATION

ISBN	TITLE	AUTHOR	PRICE	PAGES
8170088208	**3DS Max 6 Animation with Character Studio 4 and Plug-Ins**	Boris Kulagin, Dmitry Morozov	Rs. 175.00	216

Please write for a free color Firewall Media Catalog for details on the above books.

ISBN	TITLE	AUTHOR	PRICE	PAGES
8170088216	**Adobe Audition: Soundtracks for Digital Video**	Roman Petelin, Yury Petelin	Rs. 195.00	278
8170086205	**Building A Digital Human**	Ken Brilliant	Rs. 295.00	380
8170086213	**Making Digital Videos**	Ben Long	Rs. 295.00	284
8170087171	**Illustrating with Macromedia Flash ™ MX2004**	Robert Firbaugh	Rs. 245.00	366
8170082439	**Multimedia Basics-Technology (Vol. I)**	Andreas Holzinger	Rs. 195.00	312
8170082447	**Multimedia Basics-Learning (Vol. II)**	Andreas Holzinger	Rs. 195.00	326
8170082455	**Multimedia Basics-Design (Vol. III)**	Andreas Holzinger	Rs. 195.00	280
8170083532	**Maya Feature Creature Creations**	Todd Palamar	Rs. 295.00	376
8170083540	**Sound Forge Power**	Scott R. Garrigus	Rs. 195.00	344
8131800288	**Multimedia and Web Technology**	Ramesh Bangia	Rs. 395.00	878
813180044X	**Photoshop CS**	Shruti Lal	Rs. 195.00	434
	NETWORKING			
817008721X	**Networking Essentials**	Jose Dordoigne	Rs. 195.00	453
8170089328	**TCP/IP Distributed System**	Vivek Acharya	Rs. 250.00	474
8170087023	**Computer Networks**	Ajit Kumar Singh	Rs. 95.00	181
8131800148	**The Real—world Network Troubleshooting Manual**	Alan Sugano	Rs. 295.00	396
817008203X	**Telecom & Networking Glossary**	Robert Mastin	Rs. 300.00	250
8170082048	**Data Networking Made Easy**	Karen Patten	Rs. 360.00	350
8170082056	**Digital Convergence**	Andy Covell	Rs. 300.00	234
	OFFICE AUTOMATION			
8170089891	**Desk Top Publishing**	Dinesh Maidasani	Rs. 150.00	311
8170087805	**Learning Computer Fundamentals, MS Office and Internet & Web Technology**	Dinesh Maidasani	Rs. 95.00	301
8170087686	**MS-Word 2000 Thumb-Rules and Details**	Snigdha Banerjee	Rs. 175.00	390
8170089239	**Computer Accounting with Tally 7.2**	Firewall Media	Rs. 195.00	330
	ON YOUR SIDE SERIES			
8170084830	**On your Side-Powerpoint 2002**	Andrew Blackburn	Rs. 145.00	282
8170084849	**On your Side-Excel 2002**	Adrienne Tommy	Rs. 125.00	275

ISBN	TITLE	AUTHOR	PRICE	PAGES
8170084857	**On your Side-Word 2002**	Adrienne Tommy	Rs. 125.00	289
8170084865	**On your Side-Access 2002**	Adrienne Tommy	Rs. 125.00	303
8170084873	**On your Side-Frontpage 2002**	Andrew Blackburn	Rs. 95.00	245
8170084881	**On your Side-Windows XP**	Adrienne Tommy	Rs. 125.00	310

OPERATING SYSTEMS

ISBN	TITLE	AUTHOR	PRICE	PAGES
8170087236	**Linux—A Practical Approach**	B. Mohamed Ibrahim	Rs. 95.00	187
8170088623	**Red Hat Linux Study Guide**	Vijay Shekhar	Rs. 350.00	635
8170088631	**Red Hat Linux-The Complete Bible**	Vijay Shekhar	Rs. 545.00	1176
8170089581	**Unix and Shell Programming**	Archana Verma	Rs. 80.00	137
8170089131	**Operating System Concepts**	P.S. Gill	Rs. 95.00	181
8170083427	**The MS-Windows XP Professional Handbook**	Louis Columbus	Rs. 295.00	330
8170084784	**Way in-Windows XP Home Edition**	Andrew Blackburn	Rs. 95.00	183
8170086221	**Cyber Rookies—Operating System Fundamentals**	D. Irtegov	Rs. 295.00	498

PROGRAMMING

ISBN	TITLE	AUTHOR	PRICE	PAGES
8170087791	**The Art of Programming Through Flowcharts & Algorithms**	Anil Bikas Chaudhuri	Rs. 95.00	160
8170086248	**Preventative Programming Techniques: Avoid and Correct Common Mistakes**	Brian Hawkins	Rs. 295.00	322
8170083443	**Learning Computer Programming : It's not about Languages**	Mary Farrell	Rs. 295.00	375
8170086256	**Object-Oriented Programming: From Problem Solving to Java**	José M. Garrido	Rs. 295.00	360
817008931X	**Object-Oriented Programming-Concept and Implementation**	A. Rajesh	Rs. 95.00	182
8170089107	**Java: J2SE-5 A Practical Approach**	B. Mohammad Ibrahim	Rs. 175.00	332
8170089409	**Advance Java**	Gajendra Gupta	Rs. 175.00	305
8170088038	**Assembly Language Programming for Intel Processors Family**	Vasile Lungu	Rs. 295.00	577
8170088178	**The Assembly Programming Master Book**	Vlad Pirogov	Rs. 395.00	726
813180075X	**Java Messaging**	Eric Bruno	Rs. 295.00	480

Please write for a free color Firewall Media Catalog for details on the above books.

ISBN	TITLE	AUTHOR	PRICE	PAGES
	PROGRAMMING - C#, C, C++			
8170083702	**The Power of C#**	Rajiv Parida	Rs. 295.00	576
8170085632	**Mastering Graphics Programming in 'C'**	Sudhir Dawra	Rs. 145.00	286
8170088879	**Programming in C and Numerical Analysis**	J.B. Dixit	Rs. 350.00	355
8170087074	**Mastering C Programs**	J.B. Dixit	Rs. 195.00	434
8170081262	**Programming in C**	J.B. Dixit	Rs. 295.00	506
8170087619	**Unix and C Programming**	Ashok Arora, Shefali Bansal	Rs. 295.00	606
817008878X	**C Interview Questions and Answers**	J. Rajaram	Rs. 75.00	139
8170089034	**Pragmatic C**	R.K. Jangda	Rs. 150.00	258
8170086140	**Data Structure for 'C' Programming**	Ajay Kumar	Rs. 145.00	290
8170081270	**Programming in C++**	J.B. Dixit	Rs. 260.00	602
8170088194	**Hackish C++ Pranks & Tricks**	Michael Flenov	Rs. 245.00	326
8170082889	**Basics of C++ Programming**	Nishant Kundalia	Rs. 95.00	168
8170083648	**Mastering C++ Programs**	J.B. Dixit	Rs. 295.00	598
817008623X	**Cyber Rookies—C++ Programming Fundamentals**	Chuck Easttom	Rs. 295.00	417
8131800202	**Data Structure using C++**	N. Jayalakshmi	Rs. 65.00	126
8170089123	**C++ Made Easy**	T.D. Malhotra	Rs. 250.00	449
8131800393	**C++ & Introduction to C#**	T.D. Malhotra, Rajeev A. Parida, A. Rajesh	Rs. 200.00	440
8131800350	**OOPS with C++**	M. Jaya Prasad	Rs. 150.00	317
	SECURITY			
8170083419	**Computer Forensics : Computer Crime Scene Investigation**	John Vacca	Rs. 445.00	731
8131800156	**Computer Evidence (Collection and Preservation)**	Christopher L.T. Brown	Rs. 295.00	394
8170083494	**Firewall Architecture for the Enterprise**	Norbert Pohlmann, Tim Crothers	Rs. 295.00	480
8170086272	**Net Spies**	Andrew Gauntlett	Rs. 195.00	210
3826607546	**Firewall Systems**	Norbert Pohlmann	Rs. 1630.00	544
8131800504	**Homeland Security Techniques and Technologies**	Jesus Mena	Rs. 295.00	346

Please write for a free color Firewall Media Catalog for details on the above books.

ISBN	TITLE	AUTHOR	PRICE	PAGES
	ENGINEERING AND TECHNOLOGY			
817008718X	**Human Aspects of Software Engineering**	James E. Tomayko, Orit Hazzan	Rs. 195.00	338
8131800032	**Management Information Systems**	Avdhesh Gupta, Anurag Malik	Rs. 195.00	400
8170087953	**Human Computer Interaction**	Rajendra Ranjan Kumar	Rs. 95.00	210
8170088097	**Structured System Analysis and Design**	Preeti Gupta	Rs. 125.00	192
817008802X	**Autocad 2005 for Engineers**	Ionel Simion	Rs. 175.00	271
8170088054	**Digital Signal Processing Fundamentals**	Ashfaq A. Khan	Rs. 295.00	391
8131800164	**Digital Communication System Using System VUE**	Dennis Silage	Rs. 295.00	365
8170089719	**Foundations of Computer Science**	Ashok Arora	Rs. 250.00	386
817008363X	**Practical Project Management**	Ivan Bayross	Rs. 195.00	342
8131800806	**Digital Signal Processing using MATLAB and Wavelets**	Michael Weeks	Rs. 350.00	452
8131800792	**Classical Electrodynamics**	Hans C. Dhanian	Rs. 395.00	620
8131800512	**The Software Vulnerability Guide**	Herbert H. Thompson, Scott G. Chase	Rs. 195.00	368
8131800776	**Robot Modelling and Kinematics**	Rachid Manseur	Rs. 295.00	380
8131800369	**System Software**	M. Joseph	Rs. 95.00	185
	STRAIGHT TO THE POINT SERIES			
8170084601	**STTP : Word 2002**	Corinne Hervo	Rs. 45.00	154
817008461X	**STTP : Excel 2002**	Corinne Hervo	Rs. 45.00	153
8170084628	**STTP : Dreamweaver 4**	Corinne Hervo	Rs. 45.00	135
8170084636	**STTP : Flash 5**	Corinne Hervo	Rs. 45.00	183
8170084644	**STTP : Photoshop 6**	Corinne Hervo	Rs. 45.00	152
817008881X	**STTP : MS Office 2000**	Dinesh Maidasani	Rs. 125.00	290
8170086100	**STTP : MS Office 2003**	Dinesh Maidasani	Rs. 145.00	288
8170087651	**STTP : MS Word 2003**	Firewall Media	Rs. 60.00	150
8170088011	**STTP : Photoshop CS**	Firewall Media	Rs. 60.00	150
8170088143	**STTP : MS Excel 2003**	Firewall Media	Rs. 60.00	150
8170088151	**STTP : CorelDraw 12**	Firewall Media	Rs. 60.00	150
8131800105	**STTP : 3ds MAX 7**	Dinesh Maidasani	Rs. 95.00	182
8131800083	**STTP : Auto CAD 2006**	Dinesh Maidasani	Rs. 95.00	190
8131800245	**STTP : CorelDraw X3**	Dinesh Maidasani	Rs. 75.00	188

Please write for a free color Firewall Media Catalog for details on the above books.

ISBN	TITLE	AUTHOR	PRICE	PAGES
8131800253	**STTP : Dreamweaver 8**	Dinesh Maidasani	Rs. 75.00	148
8131800237	**STTP : Photoshop CS2**	Dinesh Maidasani	Rs. 75.00	172
8170088380	**STTP : Tally 7.2**	Firewall Media	Rs. 175.00	322
8131800091	**STTP : Flash 8**	Dinesh Maidasani	Rs. 95.00	180
8131800407	**STTP : My SQL 5.0**	Dinesh Maidasani	Rs. 85.00	166
8131800458	**STTP : Microsoft Power Point 2003**	Dinesh Maidasani	Rs. 75.00	142

STUDIO FACTORY

ISBN	TITLE	AUTHOR	PRICE	PAGES
8170084792	**Studio Factory—Photoshop 6**	Christophe Aubry	Rs. 175.00	364
8170084806	**Studio Factory—Flash 5**	Sami Ben Yahiya	Rs. 145.00	314
8170084814	**Studio Factory—Dreamweaver Ultradev 4**	Phillippe Chatellier	Rs. 95.00	240
8170084822	**Studio Factory—Dreamweaver 4**	Christophe Aubry	Rs. 175.00	373
8170087643	**Studio Factory—Dreamweaver MX**	Christophe Aubry	Rs. 195.00	407
8170087627	**Studio Factory—Flash MX**	Arnaud Blanche	Rs. 145.00	337
817008766X	**Studio Factory—Photoshop 7**	Cyril Guerin	Rs. 195.00	420

LAXMI PUBLICATIONS (P) LTD

113, Golden House, Daryaganj, New Delhi-110002

Phone : **011 - 43 53 25 00**

Fax : **011 - 43 53 25 28**

EMAIL : info@laxmipublications.com

Website : www.laxmipublications.com

BRANCHES

- 129/1, IIIrd Main Road, IX Cross, Chamrajpet, **Bangalore** (*Phone* : 080-26 61 15 61)
- 26, Damodaran Street, T. Nagar, **Chennai** (*Phone* : 044-24 34 47 26)
- 43/1394D, St. Benedict's Road, Ernakulam North, **Cochin** (*Phone* : 0484-239 70 04)
- Pan Bazar, Rani Bari, **Guwahati** (*Phones* : 0361-254 36 69, 251 38 81)
- 4-2-453, Ist Floor, Ramkote, **Hyderabad** (*Phone* : 040-24 75 02 47)
- Adda Tanda Chowk, N.D. 365, **Jalandhar City** (*Phone* : 0181-222 12 72)
- 106/A, Ist Floor, S.N. Banerjee Road, **Kolkata** (*Phones* : 033-22 27 37 73, 22 27 52 47)
- 18, Madan Mohan Malviya Marg, **Lucknow** (*Phone* : 0522-220 95 78)
- 142-C, Victor House, Ground Floor, N.M. Joshi Marg, Lower Parel (W), **Mumbai** (*Phones* : 022-24 91 54 15, 24 92 78 69)
- Radha Govind Street, Tharpagna, **Ranchi** (*Phone* : 0651-230 77 64)